CELIBATE LOVE

CELIBATE LOVE

Paul M. Conner, O.P.

AN OSV SOURCE BOOK

Our Sunday Visitor, Inc.
Huntington, Indiana 46750

Imprimi Potest:
Thomas Paul Raftery, O.P.
Provincial of the Western Dominican Province

Nihil Obstat:
Stanley F. Parmisano, O.P.
Censor Librorum

Imprimatur:
✠John S. Cummins
Bishop of Oakland
November 3, 1978

827

Dedicated with grateful heart to all who have helped me along the way of celibate love — to each in measure.

CONTENTS

PREFACE

For years this book has been in the making. I have always been attracted to women, a reaction which did not cease when I vowed myself to religious life or was ordained a priest. I was simply more attracted to Christ, and so entered into the two consecrating events that have definitively shaped my life. To integrate man's and woman's love with consecrated love for God remains one of my absorbing interests.

An opportunity for attempting a theological integration of these two loves came to me when I was left free to select the topic of my doctoral dissertation in spiritual theology. I wrote on *Friendship Between Consecrated Men and Women and the Growth of Charity*. This effort allowed me to grapple with essential factors in a way I found satisfying. Yet I do not view my work as an exhaustive Christian treatment of the matter. Much more could be said and different approaches could be taken. I am convinced, however, that my treatment can be of help to anyone, particularly consecrated celibates, honestly searching for fundamental understanding of chaste, masculine-feminine love as it relates to divine love. My experience with lay men and women, priests, brothers, and sisters has shown me the widespread need of basic insight into these areas of life. Many of these people have urged me to make my study available to the general public. Their prompting and a mounting, twofold pressure have brought me to publish.

The growing tragedy of pain and of shattered lives of celibates who, tortured by confronting their human hearts and their consecrated commitments, make permanent decisions out of confusion and frustration, is the first pressure. It is heightened by a profusion of popular books that offer some help but also do great disservice, because they contain a distorted or seriously incomplete understanding of love, sexuality, chastity, and charity.[1]

The second pressure is only building, like a far-off storm. I foresee a strong, negative overreaction to our present poverty in theological, moral, and spiritual depth. Signs of resurgent puritanism are already noticeable in fringe quarters. Again the baby may be thrown out with the bathwater, this time from the other side of the tub. An in-depth, balanced treatment can bring freshly into relief the ever-constant beauty of celibate love, consecrated chastity, and the sovereign goal of Christian love, and so reduce damaging effects to these values that could result from an overly narrow reaction. My contribution is one of insights and interrelationships — old and new — frequently missing today.

I have been helped by many who have given of their experience and time that this book might be enriched and brought to print. My greatest gratitude goes to Stanley Parmisano, O.P., and to Sister Mary Dominic Engelhard, O.P., whose literary counsel helped bring it to final form. For reading the manuscript and making invaluable suggestions, I owe individual thanks to Thomas Dubay, S.M., and to my Dominican brothers, Jordan Aumann and Basil Cole.

There are other friends who counseled me in diverse ways and who prayed God's favor on this work. May they all in turn be richly rewarded by Him and by the help that may come to its readers.

St. Albert's College
Oakland, California

Introduction

A NEW DAWN

"Male and female he created them . . . on the sixth day."

Dawn brings newness, another day, fresh beginnings — the chance to deepen my share in the mysteries of light, life, and love. Dawn symbolizes hope looking toward fulfillment.

Something was incomplete about the marvels of creation on the fifth day. God had been grandly reflected in the morning and evening, the sky and the waters, the seas and the earth, the seasons and seed-bearing plants, the stars and the planets, the sea creatures, the birds, and the beasts of the land. But God is spirit, and so there was need for a new dawn. "Let us make man in our own image, in the likeness of ourselves . . . and in the image of God he created them, male and female."

Completeness came to all that God had made through the dawn of humanity. Similarly, yet mysteriously, it came also to the New Creation through the birth of the New Adam and the New Eve. Jesus and Mary enfleshed fullness of Life from God's own Spirit.

Through the ages the Lord and his people live out this second New Dawn lasting into eternity. The consecrated celibate, among the people of God's choosing, is its radical witness. He or she purposes as fully as possible to incarnate this More Abundant Life.

All things human and Christian, then, that God has made possess the splendid possibility of masculine-feminine complementarity. Like the dawn, they are alive with the hope of completion. Every Christian

man or woman must sometimes wonder whether the promise of complementarity will find fulfillment in his or her life. Those who marry
experience a personal, new dawn of hope toward human completeness.
Is it possible for the consecrated celibate to cherish a similar hope for
masculine-feminine complementarity? Can he or she experience something of the fullness of the specifically human image of God in order to
realize the New Creation more fully and so give better witness to it?
Can human love between celibates help the growth of divine love in a
given man and woman? These are the questions this book intends to
answer.

Considerable interest in such questions is astir today. Contemporary celibates come from contemporary society; ours is a personalist
age that is rediscovering community on the group level and friendship
on the individual. Throughout the land we hear the cry: "Love is the
meaning of life." Social movements and academic disciplines are
championing love as the answer for contemporary man and woman.
There is abundant enthusiasm, but little discernment. Cardinal Leo
Suenens finds the popular understanding of love so fractured that he
challenges the Christian of today to reinstate the very word with its
true meaning:

> The word *'love'* is among those most used in the modern world. It
> reaches us incessantly over the air or on the screen, in innumerable
> songs or in films and literature, all of which make use of it.
>
> Unfortunately, under this magnificent word are hidden what we
> must call the counterfeits of Love: in actual fact it covers only too
> often exaltation of the sexual instinct and its supreme freedom.
>
> A Chinese sage, asked one day what he would do if he were the
> master of the world, replied: *'I would re-establish the meaning* of
> words.' An immense service, in fact, to render to mankind! Under
> the circumstances, it is up to Christians in particular not to let the
> word 'love' be profaned, to re-establish its meaning and not use it
> unless to express real love. It is urgent to set love and sexuality in
> their respective places, in order not to confuse them.[1]

It is not the contemporary discovery that lacks promise: love *is* the
meaning of life — on every level. The *variety* of loves, however, makes
more than mere discovery necessary, if lives of love are to be happy.
Experience and clear thinking are needed to weigh successfully.

Such clarity and depth of judgment are rare today, and because of what is happening in the lives of some celibates, interest in our subject mounts. Many priests, brothers, and sisters admit confusion and frustration in their personal attempts to harmonize sensitive, warm, masculine and feminine love with their openhearted commitment to celibacy for the sake of divine love. Conversations in retreat settings, theology classes, and the confessional ministry heighten my awareness of this spreading frustration. Reactions are often extreme and tragic, as media reports testify. This turmoil in the heart of the Church simply echoes the jumbled thinking and sad torment that surrounds the experience of human love and sexuality in the world at large.

After so many centuries of human thought and Christian belief, anyone searching for answers today might expect that a fairly complete array of secular and sacred wisdom on this topic already exists to help him sort out his personal confusion. Men and women in every state of life must have solved the problem before now. I have looked to the past and to the present and have found insights very helpful to me and to those I counsel and teach. But there are historical reasons why the subject has never been "mastered," at least to the point of offering a clear blueprint for today.

Lack of experience is not one of these reasons. Many saintly celibates have lived close to the perfection of love, seemingly without reflecting deeply on its concrete human substratum — manly or womanly love. They loved instinctively and intuitively in a process of accepting or excluding elements of their ongoing experience. I am certain that today, in the same manner, many live successful, consecrated lives filled with human love.

But historically, many others reflected on the issue and proposed one extreme view after the other, usually in sincere but prejudiced reaction to the extreme that preceded them.[2] Dualist distortions denied human love's connection with religion (for example, Manichaeanism, Albigensianism, Jansenism, Puritanism); opposing distortions linked love with excess (such as temple prostitution, clerical concubinage, and some forms of libertinism prevalent still in today's religious and sexual license).

Even the best of Christian tradition has not offered a wholly balanced answer. Monastic spirituality, because of the very nature of the monastic community's enclosure, fostered only brotherly or sisterly human love and excluded that between the sexes. A comparison of premodern times with ours reveals that earlier peoples developed more

13

naturally and stably at home in their human relationships, particularly in masculine-feminine knowing-and-loving patterns. Their simpler familial and agrarian society favored this, which explains in large part why many men and women of those times were able to live contented lives in the monastic setting. In our technological epoch such patterns have been disrupted to a point where a large and growing proportion of adults are psychologically less developed, especially in interpersonal relationships. Never having had sufficient human love as children and adolescents, they thirst for it as adults. This is, perhaps, an underlying reason why few committed Christians today seem able to live contentedly within the confines of strictly monastic communities.

Some Christian thinkers of the past have approached the problem intellectually. In reaction to his early, wasted years, St. Augustine struggled long in mind and will to accept conversion to continence, then to mature chastity. Unfortunately, his portrayal in the *Confessions* of the enslavement of his freedom by his "need of woman" seems to have set a wary attitude about masculine-feminine relationships outside of marriage throughout Christianity for centuries.

In his day St. Bernard spoke otherwise. He initiated the widespread medieval use of nuptial love language in describing the highest stages of Christian prayer and love. His *Sermons on the Canticle of Canticles* inspired nearly every spiritual writer for the next six hundred years to write as his most sublime treatise a commentary on the Canticle. St. Thomas Aquinas was the first to use human friendship as the root analogy for a strictly theological treatment of the Christian virtue of love. Later, St. John of the Cross tried to express his mystical experience of love in prayer and exclaimed near the end of his *Living Flame of Love*, "And now my sole experience is loving!" He did grapple, however, with the problem of integrating human and divine love, because among his writings is this pithy counsel: "Between a holy man and holy woman there should be a foot-thick brick wall!" Nearer our day, Paul Philippe and many others have searched out how human friendship both helps and hinders growth toward fullness of Christian love.[3]

In spite of advancements, the whole area of human love and its relationship to religion is still confused today, especially in theological writings and religious life, where men and women are struggling to integrate human love with their objective of full Christian love. We are in reaction to the recent past. Stemming from eighteenth-century

14

France, fear and extreme caution about "particular friendships" had spread throughout most religious communities. This stringent attitude was a preoccupation of superiors and directors until the last decade or so. Today a different distortion is growing from other quarters. Counselors of religious sometimes encounter intolerance toward friendship from community members, resulting frequently from an immature jealousy on the part of those who do not have close friends. In regard to priesthood and human love, the "celibacy debate" rages. Many priests and lay persons fail to comprehend the spiritual and psychological dimensions of either the positive or negative sides of the issue. The current confused or, at best, shallow grasp of spiritual values can be detected also in some sisters' rejection of the central theme of bridal and spousal love in their consecration to Christ. They tend to view themselves solely as serving others in Christ's ministry. More disturbing, some men and women superiors are so influenced by psychological and sociological writings that they organize "dating" experiences for their seminarians and sisters. Many more permit them. They are attempting to "balance" formation, seemingly unaware that they either have unbalanced candidates or are placing immature youth in situations highly dangerous for their yet insecure vocations. On the other hand, some religious groups still completely shelter their candidates in apostolic or conventual schools until their first apostolic work — the opposite extreme to the mean of prudence. Even among seasoned religious and priests are a few who try to justify compromising relationships by talking and writing of a "third way" between Christian marriage and consecrated chastity.

It is true, many in the immediate past saw more danger than help in friendship, especially between consecrated men and women. An elderly priest of my acquaintance is known for his kindly but prohibiting view: "If you want to love the ladies," he will tell younger priests, "love them in bunches." Some writers stressed the revealed facts of sin and the consequent propensity in us to defect from what is authentically wholesome. By way of reaction, others now stress the potential good of successfully facing the problem. Claims are being made by some theologians that Christian love and friendship, particularly that between consecrated celibates, is a great aid to attaining intimacy with the Trinity in prayer.[4] And so, for a variety of reasons, priests, religious, and others answer both "yes" and "no" to a question of foremost interest: Can mixed celibate friendship in practice contribute to growth in Christian love?

Amid the confusion and frustration, real values must be salvaged and tragedies avoided. A balanced view is needed. We must have a more detailed, scientific, and theological appraisal. The Christian must weigh all that the mind of man can discover, together with all that the mind of God has revealed, and then struggle for prudence of reason and faith in making judgments and applying them to his life. In his mental conversation, there can be balance or the predominance of one or the other source of input. Should a faith awareness overshadow reason, then pietistic or fundamentalist judgments are likely to result. Should reason so dominate that it is not adequately guided by faith, then naturalistic or rationalist judgments can be expected. In this book I hope to avoid either imbalance. I intend to gather testimony from scripture, contemporary experience, and empirical psychology. To this I will add the sanctifying experience of holy men and women and relevant areas of classical philosophy and theology. Finally, in a pastoral spirit, I will attempt a prudential evaluation and work toward general conclusions and practical norms.

To avoid any misunderstanding, I wish clearly to state that I do not hold that the model of masculine-feminine love is the only one for approaching the subject of Christian love and one's relationship with God. The Old and New Testaments have proposed the Divinity and Christ Himself to us under many models: Father, Brother, Good Shepherd, Lord, High Priest, King, Teacher, Spouse, Bridegroom, Lover, Creator, Friend, Judge, Paraclete. Each of us must meet the three divine Persons through the models that best relate to our experience. Some will grow in the love of God through most of them; others will prefer one or a few. Here I wish simply to focus on friendship in the experience of consecrated men and women to see how it can help or hinder growth in the love of God and neighbor.

If they are to avoid self-delusion, I must here voice the conviction that consecrated celibates should not presume to choose the model of mixed friendship discussed in this book unless they know experientially that their friendship is fostering their lives of prayer. Deepening personal union with God through prayer is an essential, practical gauge of this or any proposed means of growth toward the fullness of Christian love.

1

THE WORD AND THE COVENANT

"Jesus loved Martha and Mary . . ."

Who is Jesus? What is *my* experience of him? Do I know this Person who died for love of me — who is always with me?

He is "the image of the unseen God," whom both Old and New Testaments reveal as marvelously close to man. Reverently the Church attests to this truth in her Morning Prayer: All-powerful God, you made a wonderful covenant with your people Israel, and a more wonderful one with your Church, sealed with your Son's sacrifice of the cross. . . . Lead your faithful people into full, unending union with you in your kingdom.

If we have experienced God within ourselves, within his Church, his Word, his Sacraments, and have known his presence in others, we are on the way. We begin to understand his closeness, to celebrate his presence. To this celebration each of us is called. We are each to know God, each to run an immense risk, for coming to know another person involves the risk of loving, of being drawn into oneness with the other. For love does just that: it is a force drawing two persons into union.

A search into the mystery of God's love for us and its relationship to human love, especially between celibate men and women, should start with the Word of God. A true Christian outlook on any subject must incorporate the content of belief. The Christian must first learn what God has to say. God's thoughts will yield fundamental insights and the secure orientation he needs to build a helpful theology.

17

If we look to great Christians of the past, particularly to saintly celibate men and women, we find that they frequently expressed their relationship with God in terms of love and friendship. In so doing, they merely built on beginnings they had found in Scripture itself. Although they uncovered there no complete body of teaching, they clearly realized, both from what he had done and said, that one way in which the Word-of-God-made-Man proclaimed his eternal covenant with us was through loving friendships with men and women.[1]

FRIENDSHIP IN GENERAL

Human friendship is extolled in several places in the Old Testament, most strikingly in the relationship between David and Jonathan. Jonathan loved David "as his own soul" (Is 18:1; 20:17), and David, while mourning Jonathan's death, admitted that their friendship had been "more wonderful to him than the love of a woman" (2 S 1:26). It long survived in the memory of his heart. Whole speeches valuing human friendship are found in Ecclesiasticus, the author concluding, "The faithful friend is priceless" (Si 7:18). Other sayings of Proverbs proclaim the wonders of true friendship.[2]

Some friendships are illusory, however. A rich man's is frequently false (Pr 14:20), and an intimate relationship can turn traitorous (Ps 41:9-10). Though seemingly sincere, friendship can be deceiving (Jb 6:15-30), even drawing one into evil. With good reason the Word of Yahweh warned the Hebrew to be clearheaded and on his guard in the choice of friends.

The believer learned the wisdom of evaluating a friendship over a span of time: "New wine, new friend; if it has grown old, you will drink it with joy" (Si 9:10). He came to realize that authentic friendship is not offended by, but appreciates open correction (Pr 27:5f); it especially thrives in an atmosphere colored by each friend's "fear" of Yahweh: "He who fears the Lord makes for himself true friends; for such as one is, such is the friend that he has" (Si 6:16f).

One Old Testament scholar concludes his study with the statement: "Actually, the model and source of true friendship is the friendship which God seals with man. . . ."[3] Experiences of human and divine friendship interrelate and in fact illumine each other. No wonder, then, that in the Old Testament noble human friendship is used to express the relationship between God and man. Yahweh calls Abraham his friend in Isaiah 41:8, and, in the Hebrew version of 2

18

Chronicles 20:7, Jehoshaphat refers to him as the "friend whom God will love forever." Much later St. James gave us the underlying reason: "Abraham put his faith in God . . . and that is why he was called 'the friend of God' " (Jm 2:23). Yahweh similarly related to Moses and spoke with him "face to face, as a man speaks with his friend" (Ex 33:11). Solomon's experience convinced him that anyone who sought the wisdom of the Most High would "win God's friendship" (Ws 7:14), as did, indeed, the prophets.

Even at this early stage of revelation it was clear to the devout Hebrew that friendship with Yahweh was proposed to every believer. According to the exegete Philip Roets, this is the first of two great notions that the Old Testament teaches.[4]

The New Testament points to many examples of human friendship among the apostles. In the book of Acts we read that some of the Asiarchs of Rome are called St. Paul's friends (19:31), so also people he knew in Sidon (27:3). The most complete listing of his strong friendships with both men and women, however, is found in his letter to the Romans, chapter 16. The mutual love that should exist among the Lord's followers is a major theme of St. John. He himself greets a certain man in his third letter as "my dear friend Gaius, whom I love in the truth" (3 Jn 4).

These same two apostles have much to say about every Christian's friendship with God. Paul realizes that God, in sending his Son among us, has shown himself a friend to men (cf. Tt 3:4); he offers thanks to God for calling us all into fellowship with his Son (1 Co 1:9). Throughout the Gospels Jesus himself addresses people directly or in parables as his friends. John records the most moving instance — Christ speaking to his apostles at the Last Supper (Jn 15:12-16):

> This is my commandment: love one another, as I have loved you. A man can have no greater love than to lay down his life for his friends. You are my friends, if you do what I command you. I shall not call you servants any more, because a servant does not know his master's business; I call you friends, because I have made known to you everything I have learnt from my Father. You did not choose me, no, I chose you.

The apostles had shared some of the Lord's trials, and at this Supper they were being readied to face the night of his passion. Of them all, only St. John, "the disciple Jesus loved," remained faithful to the Lord until his crucifixion. He became "the type of the friend of Jesus," the one to whom the Lord entrusted his own mother.[5]

John records other friendships of Jesus: his touchingly beautiful love for John the Baptist, "friend of Christ the bridegroom" (Jn 3:29); his tender friendships with Martha, Mary, and Lazarus; and his similar love for all those who, like Lazarus, "were to rise from the tomb by faith" (Jn 11:35f).

The Evangelist John teaches further that God's friendship for man reaches a surprising depth. Jesus will lay down his life for us; he has loved us as much as the Father has loved him. He reveals that the Father also loves us. The Lord, in fact, relates all three Persons of the Trinity to the baptized in a context of love and indwelling (Jn 14:10-26). Christians are called to respond in a like spirit of love.

Clearly, biblical man was aware of the reality and the special value both of human and divine friendship. Through many figures in Scripture God had revealed himself and his relationship to those he loves: he is Father, Good Shepherd, High Priest, Teacher, Consoler, but also Friend. Indeed, friendship is a highly favored way in which the Triune God reveals and cultivates the kind of relationship each Divine Person desires to establish with man. Even friendship as a dominant feature of marriage is used to reveal added dimensions of the relationship.

FRIENDSHIP BETWEEN MAN AND GOD THROUGH THE IMAGE OF MARITAL LOVE

Marriage is certainly a specific type of friendship, characterized by aspects of love and life exclusive to it, yet sharing a core reality with any true friendship. As a *masculine-feminine friendship*, God has chosen marriage to teach us about our relationship with him. He wants us to know, on the one hand, that the spiritual core reality of conjugal love is not so distinct from a deep, chaste, unmarried, mixed friendship as it might seem. On the other, marriage is only a temporal reality. It will not exist in heaven, yet the love of friendship it contains will — as will that of any true friendship. The marital metaphor, therefore, offers any Christian, married or celibate, insights into his personal relationship with God.

Such considerations help us realize the extent of divine love, expressed to man through a variety of created figures, each conveying another facet of infinite love itself. It is a reality broader than human friendship, both married and celibate. Transcending sexuality and humanity, it includes the loves of all human relationships and can exist in and through each of them.

The marriage figure is frequently used in the Old Testament, but at this stage of revelation, the image is collective rather than personal. The prophets Jeremiah, Hosea, and Ezekiel use the image most extensively, but others also make poignant use of it. Isaiah, for example, proclaims to a despondent Jerusalem: "do not be dismayed . . . for now your creator will be your husband, his name, Yahweh Sabaoth . . . he is called the God of the whole earth" (Is 54:5). Jerusalem will exult for joy in Yahweh her God, for he, "like a bridegroom wearing his wreath," has clothed her "like a bride adorned in her jewels" (Is 61:10). The prophet concludes: "Like a young man marrying a virgin, so will the one who built you wed you, and as the bridegroom rejoices in his bride, so will your God rejoice in you" (Is 62:5).

Jeremiah, too, was told by the Word of Yahweh: "Go and shout this in the hearing of Jerusalem: 'Yahweh says this: I remember the affection of your youth, the love of your bridal days' " (Jr 2:2). The context is, however, that of an unfaithful Israel. The Word of Yahweh strengthens this image: "You, who have prostituted yourself with so many lovers . . . is there a single place where you have not offered your body? You waited by the roadside for clients . . . and you maintained a prostitute's bold front, never thinking to blush" (Jr 3:1-3). Nevertheless, love, not wrath is God's ultimate reaction: "Come back, disloyal Israel — it is Yahweh who speaks — I shall frown on you no more, since I am merciful. . . . Only acknowledge your guilt: how you have apostatized from Yahweh your God, how you have flirted with strangers" (Jr 3:12-13).

The theme of the unfaithful wife is the principal motif of the book of Hosea. Thomas Barrosse traces it succinctly in his *Christianity: Mystery of Love*. Briefly, God commands his representative, Hosea, to "Go, marry a whore, and get children with a whore, for the country itself has become nothing but a whore by abandoning Yahweh" (Ho 1:2). This grotesque action is meant to excite horror in the hardened hearts of the Israelites, causing them to see their betrayal of Yahweh in its true light. In spite of her continual unfaithfulness, Hosea perseveres in his love for his wife, exhibiting the very constancy of Yahweh's love for Israel, and wins back his unfaithful partner. And so with us: despite extensive human infidelity, God is ever lovingly anxious for our return to intimacy with him.

Ezekiel, in two great allegories of the history of Israel (chapters 16 and 23), develops the same theme even more fully. In touching but trenchant language, Yahweh teaches that in his love he will punish Israel for her unfaithfulness to him, only to draw her back to her first love: to himself.

The theme of the unfaithful marriage partner is used also in the New Testament to teach man about his relationship to God. St. James scolds quarreling Christians who have separated themselves from the unifying Spirit of God: "You are as unfaithful as adulterous wives; don't you realize that making the world your friend is making God your enemy?" (Jn 4:4). Jesus himself calls the hardhearted and unbelieving scribes and pharisees an "unfaithful and adulterous generation" (Mt 12:39); and even those of his disciples who are ashamed of his words are "adulterous and sinful" (Mk 8:38).

A positive use of the marriage metaphor, though, brings out much more fully the truth that a Christian's relationship to God must be as faithful as that to a human spouse.

In three parables of Matthew's Gospel Jesus likens himself to a bridegroom (Mt 9:15; 22:2f; 25:1f). St. John the Baptist draws the same simile about the Christ (Jn 3:23). So impressed is St. Paul with the image that he says, "You see, the jealousy that I feel for you is God's own jealousy: I arranged for you to marry Christ so that I might give you away as a chaste virgin to this one husband" (2 Co 11:2). Then, in his well-known comparison, Paul first refers to the experience of marital love to convey something of the mystery of the love between Christ and the people of God, and then to Christian faith in that mystery to penetrate the depths of the marriage relationship. As the Christian husband and wife relate to one another, so do Christ and those who believe in him (Ep 5:21-32).

One feature of the Matthean parables mentioned above is the wedding feast, symbolizing the happiness of the messianic age. In the book of Revelation, this theme concludes the whole of Sacred Scripture. In the joy of utter fulfillment, the heavenly Jerusalem has made herself ready for the eternal marriage feast of the Lamb. She is "as beautiful as a bride all dressed for her husband."[6]

Without doubt, the marital figure is powerfully used in both Testaments to present the relationship between God and man. For the human mind and heart, no image is more profound or striking. Little wonder, then, that it has been the basis for centuries of Christian mysticism.

FRIENDSHIP BETWEEN MAN AND GOD THROUGH THE IMAGE OF MIXED CELIBATE LOVE

The Scriptures do not speak emphatically about masculine-feminine celibate love as a created image of divine love, but the theme is present, both directly and indirectly, in the two Testaments. In Hebrew the terms "sister" and "bride" do not always have literal application. Often they are interchangeable. Frequently, too, "sister" can mean "friend." The context decides the meaning.

Jeremiah twice uses an unmarried relationship between a man and a woman to speak of Yahweh's love for his people: "Yahweh says this: . . . I have loved you with an everlasting love, so I am constant in my affection for you . . . virgin of Israel." Prophesying Israel's restoration from exile, Jeremiah goes on to say: Virgin Israel . . . "adorned once more, and with your tambourines, you will go out dancing gaily" (Jr 31:3-4).

The Old Testament offers some background for understanding this usage of Jeremiah. In the first place, the two Genesis accounts of the creation of man and woman teach, among other things, that God saw the distinction of the sexes as good: "Yahweh God said, 'It is not good for man to be alone. I will make him a helpmate' "; so "male and female he created them" (Gn 2:18; 1:27). Note that this is a separate, divine intention from that of marriage and procreation described in the same chapters. The distinction of these two creative intentions provides a basis in the primitive covenant for masculine-feminine friendship, whether the friends marry or remain celibate. Eugene H. Maly interprets these Genesis accounts simply as expressions of the divine intention that man and woman complement each other.[7]

Secondly, from the distinction of the sexes a mutual interest broader than genital attraction can arise between a man and a woman. The writer of Proverbs alludes to this power of human complementarity in the mysterious "way of a man with a maid." Recalling David's esteem for friendship over sexual attraction, we must recognize the possibility, at least, of a noble conception of unmarried masculine-feminine friendship. A Hebrew man and woman may well have experienced so predominantly their mutual interest in terms of personal friendship that the attraction of physical sex as such would have been minimal. In this case, the above interpretation of Jeremiah and the Genesis accounts would yield a realistic model for the Jews' approach to God, even though it might appeal only to a few among them.

Undoubtedly, the prominently proposed marriage figure would have provided most Hebrews a more accessible approach to Yahweh.

In the Song of Songs, a rich resource for our search into the Word of God, the exact relationship of the man and woman in the series of love poems is not clear. Scholarly interpretations differ widely. The two that seem most acceptable today agree that the Song is a figure of Yahweh's and Israel's love, but disagree whether it is in terms of married or unmarried love. Many Catholic commentators favor the second interpretation and, looking to the Egyptian and Arabic sources of the poems, a spiritual to a literal meaning. The Song, then, is predominantly seen as a model of unmarried masculine-feminine love that reflects divine love between God and mankind. Other arguments analyzing the very language of the lover and the beloved of the Song strengthen the possibility that their literal relationship is an unmarried one. Ardently speaking in intimate, personal terms of the power, beauty, and joy of love drawing two complementing persons into union, these poems contribute delicate and noble content to our understanding of the love between Yahweh and his chosen people. Even should the Song be interpreted as a portrait of married love, it would still serve as a richly revealing figure of divine love.

The New Testament provides two important instances of unmarried friendship: the first, St. Paul's personal experience of this relationship, which, he says, is also that of the apostles and other Christians (1 Co 9:3-5). Those who do not take the Hebraic language into account interpret this passage to mean that Paul and "all the other apostles and the brothers of the Lord and Cephas" were either married or had blood sisters serving their personal needs during their apostolic missions. This would be true, then, where Paul speaks about women collaborators, such as his "beloved sister Apphia" (Phm 1, 2), or "our sister Phoebe, a deaconess of the Church at Cenchreae . . . she has looked after a great many people, myself included" (Rm 16:1-2). The more reasonable view is that Christian friendship with women as well as with men existed in the lives of St. Paul and others he mentions. The case of Lydia of Philippi, for instance, is quite clear. She was a partial convert to Judaism when Paul arrived in Philippi. From the book of Acts we learn that she and her whole household were so moved by his preaching that they received Christian baptism. A cloth merchant of means, Lydia insisted on keeping Paul and his companions in her home (Ac 16:13-15,40). Other examples are Paul's fellow-workers, Prisca (and Aquila) "who risked death to save my life" (Rm

16:3), Mary, Tryphaena, and Tryphosa "who work so hard for the Lord . . . Rufus, a chosen servant of the Lord, and . . . his mother who has been a mother to me, too . . . Julia, Nereus, and his sister . . ." (Rm 16:7-16), and Priscilla who completed the instruction of Apollos (cf. Ac 18:26).

The second and more important instance of mixed celibate friendship is that of the Lord himself. Each of the Synoptics tells us that women followed Jesus and looked after him. St. Luke relates how, after he was no longer welcome in the synagogues, Jesus travelled through the country, village by village, preaching the Good News. "The Twelve were with him, as were certain women, who had been cured from evil spirits and from illnesses . . . Mary Magdalene . . . Joana, the wife of Chuza . . . Susanna and many others. It was their habit to minister to their needs out of their resources" (Lk 8:2-3). The Jews considered it a pious act to support a rabbi, and the fact that these women helped Jesus and the apostles was in direct line with prevailing custom. Again, we cannot be certain of the personal quality of the relationships involved in these cases, but we do know that Jesus had friendships with women that led them to know and to love his Father. St. John records that "Jesus loved Martha and her sister" (Jn 11:5). The events surrounding their brother Lazarus' death and resurrection recounted in John's gospel (chapters 11 and 12) bear this out. Moreover, the biblical commentator Philip Roets sees the significance of an earlier meeting of Jesus, Martha, and Mary to be precisely that of developing friendship with God.[8]

The living example of Jesus' celibate friendships with women is the strongest biblical basis for this kind of relationship in the lives of other Christians. If Christ in his humanity entered into friendship with women in order to draw them to his divinity, to his Father, and to the Spirit, then celibate friendship between men and women has been divinely sanctioned. Obviously, weakness and dangers, which did not threaten Jesus but can threaten men and women in such relationships, must be taken into consideration. But the Lord's personal example still stands for those who follow it in his Spirit.

2

HUMAN WHOLENESS

"God saw all he had made, and indeed it was very good."

Nothing is more attractive than to watch an athlete in champion form, or to witness a performing artist at a peak moment, or simply to meet someone personifying graciousness and wisdom. Little else is as repelling as the contorted, human features in a muscular dystrophy ward, the twisted lives in a psychotic asylum or prison facility, or the human ravages resulting from destitution, emotional starvation, prejudice, and hatred. We have these reactions because everything God has made is good, and every defection or distortion from original wholesomeness is to that extent less good, less lovable. Whatever actualizes its potential and achieves its maturity is appealing to us; whatever is stunted or deprived draws our pity.

One overarching challenge of life is to become as mature as we can, to become as fully as possible that man or woman God is creating us to be. Boundaries and barriers will limit our success, but progress is ever possible.

A Christian has more than human resources with which to work — and certainly as lofty a challenge. He must put away the old man and put on the new to become as maturely as possible the New Creation in Christ. Maturity in nature and grace; human *and* Christian wholeness — these are the goals of each baptized person. A look to the humane empirical science of today will uncover much that is useful in this twofold endeavor.

PERSONAL WHOLENESS

The findings of psychology about human love and friendship in general afford a point of departure and lead to those about celibate love and friendship between men and women. The two have important interconnections.

Contemporary psychology is particularly insistent on the crucial role of adequate human love for the healthy integration of personality.

Lucius Cervantes concludes his lengthy study of masculine and feminine characteristics by stating that love is the goal of human existence. This conclusion is clear to him from a consideration of the basic needs of children, adults, and society. Love is the specific, generic, and ultimate goal of sexual differences. The goal of each individual's life is God, but God is love. Consequently, " 'It is love and love alone the world is seeking.' "[1]

John Evoy and Maureen O'Keefe describe the integrated individual as one who senses a personal fulfillment, which "flows out of the adequacy that comes from the warm interpersonal relationships in which one both loves and is loved by the persons who really count in his life."[2] Neither achievement nor competency gives such adequacy — only an experience of love from infancy.

Ignace Lepp asserts: "Genuine love is the most effective creator and promoter of human existence. If many persons who are well (or even moderately) endowed nevertheless remain mediocre, it is often because they have never been loved with a strong and tender love."[3]

But what makes up the "genuine" or "adequate" human love these authors require? Jordan Aumann extends it beyond love of the will to the richness of emotional love, without necessarily including, however, physical, sexual love.[4] And Drs. Conrad Baars and Anna Terruwe pointedly require the full, human balance of volitional and emotional love in the formative years of priests and religious men and women if their apostolic years are to be happy and fruitful.[5]

These authorities have a lot to say about the formative influences at play in the lives of those who in fact become capable of genuine human love. Such persons normally enjoy a healthy family life, especially a wholesome balance of paternal and maternal love that young persons need in order to develop and integrate their capacities for strong volitional and rich emotional love and become adequate, mature personalities. In adult life, friendship continues the integrating work begun in earlier life by parental love. In Lepp's opinion, "The most universal and . . . the noblest of all forms of interhuman communication, the only one capable of dissolving our loneliness, is friendship. . . ."[6] "The ordinary man, at least as much as the saints and heroes, needs friendship as a condition of reaching the superior forms of existence," because "in acting with and for each other friends can accede to a spiritually elevated level of existence which they would not have attempted alone." Friendship's creative, ennobling effect results from making the self more available to the other, and so becoming more one's real self. "In friendship we discover and reveal what we are and, perhaps still more, what we are capable of becoming. . . ." The mutually enriching opportunity of penetrating the subjectivity of another also enables each friend to extend love more easily to the whole of humanity, even to all of reality.

The conclusion of Lepp's study is qualified, but strongly positive: "Its imperfections and limitations notwithstanding, friendship represents one of the most precious values of the human condition. It is certainly worth the effort to commit ourselves courageously to the experience of friendship." In the context of redeeming Christian love, a symposium of Catholic experts applied this conclusion to religious celibates, affirming that: "One does not protect and foster consecrated chastity by forbidding friendship but by promoting the right kind of friendship."

Conclusions like these should not be taken to imply that a celibate would do well to cultivate deep friendship with everyone in his life. It is impossible to have such personal love for many. The human ability to love deeply is very limited. And yet, as Baars points out, the celibate can have a *functional love* for innumerable people, a love stemming from his apostolic task, whatever it might be. Functional love is fundamentally a volitional love, yet one accompanied by feelings of compassion, kindness, and affection. To be capable of it, one must have a sufficiently developed emotional life. Functional love differs from the love of personal friendship in which the celibate receives equally the love and affection of a friend. Although in it he might indeed receive affection, the latter is based on gratitude for benefits received. How often it happens, though, that people show little or no appreciation! The professional or helping person then runs the risk of being drained emotionally, if he tries to maintain either too many merely functional relationships or too heavy a concentration of them during a given period of time. The need to be replenished emotionally is yet another important reason why anyone in the service of humanity, priests and religious, for example, should have healthy, personal friendships.

The findings of psychology go beyond stating the need for human love and friendship in every adult's life, especially the celibate's, to speaking specifically about the masculine-feminine relationship. The point of departure is the concept of complementarity, an ancient insight expressed in the Platonic myths as well as in the biblical account of Genesis. In our times it has been elaborated particularly by C. G. Jung and his followers.

Briefly, this view holds that each man and woman is an incomplete human being on all levels: biological, psychological, even spiritual. Consciously each is a man or woman as biology determines, but unconsciously each is powerfully attracted to the psychic aspects of the other sex which complement those of his own. The unconscious need in a man for the feminine counterpart is termed *anima*; in a woman, the longing for a masculine complement is called *animus*. The great strength of this unconscious need or longing derives from the human being's innate striving toward wholeness. Consequently, when a man feels attracted to a woman, it is largely his *anima* that is active, seeking in the woman fulfillment for his masculine psyche. And much of a woman's interest in a man is from her unconscious *animus*, seeking personal wholeness through him.

The Jungian theory holds, therefore, that men and women are related not as opposites, nor as uniform equals, but as complements. Many authors thoughtfully describe how the two sexes complete each other psychologically and spiritually. A representative excerpt from Karl Stern brings into relief several of the mutual benefits which may be gained through friendship between men and women:

> Thus we see that the polarity of the sexes is based on body build and organ function but not confined to it. The male principle, according to Helene Deutsch, enables us to master our relationship with reality, to solve our problems rationally. Woman, wherever she is different from man, 'acts and reacts out of the dark, mysterious depths of the unconscious, i.e. affectively, intuitively, mysteriously.' ... Woman as real or potential mother possesses the sense of creativeness by which one lets something grow, nurtures it, allows it to follow its own mysterious law of becoming. Man's sense of creativeness is that of making things work. Hence the strange 'maleness' of that entire universe of the organizational. ... However, we have seen that discursive reason, to be whole, must retain, as its soil, that form of intelligence which is derived from the world of child and mothers. To state our point paradoxically, we might say that the sci-

30

entist knows *more* about the rabbit than the painter but the painter knows *better* about the rabbit than the scientist. One form of knowledge cannot do without the other.[7]

Of the many facets of masculine-feminine complementarity that could be explored, we will focus briefly on those which shed light on the goal of personal wholeness in the lives of celibate men and women. The first might seem obvious, but is of fundamental importance for personal integration as well as the life of Christian love. Both the man and the woman in any genuine interpersonal relationship must be able to love precisely as man or woman. This is even more true if psychic complementarity is to occur between them. "Love is authentic in proportion to the degree of the authenticity of the masculinity and femininity of the partners. An effeminate man and a virile woman resemble each other too much to be truly complementary." Where expected complementarity is lacking in a given relationship, deficient love experience in the early family life of one or the other partner is frequently the cause. A boy needs a wholesome pattern of man-loving-woman, the girl, of woman-loving-man in their parents or parent-substitutes, or their attitude toward the other sex will be warped. Moral and spiritual inadequacy is often traced to early, inadequate experience of a love-life pattern. Such a deprived background can result in social misconduct, the inability to approach religious matters reasonably, or a variety of emotional and mental disorders.

Two closely connected distinctions help clarify the preceding point. The first contrasts an inadequate love experience between a man and a woman with one that is adequate and necessary for complementarity. An inadequate experience will result if either partner relates to the other with less than mature personality — if sentimental and/or genital dimensions predominate between them. This distinction has been expressed as the difference between loving as a "male" or a "man", as a "female" or a "woman." People must be authentic *as persons* in order to love as man or woman. Beyond the necessity of a favorable background, psychology finds that authenticity is fostered by the adult's striving toward a realistic self-ideal.

The second distinction refers to a man's or woman's very individuality. Each must learn to love not only as man or woman, but as *this* man or *this* woman. Such complete self-identity is established through the exchange of adequate love in friendships with persons of both sexes. Besides being necessary for any complementing relationship, it is also an important factor for progressively realizing one's self-ideal.

A prerequisite to loving God, friends, and humanity in a fully human way, and so of course to developing a friendship of complementing love, is the *capability* of loving a person of the opposite sex. This may seem self-evident, but psychologists in fact rarely find individuals capable of such love.

A major benefit of complementing friendship is the happiness it generates. Nature is always striving for utter wholeness and is never content with partial fulfillment only. Of all love and friendship, that between man and woman can, therefore, be the deepest and most satisfying. Evoy and O'Keefe speak of it as a kind of merging that still leaves each one's individuality intact:

> In *complementing love*, there takes place a psychological fusion between a fulfilled man and fulfilled woman both living authentically. While retaining completely their proper identities as individuals, they share psychologically a oneness of being. Thus, while growing even more distinct as persons, they are in a real sense, and at the same time, also one.

This love-unity in personal diversity can make for the deepest, merely human happiness:

> Love enables [a person] to relish the joy for which he is created. The deeper this love is and the more it involves one's whole emotional life, the greater will be the joy one experiences. . . . The true joys of a profoundly human friendship . . . are the most intimate when love joins two persons of opposite sex. For man and woman have a natural disposition and inclination toward one another, much greater than any which can exist between two men or two women. The union in love between man and woman provides the fulfillment of this innate disposition and, consequently, the consummation of their very being. Therefore the happiness and the joy of love are nowhere greater than in this union.

Since the human fulfillment of complementing love can best be achieved in the lifelong situation of marriage, it is evident that the masculine-feminine friendship of marriage is the most perfect human love. Nature itself is ordained to it. From this fact crucial questions arise.

Can men and women who specifically exclude the possibility of marriage from their lives enter into friendships of masculine-feminine complementing love? To insure their celibate lives, must they avoid such relationships and the human fulfillment they offer? Many critics today, having observed celibates of both sexes who as religious have become human misfits or have even developed into emotional neurotics or psychotics, assert that consecrated celibacy, of itself devoid of human love, is a sterile, unhealthy state of life. Is this claim scientifically verifiable? Several authorities in psychology have confronted these questions, acutely aware of the possible dangers. Lepp expresses their common judgment that capable celibates can avoid the pitfalls and therefore enjoy the benefits of masculine-feminine friendship:

> Friendship between two persons of the opposite sex presents more of a problem. The majority of moralists and even certain psychologists believe they are suspect, and some of them maintain that such a friendship is radically impossible. This is not my own conviction. Quite the contrary. Whatever the unquestionable difficulties attendant upon it, friendship between a man and a woman frequently is existentially very fruitful. Numerous famous pairs of friends have furnished proof of this fact . . . not all of whom were saints.

Anna Terruwe voices this same conviction in regard to priests:

> It belongs to the perfection of human existence to experience love in friendship, as the perfect man, Jesus Christ, demonstrated in his love for his friends Lazarus, Mary and Martha. Nor does a difference of sex constitute any barrier in this love of friendship: all that is required is purity in the priest who loves and in the woman to whom he gives his love and who responds to it. If their love falls short of that genuine love of benevolence, there is always the danger that the desire proper to sexuality will gain the upper hand, to the detriment of love itself. This danger is one to which priests who are not sexually mature and well balanced are bound to be exposed, for they are incapable of an integral love for a person of the opposite sex, being still too concentrated emotionally on themselves. Herein lies the danger for so many priests who have remained underdeveloped emotionally; they are not yet capable of those manifestations of tenderness in which there is no self-seeking; their emotional drives demand release in sexuality. But for those who are capable of disinterested love and self-restraint without sexual tension, the love in such a friendship will enhance the warmth and spontaneity of their functional love in the ministry.

33

An additional important quality of mature complementing love is that the man and the woman share with each other in ways not detrimental to their life commitments, but according to the values and structures of their ways of life.

Finally, psychologists affirm that for mature celibates the risks involved in masculine-feminine friendship are worth taking because of the immense richness each gains from the other in psychological, intellectual, and spiritual ways. The mutual enrichment ranges from tenderness, strength, and support to maturity's joys of self-knowledge and control.

INTERPERSONAL WHOLENESS

Contemporary psychology identifies and characterizes several types of interpersonal love. Although employing a variety of terminology, the authors selected agree on essentials. Terms from among them that best describe the reality in question will be used.

The love required by children from their parents or parent substitutes to become adequate persons can be called *affirming love*.[8] The term indicates an experience of being lovingly accepted and appreciated by father and mother in such a way that the child is made basically sound and can continue to function emotionally and willfully as a contented person throughout his life.

Love between two adequate adults can be called *fulfilling love*: a "two-way interpersonal relationship in which both persons, through exchange of genuine affection, give something of self to each other. It is marked by a genuine concern of each person for the true welfare of the other. While such mutual love is most considerate of the real needs of both persons, it is not motivated by the needs of either person." One who experiences such love is in "possession of personal fulfillment" and lives a growingly meaningful, happy, and creative life.

Fulfilling love knows various degrees; the noblest is that of human *friendship*.

> Friendship is the term used only for mutually fulfilling love at its best which has been tested and proved authentic over a period of time. There is always a recognized equality in friendship in the sense that both persons feel they can communicate as equals. Since friendship is characterized by giving rather than getting, neither person can be motivated by desires for personal fulfillment or by any other kind of self seeking.

34

In its least degree, fulfilling love is not friendship, but a unilateral love which increases the personal adequacy only of the person who offers it. Such love is called *salvific*. At this bare minimum fulfilling love need not be reciprocal, for an adequate person can add to his personal fulfillment through loving a psychologically "empty" person from whom he receives no response to his love. A teacher's relationship to a withdrawn pupil is of this sort, or the married man's to a nagging female, the woman's to an alcoholic male. "An adequate person can have salvific love for a person of either sex in the sense that his first concern in the relationship is to save the other person from some kind of hurt."

Between these two extremes fall a number of human relationships, including the *functional love* alluded to earlier, whereby one person fulfills a professional or "helping task" toward another by virtue of not only will power, but also feelings of kindness and affection. Though such a helping person may receive in return various forms of love based on gratitude, this bilateral relationship falls short of the equal exchange of selves that is true of friendship.

With regard to fulfilling love, two possible problems suggest themselves concerning the training of young men and women for living and working together in adult life. Imprudence in either direction invites danger. The first difficulty lies in the frequent assumption that if young people of both sexes are put together often enough they will develop the capacity for healthy, interpersonal relationships. This is psychologically untenable. A reasonable amount of wholesome contact is most helpful, but only on condition that in their training personal adequacy be stressed as an essential prerequisite for fulfilling love. If, individually, young men and women are taught to assume the responsibility for becoming adequate *as persons*, they will respect each other as such. They will have the strength of will as well as the warmth of feeling to honor this respect in their behavior. A reverent regard and appreciation for themselves and for each other as mature persons is the starting point for developing authentic, fulfilling relationships between men and woman.

A second current assumption is equally without justification, namely, that as necessary preparation for genuine love relationships as adults, young men and women must become deeply, even erotically involved with one another. Psychological studies of such involvements show that in fact a majority of these young people eventually become repulsive to each other. They may also experience deep-seated feelings

35

of guilt that reduce their capability for genuine love relationships later on in life.

While fulfilling love is adequate for human life and may enrich it to the level of friendship, even that between a man and a woman, *complementing love* has even more potential for personal wholeness and happiness. It is unique.

> *Complementing love* comprises all the expressions of genuine *fulfilling love* for a member of the opposite sex, including consideration, understanding, kindness, forgiveness and the other expressions [of friendship]. . . . To these expressions *complementing love adds the wholly free, mutual exchange of the communicable entirety of one's self, made in deep love between an adequate man and an adequate woman.*

This closer union of two persons in complementing love has extraordinary effects on the individual life of each partner. Their new "oneness of psychologically shared being" increases the potential for and the inclination to creativity in both the man and the woman. A surprising store of creative energy results. When needed, both persons find they can bring an almost tireless strength to their creative endeavors — in each, a combined strength.

The woman functions "in immediate possession of her potential," which can be so fully actualized only by the complementing love of the man. In addition, she draws from his masculine strength shared with her through their love. Similarly, the man experiences an urgency to become more fully what he can be and to express this better self creatively. He draws from her fidelity and sense of personal dedication.

For the inevitable hurts and disappointments of life, the man and woman find in each other a mutual support gained from sharing and understanding. Each shared event deepens their relationship; indeed, complementing love attains its greatest depth only when some severe challenge has been undergone together.

True personal communication is continuously experienced. Both the man and the woman have an ŭnrestricted trust that allows them freedom to discuss any subject. When correcting one another, the atmosphere is never threatening. It often includes humor, and always sincere gratitude for this outside, more objective help. Through such ongoing, open, and honest communication, continuous, authentic development takes place:

The man and the woman in complementing love constantly manifest their realness to each other through the consistent pattern of their overall behavior. In the man there is a constancy permeating his entire conduct which shows forth in his loyalty, trust, understanding, gentleness, strength, protection, considerateness and proper expressions of affection. The pervading honesty of his complementing love is evident in his most dependable constancy of behavior and is a continuing source of happiness and security for the woman. She is thus enabled to grow more fully as a person.

The woman in complementing love is the consistent, genuine person whose actions and reactions, once she is known, can be predicted regardless of how she happens to feel at the time. She is honest even in the mistakes she makes. In her also is a selflessness which is in reality a by-product of her genuine concern and real care for other persons. In the honesty of her love, the woman shares the relationship with the man in the matter of its overall enrichment.

But there is also an apparent contradiction among the effects of complementing love. Doesn't each person's complete freedom in sharing himself with the other bring about the end of freedom? By reason of its nature, "It is psychologically necessary . . . that complementing love as such be exclusive. This means that the complete gift of self to the person of the opposite sex which is essential to complementing love excludes such a gift by either person to a third party." This exclusive "possession" of the other is not by way of right or force, however, but by way of free gift. There is, then, no contradiction:

This exclusiveness of possession in complementing love — a kind of love shared with only one person of the opposite sex — in reality opens and further frees both persons to love many other persons with either mutually fulfilling or salvific love. Moreover, the exclusive possession of the other person proper to complementing love flows out of the mutual gift of self, and so has nothing whatever in common with the clinging, restricting possessiveness so manifest in the neurotic.

The very reason for such exclusiveness is that "each . . . increasingly understands that a person is capable of only one complementing love in his life precisely because he sees it as totally filling his capacity for such love." For this reason it follows that complementing love must also be forever.

Since complementing love tends to a complete union of persons, it will eventually arouse, most probably, biological urges to physical union — this because of the relationship that may occur between affective and sexual energy. In psychological terms, both are forms of *libido*, a general psychic energy generated by love. Libido "is absolutely undifferentiated in itself. . . . It acquires a determinate coloring only from the end toward which it is being employed. The same psychic energy nourishes erotic love, . . . filial, paternal and fraternal love, the love of science, of art, of philosophy, friendship, and even the mystical love of God."[9] Consequently, any love stimulus arouses a powerful psychic energy in the human being. That it lead inevitably to sexual union between a man and a woman, however, does not follow. Psychologists have isolated two types or qualities of love sufficient to enable the celibate man and woman to meet the practical difficulties of maintaining a complementing love along with perfect chastity: *sublimating* and *self-restraining love*.

Ability to develop sublimating love depends upon the prior attainment of a certain solid foundation:

> When a woman and a man perceive the dawn of a friendship between themselves, they should know in advance that normally spiritual intimacy will sooner or later lead them to desire physical intimacy as well. . . . If the two friends have valid motives of either an objective or a subjective nature for forbidding themselves in a definitive and radical way any sexual love, it should not necessarily be concluded that it is imperative for them to renounce their friendship. . . . Its realization is possible on condition that they are conscious of the necessity of sublimating the physical. They must sincerely desire this sublimation and have strength enough to undertake it.

The foundation for achieving sublimation, then, is a *sufficient motive*, indicating a person's ability to channel the undifferentiated emotional energy of libido that follows upon any experience of love. Once aroused by whatever object of love, a person capable of sublimation can, for a sufficient motive, direct that energy to some more lofty object. He can love art, an ideal, his country, humanity, or God more intensely by making use of the psychic energy generated in a friendship. "Psychoanalysis calls such forms of preferential (if not exclusive) love for realities of a sublime character *sublimated love*."

Not everyone has equal capacity for sublimation. Each person has a unique degree of freedom in directing emotional energy where he will, and so no general judgment can be made that applies to all men. In fact, *two* freedoms contribute to the individual's ability in practice, man's and God's. How heavily man depends for his success upon the degree of talent or genius he possesses! And yet, it is "permissible for the man of faith to believe that, in addition to talent and genius, the grace of God can act to direct affective energy toward the heights, putting it at the disposal, for example, of mystical experience."

Because of the practical possibility of sublimation, there can be no question of condemning consecrated celibacy as such in the name of psychology. "It is simply a matter of pointing out, on the basis of experience, the fact that in normally constituted human beings the *libido* cannot be channeled in a different direction without injury to sexuality unless it finds itself entirely consumed in the service of higher psychic activity." Only those people who are capable of spending a lifetime in spiritual activity — their *sufficient motive* — can hope to live consecrated chastity without developing psychological problems.

Ignace Lepp notes that in the lives of certain saints such a continuing sublimation was accomplished in the context of complementing love. But even in the case of more ordinary men and women, he has found good chances for successful sublimation provided there is freedom from neurosis. His judgment is based on scientific observation:

> I personally know a number of friendships between men and women who are not by any means great mystics or perhaps not mystics at all in any sense of the word. Yet frequently they have succeeded in experiencing a very genuine existential communion in which Eros plays perhaps the same discreet role it plays in the friendship of the saints, but where the sexual in the strict sense of the word has been completely banished.

Terruwe and others come to the same scientific conclusion, although in addition to the requirement that such a man and woman have the "so-called higher values as clearly primary . . . they must have attained to a great degree of affective maturity and to an experiential knowledge of themselves."

Some have denied that this triple foundation of adherence to higher values, emotional maturity, and self-knowledge are sufficient to accomplish actual sublimation. They maintain that even the attempt is unnatural, and so unhealthy. Terruwe confronts this disputed point in her discussion of whether or not sublimated love is psychologically wholesome:

Won't its exercise cause a repression of emotion and hence bring about an unnatural psychic condition? The answer to this question is quite simple. . . . Man's emotional life possesses a natural predisposition for the guidance of reason. As a result, the direction of reason is both natural and feasible. Reason cannot bring about psychologically harmful attitudes in one's emotional constitution.

Human reason's control of emotional experience in order to sublimate it is clearly not by way of repression, but by a willed withholding of expression, if this is what reason sees as appropriate. It is possible, for example, that the object of a person's love is good for him emotionally, but not in other respects. Think of a priest's visiting a woman with whom he is beginning to enjoy a complementing friendship on an occasion when he experiences sexual attraction to her. Both for himself and for her it is inappropriate to show his feelings in a sexual way; determinate circumstances simply require him to refrain from such sensory satisfaction. A truly human response, at the very least, is called for. Through the control of reason and will, he displays his love in the more spiritual fashion of self-restraint.

This quality or type of love called *self-restraining* allows for sublimation. In no way is it negative. "Self-restraint does not mean that I withhold something because I don't want to give it away. It is more a question of not giving in order to avoid the harmful consequences of excess or superfluity."

Each new situation that calls for sublimation by way of self-restraining love will require development in a person's reasonable control of his emotional life. At the beginning especially, a person might doubt that this positive control can occur. But to direct the emotions reasonably is a matter of growth, requiring time and enlightened, consistent effort. Given these, a basically mature person can be confident that he will eventually develop his ability for self-restraining, sublimated love.

Since self-restraining love for a sufficient motive is the psychological key to sublimation and hence to mixed celibate friendship, especially that of complementing love, it follows that this quality of love in both the man and the woman is an index of the authenticity and quality of their relationship. Terruwe discusses two possible levels of self-restraint:

When a person refrains from displaying his feelings of love because this display would not be good for the other, he is acting out of a higher, spiritual love on the basis of which he sacrifices the natural

40

desire of his own love to the benefit of the other person. For the other's good he restrains the most ardent desire of his own emotion. It is further conceivable that a display of his affection would be good for the other person emotionally, if not from the standpoint of reason, and that he or she even desires such a manifestation of love. In that case self-restraint will represent an even greater act of love for that very reason. Anyone with experience realizes that the fullness of love consists not in the abundance of the love offered but in its adequacy for the needs of the recipient. Indeed the criterion of true love is that it is proffered in the manner and in the measure suitable for the loved one. It is for this reason that human love demands an integral practice of self-restraint.

Inability to achieve self-restraining love and sublimation is not the only reason making an attempt at complementing love inadvisable. Experience indicates that when the man and the woman have unequal life commitments, it is unlikely that they can sustain complementing love, even though they are individually mature. Complementing love naturally tends toward marriage, and so where one person is free to marry, and the other is vowed to celibacy, the non-celibate party almost inevitably comes to experience the relationship as unfair. Should one person be married and the other celibate, the relationship proves unjust to the married party's spouse "because of the exclusiveness of the personal commitment made in the marriage vows, regardless of the presence or absence of love in that marriage."

Anna Terruwe elaborates on the joy that self-restraint motivated by Christian love can bring to the lives of priests. She asserts that the joy is much deeper and more genuine than nearly any other he experiences. It is primarily spiritual, since the love that engenders it is primarily spiritual. But if the priest's emotional life is wholesomely developed, his experience will also include proper emotional overtones. To the joy of Christian love will be added fulfillment of deep, human longings. Happiness of spirit will radiate throughout emotions that are tranquil and docile. Such integration can make for lifelong contentment in the priest who has given himself unreservedly to the Lord and to divine-human love in its totality.

But such joy and such love are not possible for every priest:

A priest who is not fully matured emotionally and spiritually has no business entering into such a friendship with a woman. For without the possession of a pure generous human love there is always a danger that the selfish desire which is peculiar to the sexual feeling will take the upper hand and thus harm the relationship. But a priest who does possess this pure generous human love and who therefore is able to experience this love for a woman without sexual tension, will develop an even warmer and more spontaneous functional love as the result of this personal friendship to the benefit of countless others.

That some priests are not emotionally mature is not the responsibility of dedicated celibacy as such. Lack of healthy parental influence during childhood and/or defective seminary formation in the whole area of emotional life more truthfully bear the blame.

Given the proper background and formative setting, a celibate can mature more quickly in the area of love than his married counterpart. Both have the problem of integrating a strong, fundamental drive. Both must learn to give themselves to another and to overcome selfishness. In a word, both must acquire the love of restraint. They can succeed in achieving this stage of maturity through a personal relationship with a woman, with Christ and his Church, or with both: "Whether one or the other course is for the individual man the most practical means depends entirely on his personality and vocation."

That married men have the same difficulty as celibates — even more — in attaining the maturity of self-restraining love is lucidly explained by Conrad Baars. At the outset both men must possess the qualities of affective and volitional maturity, self-knowledge, and dedication to a life ideal. For the celibate, his seminary environment

> . . . as determined by the rules, the personalities of the professors and their attitude toward love, sexuality and friendship; in short the seminary's capacity of representing the loved and loving other . . . must be such that he is not forced to repress and distort his emotional life but is invited and encouraged to unfold all the aspects of his being in a wholesome, integrated manner, not just one at the expense of the other.

Under such circumstances of training and later under similar ones in his living and apostolic setting, the celibate can successfully confront his lack of sexual gratification with his chosen priestly ideal. He will know inner struggles, especially in the thirties and forties when most men's drives and desires are the strongest. In these struggles the celibate must not minimize his sacrifice nor think of the renounced genital sexuality as something inferior to human dignity in a neurotic attempt to make the sacrifice more bearable. The challenge of facing human sexual and affective love and developing the love of restraint on the one hand, and the greater challenge of trying to fulfill his priestly ideal on the other, furnish the combined forces that can result in a relatively quicker, deeper maturity of emotional life with its accompanying joy. The married man, whose life is less demanding and less risky in some respects, for these very reasons normally requires more time to reach full maturity. Baars concludes:

> Viewed in this light, the celibate life is an inner anticipation of a mental attitude which ordinarily does not develop until a much later stage in life. . . . Of course, God's grace is an absolute necessity in this process of anticipation of a maturity which ordinarily is attained only by way of a gradual psychological process. But as God certainly intends nature and grace to complement each other, and nature matures in the redeeming action of grace, it would be incorrect to claim that this process of anticipating maturity in response to God's calling is psychologically unsound.

COMPLEMENTING LOVE AND CHRISTIAN LOVE

Catholic psychologists, integrating science with faith, have clinically studied the relationship of complementing love, facilitated by restraining and sublimating love, to the love that is called Christian.

With reference to the divine object of Christian love, God himself, Baars adds to his findings about love for God being emotionally enhanced by any genuine human friendship. He asserts that in the priest capable of experiencing complementing love, a *feeling of love* will join his spiritual love for God. Being fully capable of real human love, his spiritual love will "penetrate the rest of his being," and so take on affective qualities. This is also relatively true of priests emotionally enriched through friendships of fulfilling love with both men and women, but it is not true of priests who lack such potential. They simply cannot fully possess real human love for God.[10]

Friends can not only love God more richly, but through complementing love, the man and woman can learn each other's unique way of approaching God, and so broaden and deepen their love. To clarify, the utilitarian desire to accomplish something by one's own effort is generally stronger in the psychic constitution of a man than a woman. Conversely, the element of feeling is generally more dominant in the

43

woman. These subjective, psychic dispositions influence the unfolding of love, whether human or divine. A look at the difference between active and contemplative religious life illustrates the point. In the latter, religious strive for loving, restful awareness in the beloved: Christ and the Triune God. But prerequisite to such transcendent serenity is the ability to experience tranquil love on the natural level without being disturbed by the desire to accomplish something. No wonder, then, that women can apparently live a contemplative lifestyle more easily than men.

Complementing love also allows both the man and the woman to see better the different "faces" of God: the "masculine" attributes, such as strength, justice, consistency, fatherhood; and the "feminine": tenderness, mercy, personalness, motherhood, etc.

In complementing love a man and woman approach the heart of the mystery of the human person. They communicate and reveal their personhood to each other as fully as possible. For this reason complementing love can have a unique relationship to Christian love:

> For some Christians, the complementing love of the man and the woman — two human persons — represents in finite form the love of the Divine Persons. As such, complementing love is seen by these people as the most perfect human reflection of the infinite love of the triune God in whom there is oneness of being and multiplicity of persons.

> Both the man and the woman in complementing love find that what each knows and wants becomes increasingly identified with what the other knows and wants. More and more they come to realize that they are somehow really one in psychological being — in understanding and wanting. Hence, for the man and the woman who are Christians, it is here that complementing love most closely approximates Divine Love, with which it is necessarily associated.

Complementing friends can expect a favorable dynamic between their mutual love and their love for God:

> In effect, their complementing love for each other increases their fulfilling love for God, and this fulfilling love for God in its turn deepens their complementing love for each other. Indeed, it is impossible that in complementing love the man or the woman would in any way come between the other person and his love for God.

In this context Evoy and O'Keefe are particularly insistent that "a person's love for God ought to be his primary fulfilling love." This holds true whether he be a consecrated celibate or a Christian in secular life and whether the God-man and/or other of the three Divine Persons be the object of his love.

So closely associated is each person's fulfilling love for God and complementing love for the other that when the man and the woman have no love for God or something they consider Ultimate, it is doubtful that they have authentic complementing love for each other. The conjunction of these two loves is so inter-influential that when there is authentic complementing love the fulfilling love of both persons for God continues to grow.

One who has experienced either human friendships or complementing love can love all other men better in Christian charity. Terruwe underlines the truth that Christ's love was not just spiritual. Because ordinary human love — perfect in his case — it was richly emotional, too. She notes that the Hebrew mind, evidenced abundantly in the Old Testament, but also in the gospels and the letters of St. Paul, did not make the distinction between spiritual and sensory love typical of modern psychology. Biblical man knew intuitively that human love finds expression at various psychic levels, all intersubordinated and functioning in unison as a truly human activity. This unity of love must characterize the love of Christ in any Christian, particularly the priest or religious whose very life should radiate his love. She is convinced that only through such full Christian love will nonbelievers be led to Christ.

Terruwe's opinion could be interpreted as a call for undue emotionalism in religion. It might be helpful, therefore, to realize that psychologists themselves make the distinction between genuine and false religious emotion:

> Only a depth psychologist who is familiar with religious matters is in a position to distinguish without any difficulty between true and false mystics. . . . Just because the lucubrations of hysterics clearly proceed from repressed sexual *libido*, there is no reason at all for us to conclude that Teresa of Avila, Angela of Foligno, Henry Suso and John of the Cross were similarly projecting their frustrated sexual desires toward God and the Blessed Virgin.

Although there are today many unbalanced people who find it difficult, if not impossible, to tell the difference between their inappropriate emotional love and their authentic love of God, Ignace Lepp finds little confusion among people who have acquired sublimating love in the context of a complementing friendship.

CONCLUSIONS

The purpose of this chapter has been to determine the relationship of experience and reason to the scriptural possibility for growth in Christian love through mixed celibate friendship. Psychologists who have studied this relationship empirically and scientifically, agree that such friendship is possible and desirable, given certain conditions.

Both the celibate man and woman must be "sufficiently mature." They must, in the first place, have had the type of background which has allowed them to become "adequate persons," adults capable of satisfying, interpersonal, emotional and volitional love, including friendship with members of their own or the opposite sex. They must further possess enough self-knowledge and strength of will to be capable of self-restraining and sublimating love to the point of maintaining generosity in a fulfilling or complementing friendship. Finally, their religious vocation must give both of them a sufficient self-ideal and motive for putting these capabilities into practice.

These minimum requirements for successful friendship alone allow celibate men and women to run the obvious risks of personal, masculine-feminine intimacy, because they alone make them aware of and able to cope with its dangers. For the mature, spiritual man and woman, there is no proximate or necessary danger to chastity. For celibates incapable of the indispensable requirement of human maturity, a close relationship with a person of the opposite sex is most imprudent. Ideals notwithstanding, they do not have the internal capabilities of surviving its inevitable dangers.

Mixed celibate friendship is desirable for two reasons. In the first place, it allows men and women, already sufficiently mature, to develop many other dimensions of their human potential, some of which normally blossom only through relationships with persons of the opposite sex. Through each other, their own individualities are authentically actualized, and by the complementing richness of the other, each friend attains psychic and spiritual "fullness of humanity." As a consequence, these enriched persons are more capable of loving God and all men with genuine human love. Their Christian love expressed in

46

prayer and apostolic work is alive with the superabundance they have gained from their relationship.

For the acquiring of natural maturity, psychology does not require a friendship of either fulfilling or complementing love. On the contrary, natural maturity is a prerequisite for such friendships. Similarly, in regard to holiness or supernatural maturity in the life of grace, a fulfilling or complementing friendship with a person of the opposite sex is in no way necessary. Holiness is directly measured by the degree of divine love residing in the human will. The human will conformed to the divine will is the necessary requisite for holiness. Innumerable saints have achieved this conformation of will in spite of emotional immaturity inherited from an unfortunate human background. They often did this in and partly through great suffering caused by their arrested or distorted affective life. Christian love is above all an infused gift from God, who is not bound to bestow his supernatural gifts in direct proportion to the human disposition of the recipient. His general supernatural law, whereby grace works through nature, respects the human disposition, but, should he choose, God can heal an unhealthy disposition in such a way as to raise a particular person to great sanctity.

The school of psychology cited does not claim that mixed friendship is necessary for either natural or supernatural maturity. It does hold that, given sufficient human wholesomeness, such friendship can bring about further human development, which in turn can improve each friend's cooperation with grace in loving God and neighbor.[11]

3

TWO-IN-ONE

"That they may be one . . ."

Psychology is rich but limited. At best it can offer human insights and norms. Only personal history can furnish living proof of the concrete integration of celibate love that helps men and women expand in divine love of God and neighbor. And so we turn to men and women recognized for their holiness, and trace from biographies or original writings the workings of fulfilling, and especially complementing love in their lives.[1]

ST. DOMINIC

Is it strange to begin with St. Dominic, so little known today, and even where known often popularly misrepresented as a stern and exacting inquisitorial figure? The facts are that St. Dominic had nothing directly to do with the minor inquisition of his day, nor, of course, with those history records as occurring years and centuries later.[2] He was official chaplain and friend to Count Simon de Montfort, who headed the Toulousain crusade for the faith. Accordingly, Dominic was present during the battles de Montfort fought, though characteristically "the first warred by prayer, the other by arms." The struggle developed strong, political overtones, such that the very experience convinced Dominic that a way other than force of arms and secular power was needed for the conversion of unbelievers. His view, singular for the times, sprang from a spirit of friendliness native to him.

49

A rich historical witness of the personal side of Dominic's life is his canonization process containing more than three hundred testimonies of those who knew him during his apostolic years. These testimonies, together with the *Lives of the Brethren*, a nearly contemporary biography, and a few other documents are the principal sources for subsequent lives of the saint.

Although we have no record of a complementing friendship in St. Dominic's life, there is abundant evidence of friendships cherished both by men and women which reveal how loving his character was. History further testifies that he intentionally established his religious Order along lines of masculine-feminine complementarity to promote the twofold cause of personal sanctification and the spread of sacred truth. In their own ways, yet together, men and women of the Order were to achieve their dual goal through cooperative contemplation, penance, and preaching. This characteristic of the Dominican Order properly reflects something of its founder and encouraged complementing friendships favoring the growth of divine love both among those whom Dominic himself knew well and those who followed him. Such were the friendships of the Blesseds Jordan of Saxony and Diana d'Andalo, and St. Catherine of Siena and Blessed Raymond of Capua.

Born in 1170 in Caleruega, Spain, St. Dominic possessed the ardent nature of his kinsmen. His personal vitality seemed "to energize" those with whom he spoke, moving them "to put forth their very finest efforts."[3] As his later, incessant travels across Europe show, he had a superb physical constitution, though his frequent austerities made him subject to sickness. Through discipline he had tempered his natural disposition. "He sought always for freedom of soul, to control the flaming Spanish temperament, to hold its fervour carefully in subjection, to be unhampered and unafraid." Consistent training had liberated his deep emotions and gave him a "quick sympathy, ready generosity, and joyousness of heart — in consequence, [he was] an ideal friend and confidant." His close friend and first biographer, Jordan of Saxony, speaks of the lifelong mixture of charm and reserve that held men's hearts. In the words of Bede Jarrett: "God's greatest gift to man in the order of nature, and almost the greatest even on the supernatural plane, is the gift of making and securing friends; and judged by this, Dominic was indeed blessed by God."

Perhaps no one had a greater taste for fraternity than Dominic. One canonization witness stated concerning the ten years of his ministry in reaction to Albigensianism throughout the dioceses of Toulouse and Concerans, that it was "public knowledge . . . that wherever Dominic traveled, he stayed among religious and clerics and lay people of both sexes." Later, whether among his own brethren, pilgrims or travelers on the road, the crowds he preached to, or the communities he taught, all experienced him relaxed and friendly. "Everyone was drawn by his openness, directness, and simplicity."

His closeness to his own brothers in religion is attested to by Castiglio, who was present at his death. The brethren "had reason to mourn at the loss of their father, pastor, friend, given them by God. He had been their refuge in trouble, their resource, ever ready to console with words of counsel or compassion." Dominic enjoyed friendships of varying degrees with his followers and, like his Lord, chose from among them a "beloved disciple," John of Navarre.

Dominic always maintained a personal bond with the sisters he founded. To the first group at Prouille he styled himself "Brother Dominic, Prior of Prouille," and as such undertook their spiritual and temporal care for several years. To his second group at San Sisto in Rome, he returned nightly for instruction, which "after he had ended a busy day of preaching and working in the city, bears witness to his abiding concern for his daughters." To these same women, his "dear nuns," he carried from Spain in 1219 across half of Europe little carved spoons of cypress wood as mementos. One of these nuns, later the Blessed Cecilia, left us a valuable record of Dominic's Roman ministry. She relates that during his visits he either "exhorted them to greater spiritual effort or merely sat among them, refreshing them with the charm of his conversation and sharing with them the experiences of the day."

St. Dominic's range of friends outside the Order was extensive. The *Lives of the Brethren* records his meeting and friendship with St. Francis. "They became but one heart and one soul in God and enjoined their sons to foster this brotherly spirit until the end of time." Among his many ecclesiastical friends were his own bishop Diego of Osma, Bishop Foulques of Toulouse, the Norbertine Abbots John and Navarre d'Acqs, and Popes Honorius III and Innocent III. Cardinal Ugolino, who as Gregory IX canonized Dominic in 1234, was also his longtime friend. The Bull of canonization itself affirms the pope's intimate knowledge of Dominic,

> . . . bound to us by ties of deep friendship, before we were raised to the Pontificate; his life carried with it in our eyes certain proofs of

heroic holiness. . . . We are convinced, as also are our people, that through his prayers God may do us mercy, and that one who was our friend on earth will still in heaven hold us in no less affection. Wherefore . . . we have determined to add his name to the number of the saints.

Such testimonies reveal a character anything but harsh and forbidding. They demonstrate that Dominic possessed the affective and volitional maturity that contemporary psychology demands of an adequate personality, one capable of fulfilling love with persons of both sexes.

The earliest recorded instances of friendships with particular women occur during his apostolic years in southern France. He would stop to eat and sleep "in the houses of friends," and the "devout women of Toulouse did all they could to ease and comfort his busy life. . . ."[4] At his canonization process three of these women told of their personal relationships with Dominic.

"Willelma, the wife of Elias Martin, was one of these young women whose hospitality was always given him." She said that "she had known Dominic very well. She had made hairshirts for him and fed him more than two hundred times during those years in France," though she "had never got him to eat more than a quarter of a dried fish for dinner or at most two eggs, and his wine was always two-thirds watered." Dominic was often exhausted and sick when he arrived at her house. She would put him to bed, but whenever she returned she found him lying on the floor. "Though she saw that he needed someone to take care of him," he simply didn't have the habit of sleeping in beds, and "so there was little she could do to help him." It was her conviction — and she swore to it — that Dominic was always a virgin.

Noguenza confirmed what Willelma had sworn. She, too, had sewn hairshirts for him and believed him always to have been a virgin.

Another young woman who befriended him later became Sister Beceda of the Holy Cross. . . . More than two hundred times he had [also] dined with her, and she had never got him to take more than a couple of eggs. . . . She [too] had found him asleep on the floor of her house several times, and had always had to cover him up with a cloak. . . . She certainly took every care of him that she could, and as he was nearly always dead-tired when he came to her, she found little difficulty in managing to get him to do what she wanted.

52

Beceda testified that "she had a great solicitude for him. . . . She had lived much in his intimacy," but had never heard him speak a vain word. She had made hairshirts for him, and "she knew that Dominic was always a virgin."

One modern writer sees that "the solicitude of these three ladies for the holy man, the way they took care of him, demonstrated their love for him. He possessed a quality that won the confidence of women. They loved and trusted him."

A chronicler records that during his years at Fanjeaux "an intimate friendship bound St. Dominic to the Count Simon de Montfort and to his family, especially to his oldest daughter Amicia of Joigny and to his youngest, Petronilla," later to become a nun of Saint-Antoine in Paris. Amid all his activity in the Eternal City, "we [also] see him visiting, encouraging, and instructing the women recluses who at that time lived solitary lives in little cells built here and there into the city walls." Sister Cecilia has recorded these regular visits and two miracles he worked to relieve his friends' sufferings. By touching the diseased breast of a Sister Jacobina on one occasion and the gangrenous arm of Sister Lucy on another, each was healed at his leaving. Bologna affords "another occasion for the exercise of his particular gift of ministry to women." Young Diana d'Andalo had become "attached to the founder with all her affection and opened her soul to him." Her desire to become a Dominican nun had so impressed Dominic that, even against the prohibition of her noble family, he allowed her to consecrate her life to God through the vow of virginity, promising under obedience to enter the Order of Preachers as soon as a Dominican priory was established in Bologna. In the meantime, "while she was being restrained in her family castle, he sent her letters in secret," to encourage and console her. Unhappily, Dominic died before her family relented, leaving Diana plunged in affliction by his loss. Another of several women whom Dominic directed to the cloister is Béné, a prostitute, converted in 1220 to a life of penance, prayer, and Christian works of charity. After she had become Sister Benedicta, he continued to visit, comfort, and instruct her.

On his deathbed, while making his general confession to Father Ventura in the presence of several brethren, Dominic mentioned two things concerning his association with women. "Though God's grace has preserved me from all stain until this moment, I must admit that I have taken much more pleasure in conversation with young women than I have with old." Then, scrupling over his admission, he said later to Ventura, "Brother, I think I did wrong in speaking of my virginity aloud. It would have been wiser to be silent." And so, from Dominic himself we know that he especially enjoyed the company of women and that he had successfully integrated this pleasure with his consecration to God in chastity. Throughout the centuries, his sons and daughters have hailed this side of their founder's character in the liturgical hymn which closes Night Prayer. A recent commentary on the hymn speaks of the phrase in question:

> When men began to reconstruct Dominic's life they were struck by the fact that he enjoyed the company of women, especially of young women, and did so without ever sinning. Observers began to perceive how fine and noble and true a life he had led, and in the end expressed their admiration by calling him an *Ivory of Chastity*.

The foregoing documentation brings to light the features of a man who, in terms of contemporary psychology, was not only an adequate person capable of friendship with both sexes, but mature enough in self-restraining, sublimating love to have the rare freedom of close association with nearly everyone — an association of human friendship which led to growth in the love of God.

Another woman at the process of canonization, a certain Berengaria, relates the beginnings of the Dominican Order.[5] In 1206, soon after a miracle had confirmed his defense of the faith in a public dispute with Albigensian leaders, Dominic preached in the marketplace to "women who had lapsed from the faith or who had been born and educated heretics." Berengaria and eight others were converted and decided to approach him as he prayed in a neighboring church. They pressed him for further instruction. Perhaps it was at this time that having experienced their tireless interest, "loyalty, fortitude and selfless love," Dominic conceived of "an auxiliary of women to aid him in his campaign for the faith." In view of his own long and seemingly fruitless toil the "employment of converted women as envoys to the Albigensians" must have suggested itself as an answer to his problems. Praying over the possibility, Dominic was given three nights in succession a vision which convinced him that he must establish a convent of nuns in the abandoned church of St. Mary at Prouille.

As result, in 1207, he founded his first convent of women of which he was the prior, although he delegated "certain authority to a prioress appointed to govern in his name." He had one assistant, Brother William Claret, with whom he occupied an "adjoining shack." "It is clear that St. Dominic had founded not only a convent of nuns, but a priory also of his friars; he had . . . quite consciously established a 'double monastery,' where dwelt side by side the preachers and the nuns each with their separate establishment, yet joined in one common life." "They were, and are still, two branches issuing from the same trunk."

As a canon regular in Osma, Spain, Dominic was familiar with the "double monastery." It took great conviction, however, to found one in southern France under the very eyes of the censorious Albigensians whom he hoped to convert — and, even more, to found one from among their own women. Yet,

> wisely and patiently the saint was finding his way, trying one plan after another, till he had made trial of what would really better secure the purpose to be achieved and the due order of the communities which he established. All this is characteristic of him. No one saw more clearly than did he what was needed; and no one was quicker than he, once the best means were discovered, in getting the work done. He knew always what he wanted. . . . Thus it will be seen that St. Dominic established contemporaneously his Order for women and for men. . . . Prouille is the center of both.

The nuns were to pray and do penance; the friars were to preach: as Preachers and Preacheresses, they were to spread sacred truth together. Gerald Vann explains the complementarity envisaged:

> In St. Dominic's scheme, the friars were meant to be busy men, to undertake teaching or preaching in its various forms. . . . The practical difficulty is obvious: if they are to be so active how will they find the time to be contemplatives? The answer lies in the organic unity of the Church, Christ's Mystical Body: the light and the power necessary to supplement their own attempts — perhaps even, where necessary, to make good their failure — to be men of prayer should be provided for them by their religious sisters. As Adam needed and was given a helpmate like to himself, so — the analogy is Père Cormier's — the first Order needed and was given a helpmate to share its work and its life, and a helpmate like itself because stamped with the same family spirit, the spirit of Dominic. The convents would be the Order's centers of energy; at all costs therefore they must be provided.

Dominic established the feminine counterpart later wherever he had friars. "The nuns of Madrid, like those of Prouille, were known as Sisters Preachers, or Preacheresses. Other foundations made in Spain during this journey (1218) were at Segovia, Saragossa, and Palencia." He founded the convent of San Sisto in Rome in 1221, and hoped to do the same with Diana and her friends in Bologna when he died.

His successor as Master General of the Order, Jordan of Saxony, continued Dominic's pattern and averted an attempt during a General Chapter to free the friars from involvement with the rapidly increasing number of nuns by turning their convents over to the jurisdiction of the local bishops. He made it clear to these capitular fathers that they had not understood Dominic's plan of complementarity. Their effort "meant in effect abandoning [the nuns] and destroying the organic life of the Order as Dominic had envisaged it. Jordan, though deeply concerned for the teaching and preaching work of the friars, was against any such abandonment."

> Following the example, and with the blessing of their father, Dominicans have ever since maintained this ideal of unity. Brothers and sisters of the Order are united as in family life. The bond of union is centered in a devoted loyalty and love: loyalty to the quest for truth which their Father had entrusted to them and by which they must bring Christ to all mankind; and love for, and intimacy with St. Dominic himself, who, as an inspiring presence, lives amongst them. . . . 'Seven hundred years of trial have done nothing to break the unity of Dominic's family, because in every crisis which threatened to break them apart, they have remembered their Father and were one.'

BLESSEDS JORDAN OF SAXONY
AND DIANA D'ANDALO

> Historical documentation relative to the life of Blessed Jordan of Saxony not only lets us know the multiform works he accomplished but also allows us to enter intimately into his personality. . . . We owe this privilege largely to the important series of letters from him . . . they reveal to us the profound depths of their author's soul, his qualities and his character . . . the intensity and firmness of his religious faith, his detachment from earthly things and his heavenly aspirations, and his solid and deep affection which he felt for his spiritual daughters and his friends. Jordan of Saxony has left us the first collection in Christian Europe of letters of spiritual direction ad-

dressed to a woman — Blessed Diana d'Andalo. In this respect he marks an epoch.[6]

From this collection of thirty-seven letters we learn of a complementing friendship that helped two people arrive at sanctity. The characters of Jordan and Diana stand revealed in the correspondence, as well as the quality of their friendship and the help, natural and supernatural, it allowed them to be to each other.

Of all the early Friars Preachers, "Jordan most nearly resembles Dominic particularly in those gifts by which as a master he would have to hold the Order together." He had the same physical endurance for endless travel, the same personal vitality, and a similar austerity, "tempered with . . . Dominic's own joyousness." He was a man of "charm and tact, to whom, as to his master, friendship was the real support of life."

Jordan came from Westphalia. He was a student and then Master of Arts at the University of Paris, where he met St. Dominic. Soon after he entered the Order, Dominic appointed him the first prior provincial of Lombardy, and upon the founder's death a year later (1222), he was unanimously elected Master General. As head of the Order during its formative years until his own death in 1237, it was Jordan more than any other after St. Dominic who moulded the essential character of the Order of Preachers. The historian, Père Mortier, credits him with the founding of 240 priories and four provinces during his fifteen years of generalship. This phenomenal achievement was due in part to the idealistic, but also practical breadth of his character. "More perhaps still than Dominic, the Master of Arts . . . knew the world, the business of human life, the characters of men, their passions, their motives and their weaknesses." He understood how to gain the confidence of men in every station of life. He was counselor to the political and ecclesiastical powers of his day; at the same time the sought-out advisor of those of low class. As he himself said, he was able to "become all things to all men."

Master Jordan was "a ready and flaming preacher whose particular fortune it was to gather to him the younger members of whatever congregation he addressed." A chronicler states that no one recruited as many novices to any religious order from among the students and professors of medieval Europe as Jordan of Saxony. For this reason he was nicknamed by his contemporaries "The Siren of the Schools." His modern biographer surmises why:

57

The most intimate pages of *De Initiis Ordinis* and the letters to Diana still bring to us a certain human grace, tender, alive and lovable. Jordan has the gift, rare among intellectuals, of perfect naturalness which being without formality frees the sentiments and emotions. It was doubtless by his open-heartedness, no less than by the authority of his knowledge, that he remained even in his old age so close to young men, so beloved by them, and so truly their friend.

The style and content of his writings reveal the humanist, the man of culture, the theologian, the biblical scholar, and the wise director of souls. His evident poetic ability made his erudition "featherlight" and most appealing.

There is one adjective in particular which all who knew Jordan and wrote of him seem to regard as peculiarly fitting to his character so that it becomes indissolubly linked with his name: it is *dulcis*, gentle, sweet-mannered. He was a man of manifold gifts, but his sweetness and charm seemed to colour all his other gifts, and to be the secret of his amazing success in his work for souls.

Jordan had a wide range of friends. Besides being the confidant of innumerable students, his early biographers speak of him always as "so kind and gentle towards his own brethren." Pope Honorius was his "personal friend," as was the bishop of Paris and several princes. In short, Jordan was "beloved of God and man." His affection could be profound. This was the case for Henry, a student companion of his in Paris who had followed him into the Order. Upon his death, Jordan wrote to Diana: "Wherefore I have wept, and still sometimes now I weep. I weep for my most faithful companion, my sweetest friend, I weep for the brother who loved me so much, I weep for my dearest son, Henry, the Prior of Cologne."

In addition, Jordan had an extensive, personal apostolate with women. This was a feature of his continuous travels to his brethren throughout Europe. From Paris, for example, he writes to Diana that "the Queen," Blanche of Castile, had "talked with me personally and in private about her affairs." On a trip to the north, in Brabant, he became the spiritual director of the saintly and celebrated Flemish nun, Lutgarde. He corresponded with her and must have seen her at each passing thereafter, for the *Lives of the Brethren* says that "Father Jordan knew her well, and she was greatly devoted to him." At Trier he also directed sisters who were friends of the Order. One became especially close to him, "a certain Marie . . . learned, of a fine intelligence and delicate sensibilities." In his letters to Diana, Jordan nearly always asked to be remembered to his friends in the community or the city of Bologna: "Greet for me all those whom I love and who love me, especially those whom you know to be especially dear to me." These and other texts "throw a brief but intense light on the ministry of Jordan; his travels consisted not only of visiting priories and official preaching to students, but also in a more intimate apostolate to certain select souls, in particular religious women."

Jordan's was, without doubt, a talented and developed personality, certainly "adequate" in the judgment of empirical psychology, eminently fitting him for all forms of fulfilling love.

Of the childhood of Diana d'Andalo we know nothing.

> But we know a good deal about her as she was when she first came into contact with the friars (age 18). She was of outstanding beauty . . . says the contemporary chronicle, 'lovely of face and charming to behold.' . . . Her contemporaries also speak of her as eloquent and learned; and there is no doubt about her charm, her high spirits, her courage, and that faculty of making swift and sure decisions. . . . She was full of the joy of living.[7]

Another description discloses a young woman with "an active spirit, a vivid imagination, deep emotions, an ingenuous and sympathetic heart, and a will firm in the pursuit of all that is good, true and beautiful." In addition to these natural qualities, "like Dominic . . . Jordan also discerned in her the sovereign flame of the contemplative vocation, the thirst for a transforming union, for a life hidden in God and with God." Her spiritual purpose was so intense that Jordan often in later years had to restrain her eagerness for physical austerities.

All her life Diana cultivated friendships with both men and women. She was socially influential in Bologna, and from among her many friends a small group came with her to found the convent of St. Agnes. To these religious sisters, even when she was not the superior, she was, in the phrase of Père Cormier, the "heart of the community." Jordan refers to several of her friends among the friars. When he himself could not come, he sent Brother Bernard the German, "an old friend," to comfort her on one trying occasion. He would often send her messages from absent friars: "The brothers who are with me, Archangel and John, send you very affectionate greetings. Archangel is very sad that he did not see you before he left Bologna . . . he is very fond of you, so forgive him." In two letters, another friar added a postscript in his own hand: "Your brother Henry greets you very affectionately and sends you his deep sympathy in your sorrow." (Her favored blood brother, Brancaleone, had just been killed in a political skirmish.) "I, brother Henry, salute you Diana with all my heart."

In these few sources Diana stands clearly portrayed as a fully matured personality, one particularly capable of human friendships. It is not surprising, then, that her personal association with Jordan was deep and intimate. Indeed, the most thorough of their recent biographers thinks that their friendship was unique in history:

> Jordan's tenderness for Diana, Diana's affection for Jordan, is one of those rare flowers which Christian holiness alone can cause to grow from the depths of the human heart. The ancient world never dreamed of anything like it; and if the modern world has known the love of St. Francis of Assisi and St. Clare, that of St. Francis de Sales and St. Jane de Chantal, it can be said that in ardour and in closeness . . . the friendship of Jordan and Diana seems to have surpassed them.[8]

This relationship began when Jordan, the newly elected Master General, came to Bologna in 1222. Diana confided to him the dream of a convent of nuns she had shared with St. Dominic. Jordan "was able to inspire in her a renewal of confidence and hope, . . ." while at the same time constraining her ardent temperament which could tend to extremes. Soon, "she could not but give herself up to his prudent guidance. . . . From this moment Jordan became the director of Diana's conscience and her spiritual father."

Because of Jordan's constant travels, they could be together only rarely, and so they communicated by letter. This correspondence, lasting over a period of fifteen years, ended with their deaths. Both died within a few months; Diana, first, sometime in 1236. Jordan, it seems, never learned of her death. In February, 1237, he was shipwrecked and drowned on his way to Jerusalem. Today only Jordan's letters to Diana are extant; all of hers to him have disappeared. In themselves, however, Jordan's suffice as a dialogue. They "were obviously written without any thought for posterity. There is no 'literature' in them to alter their absolute sincerity. There is nothing in them except what came spontaneously from the tender soul of the father and friend." From the pervading "familiarity" and the simple use of the intimate "thou," "there is born an unplanned lyricism, a wonderful freshness, an indescribably deep vibration which, at seven centuries' distance, grips and moves us still."

Commentators have always remarked on the human intimacy these letters reveal. "Always there is the same underlying depth of feeling for her which the constantly recurring *carissima, carissima mea,* only serve to emphasize." In Jordan's heart, Diana had been "chosen above all others." On one occasion he even addresses his letter from "Brother Jordan . . . to his beloved bride and daughter in Jesus Christ, Diana." The letters show that from the day of their meeting, "they were never very far from each other's thoughts." Père Mortier notes how this abiding presence to one another touched their lives:

> With Diana his thoughts are incessantly occupied. Whether he is staying at Paris or at Padua, or trudging the roads of the world, the image of his beloved daughter follows him, haunts him, stirs him. If his efforts meet with success, if the students flock into the Order, if his preaching wins to it famous doctors, he writes to tell Diana. He tells her all: his joys and triumphs, his sorrows and disappointments; for he knows how keenly it will all interest her. Nor is it only of the things of the spirit that he tells her. This great man, so full of goodness of heart, descends to the minutest details of his life. He knows well enough how a woman's heart, however unworldly she may be, is made anxious by any suffering, physical or mental: it longs to know all that it may share all. If Jordan delays his letters, Diana is sad or indeed impatient, and often he has to restore her serenity and peace of soul by tender reproaches. His long, perilous journeys, his delicate health make Diana always frightened for him: at the least onslaught of fever her whole soul is troubled. She knows the Master's austerity with himself; she knows that fatigue never stops him; and all the time she is frightened for his life. So these letters, these wonderful letters that one cannot read without deep emotion, follow one another at every halting-place, to reassure her and console her.

Excerpts from the letters themselves will best show not only how abidingly present they were to each other, but also how real were other aspects of their love. Little comment will be needed, but in each case the supposed date will be given to facilitate tracing the development of their relationship over the years.

> (1227) Since it is not given to me, my beloved, to see you with my bodily eyes as often as you would wish and I would wish, nor to find

comfort in your presence, my heart finds some slight solace, and a tempering of its longing, when I can visit you by letter and tell you how things are with me; at the same time I would gladly hear more frequently how you are faring, for your progress in the way of the Lord and that of the other sisters is a joy to me.[9]

(1232) Yet, though I do not at the present time come in the flesh to visit you, still I am with you in spirit; for wheresoever I go I yet remain with you, and though in the flesh you remain behind, in the spirit, I carry you with me. . . . May the grace and the bondage of Christ Jesus be with your spirit, beloved to me for ever, Amen.

(1236) Beloved, since I cannot see you with my bodily eyes nor be consoled with your presence as often as you would wish and I would wish, it is at least some refreshment to me, some appeasement of my heart's longing, when I can visit you by means of my letters and tell you how things are with me, just as I long to know how things are with you, for your progress and your gaiety of heart are a sweet nourishment to my soul.

Jordan often speaks openly of their mutual anxiety and love:

(1225) I do not requite your love fully; of that I am deeply convinced: you love me more than I love you. But I cannot bear you to be so afflicted in body and distressed in mind by reason of this love of yours which is so precious to me: and I have indeed heard that you are too oppressed and troubled because of my illness. . . . But I am anxious about you . . . anxious to know what things are against you.

(1228) You are so deeply engraven on my heart that the more I realize how truly you love me from the depths of your soul, the more incapable I am of forgetting you and the more constantly you are in my thoughts; for your love of me moves me profoundly, and makes my love for you burn more strongly.

(1229) [One Christmas, after speaking to her about the Incarnate Word . . .] There is another word that I send you, small and brief: my love, which will speak for me to your love in your heart and will content it. May this word too be yours, and likewise dwell with you forever.

His last letter to her specially reveals the intensity of their affection:

(1236) Yet whatever we may write to each other matters little, beloved: within our hearts is the ardour of our love in the Lord whereby you speak to me and I to you continuously in those wordless outpourings of charity which no tongue can express nor letter contain.

O Diana, how unhappy this present condition of things which we must suffer: that we cannot love each other without pain and anxiety! You weep and are in bitter grief because it is not given you to see me continually; and I equally grieve that it is so rarely given to me to be with you. Who shall bring us into the strong city, into the city of the Lord of Hosts that the Highest himself has founded, where we shall no more have to long either for him or for one another?

Partings and the long separations always caused Jordan and Diana deep pain of heart:

(1229) Let it not be a heavy burden on you, beloved, that I cannot all the time be with you in the flesh, for in spirit I am always with you in love unalloyed. Yet I cannot wonder that you are sad when I am far from you since, do what I may, I myself cannot but be sad that you are far from me; but I console myself with the thought that this separation will not last forever: soon it will be over, soon we shall be able to see one another, endlessly, in the presence of God's Son Jesus Christ who is blessed for ever, Amen.

(1231) When I have to part from you I do so with a heavy heart; yet you add sorrow to my sorrow since I see you then so inconsolably weighed down that I cannot but be saddened not only by our separation which afflicts us both but also by your own desolation as well. Why are you thus anguished? Am I not yours, am I not with you: yours in labour, yours in rest; yours when I am with you, yours when I am far away; yours in prayer, yours in merit, yours too, as I hope, in the eternal reward?

(1235) The longer we are separated from one another, the greater becomes our desire to see one another again. Yet it is only by God's will that so far I have been prevented from coming to you.

Clearly theirs was the experience of unity peculiar to complementing love. In spirit they were two-in-one:

(1232) As I wish for strength and good health for myself, so do I for you, my beloved daughter, for my heart is one with your heart in the

Lord; rather, that part of myself which is yourself is by so much the better part that I would much prefer to suffer anything burdensome myself than allow it to fall upon you. . . . For the rest, be of good heart, for soon by God's grace I shall see you with my bodily eyes, you whom in spirit I never cease to see.

(1234) [Once, when Diana had injured herself, Jordan wrote:] Your poor foot, which I hear you have hurt, hurts me too; and makes me the more anxious that you should take more care not only of your foot but of your whole body.

These extracts demonstrate beyond doubt that Jordan's and Diana's love was human and complete, exhibiting the characteristics of complementing friendship. From their love, integrated with consecrated chastity and divine friendship, flowed mutual benefits both natural and supernatural.

In the first place, the help they gave each other was deeply human. Besides establishing and protecting her convent of St. Agnes and counseling her constantly concerning it and the community, Jordan sought especially to console and to encourage Diana.[10] Throughout his letters, he writes in similar vein:

(1223) Brother Jordan . . . to Diana, his beloved in Christ. . . . Be consoled therefore in the Lord, that I thereby may be consoled also, for your consolation is a joy and gladness to me before God.

(1226) But if the Lord is willing I shall come later on this year and then we shall see each other again and our hearts shall rejoice.

(1229) My Beloved, be in all things confident and gay; and what is lacking to you because I cannot be with you, make up for in the company of a better friend, your Bridegroom Jesus Christ whom you may have more constantly with you in spirit and in truth, and who speaks to you more sweetly and to better purpose, than Jordan.

(1231) Soon, if the Lord grant it, we shall be able to console one another.

On her part, besides willingly being at his disposal when he was in Bologna, "she had done her work . . . as the Diana of the letters: her love had given Jordan strength, comfort, joy through his many cares and troubles. It had done more: it had called forth from his own heart a flowering, a fullness of life, which helped to make his greatness, helped to make him what he was, what the Order needed, and God wanted him to be."

As he confided to her his work and concerns, Jordan received understanding and support from Diana; as he gently restrained her ascetical enthusiasm, she communicated to him her fervent belief in the mission of the Friars Preachers and his part in it.

Secondly, it is equally evident from the letters that they also helped each other in the realm of grace. For Jordan, Diana's convent "is the holy reservoir upon which he relies for his preaching; it will not be either his talent or his prestige, but the unremitting sacrifices and valiant faith of this handful of religious women that will bring down divine grace and win the victory." He entrusts himself to her prayer in view of his faults and when he himself cannot find time to pray. From his first to his last letter he seeks her intercession for his projects and her thanksgiving and praise to the Lord for his successes.

In agreeing to be her spiritual director, Jordan on his part "wished to help this soul, so exalted but at the same time so realistic . . . in all that she sought, to climb step by step the mystical mountain." And once he had become aware of her capacity to love, "it was that power of love, strengthened, deepened, hallowed by the divine life within her, that Jordan was most concerned to guard and to guide."

The fundamental spiritual direction he gave her was "to live in heaven." Diana is to live entirely turned toward Christ her Bridegroom. In nearly every letter — thirty-one times in all — he addresses her as the bride of Christ and often instructs her in the meaning of this beautiful title. She is to make her heavenly Spouse present to her by holy desire; in faith and in hope she is to seek the things that are above in the "abiding city"; in her weaknesses she is to find strength only in her Lord.

In his very first letter Jordan clearly set the tone:

(1222) Dearest sister, the longing of the patriarchs of old invited Christ, your Bridegroom, God's Son, to suffering: and he came. How then should he not come when your longing invites him to joy? Therefore let all your longing be fixed on heaven. . . . You, then, beloved, if you would learn the language of heaven must dwell in heaven by desire. . . .

Since the body must eat earthly food, lest it die . . . Do not then, beloved, be less concerned for the soul, but on the contrary send it forth sometimes to seek its food in the land of the spirit, that food which is not to be found in the earth and which is bought not with silver but with loving desire.

Who would be so foolish as to allow himself to die for lack of a food which he could have simply by desiring it? Say then with the psalmist: My eyes are ever towards the Lord.

Jordan's direction is:

. . . the pure doctrine of divine love, such as was expounded by the great doctor of the Church in the twelfth century, St. Bernard. . . . In his letter Jordan showed his daughter how to buy the supreme good, the sole necessity. He gave her the secret of union with God. He gave her, in this simple manner, which was above all concrete and alive, something of his own, the fruit of long and rich meditation. This teaching was of the clearest and most concise, most profound and most opportune, since they were then and for a long time separated from one another.

His constant theme thereafter was that Diana's eyes "should be ever towards the Lord." It occurs in his last letter. Speaking of the endless miseries they both had to suffer, he concludes: "these things we must bear with patience and, so far as our daily work allows, dwell in mind and heart with Him."(1236)

In regard to their own relationship, the essential and principal thing for Jordan is the love of God:

There is never any uncertainty in these letters as to who must come first in Diana's heart. It is not Jordan himself, it is that 'better friend.' . . . The love of God comes first for both of them, though it brings them the sorrow of separation and of constant anxiety for each other. But at the same time it is precisely their shared love of God which binds them so closely together: 'He is the bond whereby we are bound together: in him my spirit is fast knit with your spirit, in him you are always without ceasing present to me wherever I may wander.'

In the words of Marguerite Aron, his leading modern biographer:

Tenacity, endurance, a lasting serenity of faith, in these we have Jordan's spiritual direction at its most intimate. It is in the counsels

66

addressed to Diana d'Andalo personally that its depth is best revealed; to touch upon it we must . . . cross the threshold of the friendship which united . . . them in this world and for eternity. . . .

The most precious things of his spiritual life he gave to her, if only in a few lines. . . . Thus, directed by Jordan, Diana ran with all generosity in pursuit of the divine Spouse; and she, in her turn, drew him along. Being both vowed to the service of God, both immolated for the salvation of souls, . . . it was in God that they were united, in God that they loved one another, and, while sighing for one another when they were separated, it was for God they sighed.

Jordan and Diana offer the first, and perhaps the most perfect, personal exemplification of the masculine-feminine complementarity characteristic of the Dominican Order to which they belonged.

ST. CATHERINE OF SIENA
AND BLESSED RAYMOND OF CAPUA

Two other Dominicans exemplifying the masculine-feminine character of their religious Order are Catherine of Siena and Raymond of Capua. One of them, Catherine, now proclaimed Doctor of the universal Church, has even left a concise teaching about "spiritual friendships" in her principal writing: *The Dialogue of Divine Providence.* Amplified by features of the numerous friendships revealed through her letters, the teaching in this work is specially powerful because presented as the very words of God the Father, heard by St. Catherine in prayer.

In early sections of the *Dialogue*, human friendship is given very positive temporal and eternal values. In chapter 41, for example, Catherine learns that we do not lose our human friendships in eternal life. While all the saints in heaven are united in divine love and so are fully happy, each according to his capacity, they also share in a special way the happiness of "those whom they have loved more tenderly here below." Not that their eternal happiness can be increased; it is colored, rather, by "more abundant . . . delight, contentment, jubilation and joy" renewed at each fresh vision of the good the Lord has brought about in their friends. Since in heaven this will be the happy result of the "friendship of her friends," so on earth Catherine looks at the "reciprocal love between those who share the same sentiments" as "consolation, sweetness, comfort, and joy." Furthermore, through this love here below, friends "grow in grace and virtue," and provoke each other to honor and glorify the heavenly Father.[11]

At other times, Catherine records the serious dangers of human friendship. Even that which begins as spiritual love may slowly become sensual, a result which the satanic spirit insidiously pursues. In consecrated persons, Satan first engenders a distaste for religious life, inducing them to search for pleasurable compensations in their friendships. Prayer is then judged in terms of self-satisfaction, and its practice is eventually dropped. Worldly conversations become more and more appealing and help stifle any former desires for prayer, purity, suffering for God, and fraternal charity.

In chapter 144, the heavenly Father gives Catherine an explanation of spiritual love that places the positive and negative aspects mentioned above in coherent context. In his goodness, he occasionally chooses such friendship as the means of exercising a person in virtue, while liberating him from his unrecognized imperfection of loving creatures with a love predominately "passionate" or "sensible." How does this happen?

When the Father bestows the gift of friendship on someone who becomes aware that he "loves a particular creature with a singular love," the delight and consolation he has become accustomed to might diminish. The person might perhaps observe that his friend pays more attention to others than to him. In any case, the result is disappointment and suffering. Two possible outcomes front him. His suffering can bring deepened self-knowledge through the discovery that he has been seeking self in a love he thought wholly generous — the Father's hoped-for outcome. The new insight will give birth to distrust of self and "hatred" of selfish satisfaction, liberating him from his unknown imperfection. In place of the latter arises the opposite perfection: a "greater and more perfect love," namely, "charity" for all persons, including his particular friend. He comes to perceive that perfect human love depends in strict proportion upon the fullness of his love for God; that he must love others with the same love with which he loves God. Thereafter, he loves both his friend and all people predominately in God and pursues with preference this new perfection God has brought him to by means of an individual "spiritual friendship."

This is the happy outcome. It can occur only in someone "enlightened by faith," who desires "to walk in the virtues . . . especially prudence and discernment." Such a person will already be accustomed to supporting the sufferings of life humbly, for the praise and glory of

God, and so will make the discoveries described above and progress in perfection. On the other hand, a person who is "ignorant" of the faith and not striving to walk in virtue, a person who "has no life" will find the experience of diminishing sensible satisfaction a great danger. He may well follow Satan's lead and give himself up to "confusion, tedium of mind and sadness of heart, abandoning any virtuous exercises." To such a person, friendship will eventually mean ruin and inner death.

St. Catherine's general teaching on spiritual friendships is clear: they are good if their result is not self-love. In people with the requisite spiritual disposition, they can be providential means for bringing to greater fullness their yet imperfect love; in unspiritual persons, they are likely to lead to disaster. In the former, friendship is a present source of joy and consolation and an eternal feature of their beatific happiness; in the latter, it results in grave harm here and spiritual death hereafter.

Catherine's Friendships:

As Catherine herself became known for her spiritual stature, a "little circle of admirers and friends" began to form around her.[12] She referred to them as her "family" or more familiarly, her *bella brigata*, comprising her old friends the Dominicans, her first companions, and several newcomers, including for awhile only one other woman, Giovanna Manetti. As spiritual head and mother of these, her "own chosen friends," Catherine's twofold concern was for their spiritual advancement and their calm and cheerfulness amid the continual political agitations surrounding them.

We know the names of some of her women friends. Alessia dei Sarracini was the "most dearly loved," to whom Catherine later wrote many letters, still extant. Widowed early, Alessia became a Mantellata, or tertiary Dominican sister, with Catherine and was her "inseparable companion." To her we owe much of Catherine's personal history, for at times she shared even in her spiritual mother's private devotions. Upon the request of Alessia and other most intimate friends, Catherine "dictated from memory a record of much of her soul's experience, including the directions and revelations she received from her Lord." Other close women associates were Lisa, the two Catherines, and Francesca Gori.

The greater number of Catherine's closest friends were men, however. One biographer states that she favored their company. Witness to this predilection was her relationship with the English

Augustinian hermit, William Fleete, who lived in the monastery of Lecceto about three miles outside Siena and received frequent visits from Catherine after their initial meeting in 1374. "He became her firm friend and ever ready servant." Their temperaments were quite different, but their "identity of spiritual aims" caused William to admire Catherine, and so began their "close friendship." William was a learned, contemplative man, "moderate in judgment, and well-balanced in character . . . who understood and practiced Christian charity." Catherine on her part developed a "great affection and regard for him." Much of the Augustinian teaching in her writings "came to her through her friends, the hermits of Lecceto, and especially from Father William." That their mutual influence was considerable is evident from the fact that when she was dying, Catherine chose to entrust to this Englishman the care of her spiritual family at Siena.

"The friendship between Catherine and Fra Bartolomeo de Dominici . . . arose quite spontaneously, through a mutual spiritual sympathy fostered by his admiration for her sanctity and her admiration for his learning." The Dominican became a regular visitor. Catherine was happy to receive this knowledgeable friar who understood her and with whom she could have theological discussions. "Thus began a mutual exchange of help." Fra Bartolomeo instructed her, and she, through "her intuition and tact, made him 'a soul enamoured and strengthened in the blood of Christ.' " From him we have two touching statements about their relationship. " 'When I made her acquaintance, she was young and her face was sweet and gay; I was also young, but nevertheless I never experienced the inner confusion I used to feel with every other young girl, and even the more I talked with her the more the human passions quieted themselves in my heart.' " Then much later, "Till the last years of her life our Lord granted me the grace of being united to her by the bonds of a pure and holy affection."

Catherine's virile character often attracted men of a delicate nature, so that she developed strong maternal relationships with many of her disciples. The most striking instance is that with Fra Simone de Cortona, her "favorite little son." He was "as shy as a young girl, and very easily hurt." Catherine sensed his silent needs, saw his touchiness and tendency to jealousy, and "guided him into spiritual paths with exquisite tact." When he was oppressed and remained away, she would send him tender messages: " 'Bless my little son, Fra Simone; tell him to open the mouth of his desire to receive the milk that his Mother will send him,' " or " 'Tell Fra Simone that I shall take the cord of love, and bind him to my bosom like a mother and her little son,' " and finally, " 'Tell Fra Simone, my little son in Jesus Christ, that the son is never afraid to go to his mother, but runs to her, especially when he is hurt, and his mother takes him in her arms and lifts him up to her breast and feeds him; even a bad mother will always lift him up to the breast of love.' "

Fra Stephano Maconi used to address her as "my very dear mother." His greatest desire was to remain near her; he was able to do so by acting as one of her secretaries. As such he accompanied her to Avignon in her effort to bring the pope back to Rome. He came to know Catherine intimately not only through writing her letters over a period of several years, but also because she "consulted me about her thoughts and movements, and dictated to me a portion of her book. She loved me with the tenderness of a mother. . . ." As she lay dying in Rome, Catherine's desire to see Fra Stephano was so strong that he, in Siena, heard a voice bidding him to come to her. He arrived in time to be with his mother during her last days.

Still another example is that of an old hermit, Blessed Giovanni of the Cells. He was a seasoned ascetic, living happily in austere solitude "among the rocks and stones." But apparently there had been contact between him and Catherine, if we may judge by the cries he uttered upon being told of her death:

> How ever shall we live any longer, now that our Mother, our conso-
> lation, is dead? What else remains for us to do now, but mourn our
> desolate state? I weep for myself, orphaned and abandoned, for the
> joy of my heart that has been reft from me; therefore my eyes are
> darkened and dimmed with tears; and in truth there is no remedy or
> consolation.

Only heaven was happy that day, because the "soul of his friend and teacher" had been received there.

Catherine's friendships with consecrated men and women show her unusual ability for relating to a wide range of people. Loving them either as friend or mother, she led them to grow in Christian love. In psychological terms these relationships exemplify the several degrees of fulfilling love, including friendship. With still another Dominican, Raymond of Capua, Catherine enjoyed a complementing friendship.

After their first meeting in 1374, Raymond became the most important figure in Catherine's "family." She had prayed for a confessor capable of guiding her in her evolving mystical experience. Raymond, appointed to investigate her life and to direct her, was to meet that need.[13] In letters written to him later, Catherine twice referred tenderly to that signal grace accorded her by the Blessed Virgin which "had given you to me." She promised obedience to her new confessor, who, after testing her authenticity, came quickly to understand her and her spirituality. Their friendship, to become firm and profound, was "strengthened by constant mutual admiration. Fra Raimondo instinctively recognized in Catherine the woman of lofty intellect, the great saint and tireless apostle; Catherine admired his intelligence, tact, breadth of understanding, and straining after perfection."

That the two came to know each other intimately is a frank admission in some of their writings and a necessary deduction from events and biographical documents. Even in the initial three-year period "they had spent together . . . the sage Dominican had become her most intimate friend and her most secure support." By his wise, deeply personal counsel and his authority over her, he had helped her more than anyone previously to come to self-knowledge. At the same time, Raymond "acquired a profound knowledge of her, for she had revealed her whole soul to him."

Quickly their relationship assumed great importance for each of them. In 1377, the pope called Raymond to Rome as prior of the convent of the Minerva, and from her letters to him there we can tell how harsh a privation it was for Catherine to be separated this first time from her "intimate friend." It was such a "torment," that she could only resignedly accept it from the divine will as a "particularly hard and painful" purification. Raymond had become her "last and perhaps most vital earthly consolation." In this "cruel separation" from him, she saw only "pure suffering, the crown of thorns, the way of the cross." She wrote: "It seems that my Spouse, who is eternal Truth, has wanted to impose upon me a royal and very poignant trial . . . may he then strengthen me in this privation which language is so incapable of expressing." Understandably, news from her "absent friend" always brought her joy.

Their later correspondence and experience of separation give further indications of the quality of their love. Catherine knew that Raymond, though very influential in secular and ecclesiastical politics, lacked the virile courage to risk his life for the Church. He sought, rather, peaceful and secure ways of serving it. Once, when he had turned back from a mission to Avignon because of impending ambush, Catherine affectionately reproached him. Though "she loved him and understood and excused his weakness, she wanted him to be more courageous in the future." In his turn, Raymond "loved and admired Catherine"; yet he must have thought her admonition unfair, because a letter from her reads: "My dear Father in Jesus Christ . . . you have thought that I have judged you by too high a standard of my own. You have thought also that my affection for you had diminished; but you are mistaken. . . . I love you as I love myself; and I have hoped that the goodness of God would also make your affection perfect." On another occasion she writes: " 'Pardon me if I have ever written anything to give you pain. I never wish to give you pain. . . . Do not be grieved because we are separated; your presence would certainly have been a great consolation to me.' " She would customarily address Raymond as her "beloved Father" or "friend of predilection," or by the pseudonym that so pleased her, *il mio Giovanni singolare*. During the last months of her life, in extreme weakness and suffering, she wrote a long report to "the man who was a father and son to her, master and disciple," telling him about the painful mystical experiences she was undergoing. She says, " 'Amid these torments . . . I am deprived of the comfort of having my spiritual Father with me.' " In this separation, "she could only think of him lovingly and write over and over again: 'Most sweet Father,' as if to express to him all the tenderness of her . . . heart. As a last instance of her sublime love for him . . . she gave him some loving advice," for she had foreseen in a vision that he would be elected the next Master General of the Order. Another vision she had is recorded in Letter 232. By love and desire she sees herself entering into Christ through the wound in his side, "accompanied by my Father St. Dominic; Giovanni, my friend of predilection; and all my spiritual children."

Before their last meeting, it had been revealed to Catherine that the pope would send Raymond to King Charles of France to induce him to renounce schism, and that she would die before he could return. Knowing that it would be their final conversation, Catherine took Raymond into privacy and "talked and talked continuously, her large eyes shining . . . saying such strong and beautiful words." Often she would "grasp his hand and smile beautifully." Then, she accompanied Raymond to the port of Ostia, saying: " 'All is over; you will never see me again in this world.' " As the ship left the shore, she "knelt, and crying, made the sign of the cross."

In their few years together, Raymond and Catherine collaborated in many undertakings, helping each other both naturally and supernaturally. Raymond, for example, was cured from the plague which decimated Siena in 1374 by Catherine's prayer and joined her in her unremitting relief work among the city's victims. Afterwards they went together in retreat to the tomb of St. Agnes of Montepulciano. In these early days, they frequently enjoyed "friendly evenings" while conversing and "contemplating the Sienese countryside." Later, in Pisa, Raymond was with Catherine in the Church of St. Christina when she received the stigmata from our Lord. He had been chosen to bear public witness to the miracle. In 1376, they met in Avignon in a successful attempt to persuade Pope Gregory XI to come back to Rome; afterwards, they returned together to Italy. In Rome itself, they were able to spend some little time together before Raymond's departure.

During all their political activity, Catherine and Raymond leaned upon each other for support. She admired his political wisdom and most often followed his advice. Through him new dimensions and possibilities were opened up to her. Together they promoted the crusades, prayed and worked for the reform of the Church, and gained, as indicated above, the return of the papacy to Rome. When needful, Catherine would "exhort him to act bravely and with courage," and Raymond, "her spiritual director . . . friend and disciple, [would] clarify and strengthen [her ideas and] inspire her to action on a great scale. . . . Thus, Catherine and Fra Raimondo were both working for the same ends, and aided each other with a mutual exchange of ideas, energies and counsels."

In the realm of grace, Raymond "received from her precious instruction for his spiritual progress." In prayer, too, Catherine was ever "mindful of him," "presenting this Father of her soul before the throne of heavenly mercy." Even after her death, Raymond realized that his spiritual stamina came from his continued communications with Catherine. Similarly, years after their last earthly conversation he admitted that her urging him to defend the true pope had always consoled him in the trials and sufferings experienced during the Western Schism.

In return, Raymond "omitted nothing . . . to procure Catherine's glory and to accomplish all that she had entrusted to him." He worked successfully to promote her canonization and preserved, according to her instructions, all her writings: "I beseech you to collect into your own hands any writings of mine which you may find and the book [the Dialogue]; do with all of them whatever you deem is most for God's honour and glory." Even in his overbusy life as Master General,

Raymond found time to write her first biography, a task that took him fifteen years. Written by "her intimate friend and companion," one who had "acquired a profound knowledge of her," the work is a surprisingly objective account, dealing principally with her personal rather than public life and bringing to light the most touching incidents and most characteristic traits. Raymond's was her first " 'official' life, from which all other biographers, even those who affect to despise his sincerity, have drawn their material."

Without doubt, in their close knowledge and love of one another and in the cooperative ministry they exercised, Raymond of Capua and St. Catherine of Siena personified the masculine-feminine complementarity of their Dominican Order. Their complementing friendship helped both of them toward sanctity.

ST. TERESA OF AVILA
AND FATHER JEROME GRACIAN

Teresa of Avila lived a life rich in human and divine friendship. Recently proclaimed a Doctor of the universal Church, along with Catherine of Siena, she has left, in addition to many statements of a personal nature, some general teaching based on her experience.

Teresa speaks of her own relationship with the Lord in terms of friendship that has many stages of development. In her *Conceptions of the Love of God*, when commenting on the Song of Songs, she briefly treats each stage as a different type of friendship. Everyone, she maintains, is called to friendship with God and should prepare himself for it, even asking for that perfect type exemplified by the bride of the Song of Songs who asks for Christ's kiss.[14] "For the kiss is a sign of great friendship and peace between two persons." To arrive at this stage of "close friendship," however, requires great suffering — eventually receiving from Christ his own cross to bear. "It is clear that, since God leads those whom He most loves by the way of trials, the more He loves them, the greater will be their trials." For, "what better sign of friendship is there than for Him to give you what He gave Himself?"

Teresa considers certain human friendships very helpful for progress in divine friendship. Beginners in the life of prayer, who earnestly desire true friendship with the Lord, can avoid many pitfalls with the help of human friends. In fact, "it is a great evil for a soul beset by so many dangers to be alone." She points to vainglory as a concrete example. To be able to discuss this or other spiritual dangers

75

with a friend would help Teresa not to fall again, "if only because I should have been ashamed in his sight, which I was not in the sight of God." She concludes:

For this reason I would advise those who practise prayer, especially at first, to cultivate friendship . . . with others of similar interests. This is a most important thing, if only we can help each other by our prayers, and it is all the more so because it may bring us many other benefits. Since people can find comfort in the conversation and human sympathy of ordinary friendships, even when these are not altogether good, I do not know why anyone who is beginning to love and serve God in earnest should not be allowed to discuss his joys and trials with others.

These benefits of comfort and intercession, mutual enlightenment and restraint from sin result from truly spiritual friendships based on unselfish love. And Teresa is not here speaking of dispassionate love. She distinguishes three kinds of affection. "Illicit affections" she excludes, calling them "a very hell," and finding no need to discuss them further. The second type are "lawful affections" which we have quite naturally for those we love — "relatives and friends." These earthly affections make us either joyous or sad over a natural, human good or evil that has come to our loved ones. "If their heads ache, our souls seem to ache too; if we see them in distress, we are unable to sit still under it, and so on." "Spiritual affection," however, looks beyond this physical reaction of nature. We "reflect whether our friend's trials are not good" for him, whether he is bearing them with patience, and so becoming richer in virtue and merit. We ask this patience of God, and if we see it in our friend, his trials give us "no distress"; rather, "we are gladdened and consoled."

Teresa tells us in her *Life* that she experienced this spiritual affection for any person "whom I like very much" as a yearning for his spiritual advancement so strong that at times "I am powerless against it." In the *Way of Perfection* she says: "It is strange to see how impassioned this love is; how many tears, penances and prayers it costs; how careful is the loving soul to commend the object of its affection . . . [to God]; and how constant is its longing, so that it cannot be happy unless it sees that its loved one is making progress." If, however, the loved one seems to have regressed spiritually, his "friend seems to have no more pleasure in life." This third type of affection is "love without any degree whatsoever of self-interest." And Teresa sings a canticle to

76

it: "O God my Lord, wilt Thou not grant me the favour of giving me many who have such love for me?"

Teresa is convinced that such spiritual friendship is a gift the Lord will provide. Those religious who serve as they should their "true Friend and Spouse, Christ . . . will find no better friends than those whom His Majesty sends you." They will be there, when and "where you had never expected to find them."

These friends do not look for rewards from us for their help, but "look for their reward only from God." This kind of love Teresa wishes for her religious. In seeking to obtain it, they should not fear a mixture of some earthly affection: "It is sometimes good and necessary for us to show emotion in our love and also to feel it and to be distressed by some of our sisters' trials and weaknesses, however trivial they may be. . . . At first, it [their spiritual friendship] may not be perfect, but the Lord will make it increasingly so." This is why she directs superiors contrary to their usual inclinations:

> When you make the acquaintance of any such persons, sisters, the Mother Prioress should employ every possible effort to keep you in touch with them. Love such persons as much as you like. . . . When one of you is striving after perfection, she will at once be told that she has no need to know such people — that it is enough for her to have God. But to get to know God's friends is a very good way of 'having' Him; as I have discovered by experience, it is most helpful. For under the Lord, I owe it to such persons that I am not in hell. . . .

Teresa herself must have learned early in life to concentrate on such spiritual affection, generous and ordered to God, but at the same time fully human and emotional. She discloses in her *Life* that after a certain point "never have I been able to maintain firm friendships save with people who I believe love God and try to serve Him, nor have I derived comfort from any others or cherished any private affection for them."

Teresa's Friendships:

That St. Teresa's life was enriched by her extraordinary capacity for friendship with a wide range of men and women is apparent in all her writings, especially her numerous extant letters. Some of her friends were P. Daza, Don Francisco de Salcedo, Dona Guiomar de Ulloa, P. Ibanez; Dr. Velazquez, the Bishop of Osma; Hernandez; Don Teutonio de Braganza, the Archbishop of Evora; M. Ines de

Jesus, the Prioress of Medina; Fray Bartolome de Medina, O.P.; Diego de Yepes, a Hieronymite and later the Bishop of Tarazona; and, of course, Fray John of the Cross. These are but a few of her many relationships of fulfilling love; of them all, it is popularly thought that the most intimate was with St. John of the Cross. He and Teresa certainly did enjoy a spiritual friendship, but a close knowledge of her writings, particularly her letters to Jerome Gracian, shows clearly that her greatest affection was for the latter friar, not for John of the Cross.[15] This is the conclusion of those who have studied the question — of Allison Peers, for example, who in his introduction to Teresa's *Spiritual Relations*, speaks of the many "allusions to her friends and acquaintances, pre-eminent among whom is P. Jeronimo Gracian." Documentation for this judgment is so considerable that the remainder of this section will concern itself only with Teresa's relationship with Gracian.

Teresa had heard such favorable accounts of Father Gracian that she was "extremely anxious to see him," and "simply delighted" when she heard of their possible meeting at Beas in 1575. Of her first reaction to him — thirty years her junior — she writes: "When I began to talk to him I was happier still, for he pleased me so much that it seemed to me as if those who had praised him to me hardly knew him at all."[16]

Like Catherine, she had long looked for a confessor who could guide her in her developing mystical experience. After her initial meeting with Gracian, she returned to him several times for confession, but had not yet given him full direction of her soul. Teresa then had a brief vision, which decided her in the matter. Christ appeared to her in his customary way, but "on His right hand was Master Gracian, while I was on His left. The Lord took our right hands, joined them and told me that He wished me to take him in place of Himself for my whole life long, and that we were to agree together in everything, for it was expedient that we should." She felt sure that this was the voice of God, and was utterly convinced after the Lord on two other occasions repeated the same thing in different words. From then on she determined to follow Gracian's opinion in all things. She sensed no fear at this prospect, because all she had heard about Gracian made her believe that his aim was the same as hers: "to follow what is most perfect in everything." The consequent "great peace and comfort" she experienced could not have come from the devil, but only from God. And so praying that her decision would indeed mean following the Holy Spirit more completely, and reflecting on the restriction of her personal freedom that such a promise would entail, she hesitated until the Lord gave her "a great confidence" that it was for the sake of the Holy Spirit, who would enlighten Gracian, "so that he in turn might enlighten me." Teresa is careful to state her pure motive: "I did not reflect how much I loved him [Gracian]: indeed, I was not thinking of him at all, or of his talents, but only if it would be a good thing for me to do this for the Holy Spirit's sake. . . . I also remembered that he had been given me by Jesus Christ our Lord. Thereupon I went down on my knees and promised God to do whatever he ordered me all my life long." She made certain stipulations "to save myself from scruples," but "promised, in fact, that both inwardly and outwardly I would put him in the place of God."

Gracian himself knew nothing about this vow until several days after it had been made. Teresa was left with "a great satisfaction and joy," which always remained with her. Instead of the oppression she expected, she experienced a "greater freedom." Confident that her action would bring divine favors to Gracian and to her through him, she praised the Lord, who raised up someone to satisfy her needs and gave her strength to promise obedience to him. A few days later she wrote:

> I must tell you that, without exaggeration, I think these have been the best days in my life. For over three-weeks we have had Father-Master Gracian here; and, much as I have had to do with him, I assure you I have not yet fully realized his worth. To me, he is perfect, and better for our needs than anyone else we could have asked God to send us . . . anyone so perfect, and yet so gentle, I have never seen. . . . I would not have missed seeing him and having to do with him for anything in the world.

Such a beginning set Teresa's and Gracian's relationship on firm foundations, paving the way for further development. Gracian became her "intimate confidant," both in the internal experiences of her soul and the outward events of her life. At his advice, she either wrote or did not write books, and submitted everything she did write to his judgment. In censoring the *Interior Castle,* for instance, he found no "erroneous teaching," but deleted passages "too advanced and too difficult to understand." His motive was personal: "for such was the zeal of my affection for her that I tried to make certain that there should be nothing in her writings which could cause anyone to stumble."

79

Teresa and Gracian also cooperated in several reform ventures, he as provincial and she as foundress, thus deepening their relationship through common efforts. They often traveled in the same party while making arrangements for new foundations. Later in letters, Teresa would recall the happiness these trips caused her: "How well I remember what a good time he and I had together on the journey from Toledo to Avila." Or the sadness: "Now do you not see how short-lived my happiness has been? I was looking forward to the journey . . . with the companion I was expecting to have this time [Gracian] . . . and what has happened has made me sadder than I could have wished to be: It has been a great blow to me." She also recounts the harsh trials they suffered together in the reform.

Through all of this Teresa came to know Gracian intimately. In several places she characterizes him. "He was a man of great learning, understanding and modesty; and to these qualities had been united such great virtues. . . ." She speaks of his humility many times. Because of the confidential nature of their work and correspondence and the unsure mail delivery of their times, Teresa and Gracian often used pseudonyms. For him she particularly favored "Paul" and "Eliseus," while for herself, "Angela" or "Laurencia." Accordingly, at a time when he was overcome by troubles in the Order, she wrote: "Oh, how well my Paul's name fits him! Now he is up in the air, now in the depths of the sea." Comparing Gracian and another confessor she well appreciated, Fr. Nicolao, Teresa avowed: "He has not that graciousness and serenity that God has given to Paul — there are very few to whom He has given so many gifts all at once as He has to him." Once, when she heard that Gracian's sermons had borne much spiritual fruit, she replied, "He is so saintly that I am not at all surprised at the good he has done their souls." At another time she declared tersely: "I have the saintly Paul with me and no one can make me break my promise to that saint [her vow of obedience to him]." Teresa noted among Gracian's qualities such a "pleasant manner, that most people who meet him love him at once and so he is greatly loved by all who are under his jurisdiction, both friars and nuns."

Teresa also knew Gracian's interior life. As he confided his prayer experience to her, she analyzed it and gave him advice. In one letter she expresses happy surprise that "in spite of all he has to do, Paul can commune with Joseph [pseudonym for Our Lord] so tranquilly." After counseling him that the best prayer is one which leads from desire to action, she gives this warning: "The greatest caution is necessary, for I am positive that the devil will not omit to think out all the tricks he can so as to harm Eliseus."

Gracian must have revealed even his most inner spiritual experiences to Teresa. She knew of his lifelong purity, which she judged Mary had bestowed on him because of "his great desire to serve His glorious Mother." She talks about his exceptional caution with regard to women, relating the case of one "young . . . and good-looking" woman who, "a dozen times or more," had asked without success for him to hear her confession. Teresa regarded his refusal "very prudent." Such an attitude must have been part of his acquired asceticism, for Gracian once gave Teresa what he had written "while struggling with these severe temptations." She reflects: "It may seem an improper thing that he should have spoken to me in such great detail about his soul . . . for I know that he has made such revelations neither to his confessor nor to anyone else." And yet, she finds justification for his action on grounds of her age and experience and her praising the Lord in her writings for his victorious grace in one of his creatures. Teresa does not, however, reveal "other things of which I should have a great deal more to say were it not unsuitable for me to write of them." Concluding this account, she admits: "I have certainly restrained myself a great deal here, for otherwise, if this should ever reach his [Gracian's] hands, he might be troubled by it."

Knowing each other so intimately gave rise to a singular, mutual affection attested to by history. None of Gracian's private letters to Teresa are extant, only his brief declaration in *Dialogo XVI* of his *Peregrinacion de Anastasio:* "She loved me, and I her, more tenderly than any other creature on earth." Contrariwise, in addition to Teresa's autographed vow of obedience which he always carried on his person, Gracian conserved her letters to him with utmost care. Forced to destroy some during the persecution, he relates in *Dialogo X* that he "sewed together those that were left" which "made a book four inches thick." He kept these with him until about a year before his death, when he sent them from Brussels to his sister in Spain for safe keeping.

A great deal of evidence on Teresa's side supports the fact of their friendship. An interesting series of visions of Christ or Gracian himself reveal both his place in her life and her affection for him. She recounts them in her *Spiritual Relations.* Once, deeply recollected and commending Eliseus to God in all the troubles he was having in the reform, Teresa heard the Father's reply: " 'He is My true son: I will not fail to help him.' " On another occasion, receiving additional news

81

about dangers threatening him, she relates: "I was making very earnest petition to Him that, as He had given him to me, I should not be deprived of him, when He said to me: 'Have no fear.' " Two other visions, separated in time, are connected in meaning. After communion one day Teresa was inwardly filled with a great light. "I thought I was in another world, and my spirit found itself inwardly in a most delightful rustic garden, so lovely that it recalled to my mind those words in the [Song of] Songs. . . . I saw my Eliseus there, looking not in the least unattractive but having a strange beauty; around his head he had a garland of precious stones. . . ." She heard Christ praising Gracian's virtue and foretelling that he would proclaim a great festival in honor of Mary. "The experience lasted for over an hour and a half, and, as seldom happens with visions, I could not take my eyes from it, so great was my delight. What I gained from this vision was love for Eliseus and I came to picture him more frequently amid that beauty." Later, Teresa became seriously worried because Gracian was in danger from a certain group of friars. The day was the feast of the Presentation. In praying to Mary and Christ for him, she heard these words: " 'O woman of little faith, be still; things are going on very well.' " She thereupon resolved to have Gracian establish a feast in the Order celebrating his freedom and only afterward reflected that this might be the fulfillment of her vision. Later, when she was "suffering greatly" from not having heard from Gracian, even more from his fresh difficulties ("I have never known any distress like that"), he appeared to her in her anxious prayer. "It could not have been imagination, for I became conscious of an inward light and he himself was coming gaily along the road, with a bright countenance." She wondered if this was a portent of heavenly glory and heard a voice: " 'Tell him to begin at once and not to be afraid, for his is the victory.' " When, after a visit from Gracian himself, Teresa was praising the Lord for all these favors, she heard the divine acknowledgment of their extent: " 'What dost thou ask of Me that I have not done, my daughter?' "

Above all in her letters Teresa openly reveals her love and concern for Gracian, her need for him, and the help and comfort she receives from him. Quoted here are only the most remarkable of many touching passages. Each speaks for itself better than could any commentary. The passages appear in chronological order within each grouping to point out any development in the relationship that has occured. Unless otherwise noted, all citations are from letters written to Gracian personally.

Teresa is quite candid about her friendship and love for Gracian. Not long after they had met, she writes to a third party:

— As concerns . . . my friendship with him, you would be amazed at what is happening. I have been unable to do otherwise, and I am not at all repentant. . . . I assure you he is a saintly man, and not in the least headstrong, but very cautious. I know this from experience . . . of his friendship that involves attachment to nothing but things of the spirit. It is like having to do with an angel, for this is what he has always been.[17]

— I have been wondering which of the two your Paternity [Gracian] loves better — Senora Dona Juana [Gracian's mother], who, I reflected, has a husband and her other children to love her, or poor Laurencia, who has no one else in the world but you, her Father. May it please God to preserve him to her.

— For many reasons it is permissible for me to feel great affection for you and to show it in the dealings we have together. . . . I confess, too, I have tried to conceal my imperfections from them (the nuns), though these are so numerous that they must have seen a great many of them as well as my love for Paul and the concern I have for his welfare. . . . Realizing, as you do, with what love I am addressing you, you will be able to forgive me, and to do me the kindness, as I have begged you, of not reading in public the letters I write you. . . . There is a great difference between the way I treat your Paternity privately and the way I talk of you to other people, even to my own sister. Just as I should not like anyone to overhear my conversation with God or to disturb me when I am alone with Him, so it is with Paul.

— O, Jesus, how wonderful it is when two souls understand each other! They never lack anything to say and never grow weary (of saying it).

— I must explain to you, my Father, that I am quite clear that the desire I have had to see you free [i.e. from the office of Provincial] has sprung from the love I have for you in the Lord rather than from my concern about the good of the Order. This love produces a natural weakness in me and makes me very resentful that everybody should not realize what they owe you, and how you have laboured, and [it makes me] unable to stand hearing a word against you.

Teresa's love for Gracian prompted her to a fully human and Christian concern for his welfare.

83

— I am worried about whether you have thought to put more clothes on, as the weather is getting cold now. Please the Lord you have not done yourself any injury [in falling off his donkey].

— My great comfort is to think that God will protect your Paternity for me and make you very holy.

— Oh, how Angela would have loved to get Paul a meal when he was hungry like that — so she tells me! . . . Your Paternity must scold him, please, and also thank him from me for all the care he takes to write to me.

— Oh, my Father, if only I could be with you now that you are having such an anxious time! How right you are to tell your troubles to one who has a fellow-feeling with your distress! . . . I have always had the deepest affection for the nuns at Seville, and I love them more every day for the care they are taking of one whom I wish I could be always cherishing and serving and taking care of, too. God be praised for granting him such good health.

— When he [Fray Antonio] casts reflections upon me, he also casts them upon my Paul, I can't bear it. What he says about me doesn't matter in the least.

May God watch over you, my Father. It is a great favour from him that you should be putting on weight — in spite of all you have to do.

— I must tell you that I felt so overcome at seeing your Paternity that all yesterday, Wednesday, my heart was aching, for I could not bear to see you worrying so.

— The life your Paternity is leading [overwork] worried me dreadfully. God forgive you: you have given me such a time with your attacks of fever, and with the haemorrhage, of which I am told you have had a great deal. I cannot think why you have told me nothing about it. I declare, my Father, you exasperate me so much that I don't know how I manage to write nicely to you.

Another more frequent expression of Teresa's relationship to Gracian is the human and spiritual need she has of him.

— That was a great relief to me [the re-reading of a letter from Gracian] but it was not sufficient; indeed, on the next day I was greatly distressed at finding myself without him, for I had no one to betake myself to in this trouble, and I seemed to be living in very great loneliness. And what made it worse was that I find no one else who can give me relief, and yet for the most part he has to be away: this is a very great torment to me.

— When I reflect that I shall have news of you only occasionally, I do not know how I shall bear it. . . . For love of Our Lord, do try to write to me soon . . . even a few hours has seemed a long time to wait to hear from you! And now, as your Paternity knows that, it will be very cruel of you if you fail to write: even if you cannot send me a long letter, just let me know how you are.

— I . . . should like to have news of him [Gracian] every day. How I envy your having him with you! [Superior of the convent at Seville.] Please do not treat me like this, and do not omit to write and tell me about everything that happens, for our Father's letters are short, and if he has not chance to write, you must not fail to do so instead.

— [To Gracian:] I am extremely envious of the souls whom it is his (Paul's) duty to help.

— I can see there have been causes for your silence, but, as it has been such a cause of suffering to me, nothing should have kept you from writing.

— Oh, how much lonelier my soul gets each day when I am so far from your Paternity!

— Angela's mind is still not entirely at rest about the suspicion she was entertaining. That is not to be wondered at, for she has nothing else to console her (but your friendship), and she wants no other consolation than that. And, as she herself says, she has a great many trials and is weak by nature, so that she becomes distressed when she thinks (her affection) is not repaid. Your Paternity must please tell that gentleman [Gracian himself] that, careless though he may be by nature, he must not be so with her: for, where there is love, it cannot slumber so long.

— Oh, how tired poor Laurencia is of everything! She commends herself earnestly to your Reverence, and says her soul can find no peace or quiet in anyone but God and those who understand her, as your Reverence does. Everything else is such a cross to her that no one can adequately describe it.

— I am really feeling your being so far away very keenly: I do not know why it has affected me like this. May God bring you back safe and well.

When Gracian could be with her or did write, Teresa experiences help and comfort.

— Laurencia finds herself quite unable to be on her old terms with her confessors, and that was her only comfort; she is now without any comfort at all. [A note explains that Gracian is away. Thus her discomfort, "since she can open her heart freely only to him."]

— So Angela is very happy, my Father, now that she has made her confession to him [Gracian]; and she is happiest of all because, since first she saw Paul, her soul has found relief and happiness with no one else.

— In reality her greatest pleasure is to be with her confessor Paul.

— I shall never have a better time than I had there [at Beas] with my Paul. I was so delighted when he wrote to me, 'Your dear son.' 'How right he is!' I exclaimed — I was alone at the time. I was so glad he wrote that, and I should be still more so if I could see his work being such a success that he could return here.

— May God preserve you for me: you make me so very happy! I wish I were very good, so that I could commend you a great deal to God: I mean I could get my desires granted if I were. In courage I never find I am lacking, glory be to God, unless it be in matters relating to Paul.

Oh, how happy Angela felt when she read the sentiments which he expresses on a separate sheet at the end of one of the letters which he wrote her! . . . Your Paternity is to tell him that he can be quite easy about it [the separate sheet] in his mind, since the work of bringing about the union was so well done [our Lord's work through her vow to Gracian], and the knot was so tightly tied, that only death will break it — nay, after death it will be firmer than before, and no foolish notions about perfection could do as much as that [her vow, in unifying her to Gracian and ultimately to God]: the very thought of it helps her to praise the Lord. That freedom which she used to have has been nothing but a hindrance to her. Now she thinks her

86

present bondage better and more pleasing to God, for she has found someone to help her bring souls to Him who will praise Him. And such is the relief and joy which overflows in her that a large part of it spreads to me [Teresa herself].

— God keep you, for if anything could give me any pleasure, it would be to see Paul.

— Oh, my Father, how oppressed I have been feeling lately! But the oppression passed off when I heard you were well.

Testimony of such intimate knowledge, trust, cooperation, and love in nature and grace indicates a complementing friendship between St. Teresa of Avila and Father Jerome Gracian, which contributed to their personal holiness. Teresa's life corresponded perfectly with her doctrine on human and divine friendship, showing that she both drew her teaching from experience and adhered to its truth throughout the development of that experience.

SAINTS FRANCIS DE SALES AND JANE DE CHANTAL

When Francis de Sales and Jane de Chantal first met and became friends, neither was a religious. Francis had been Bishop of Geneva for nearly two years when, early in 1604, he was introduced to Jane de Chantal, a baroness, widowed for some three years and mother of four young children. Six more years were to pass before Jane became a religious. Her relationship with Francis, then, had become well established before the two assumed a similar state of life. History attests to the fact that this earlier difference posed no difficulty in the development of their friendship or their Christian love through it.

During her brief marriage, two loves had consumed Jane de Chantal: love for her husband and love for her God.[18] After the baron's accidental death in 1601, her religious interest more and more dominated her life. She increased her customary prayer, penances, and charitable works, and within the year began to have supernatural visions which at first frightened her. For two years she ardently prayed to God "to give me a man to guide me spiritually, who is truly holy and your servant, who will teach me your will and all you want of me, and I promise and swear to you that I will do all that he tells me in your stead." One day, while riding in a valley near Bourbilly, Jane had a vivid vision of a priest she did not know. Interiorly she heard a voice say: "There is the man into whose hands you must entrust your conscience." Several months passed before her father, Monsieur Frémyot, invited Jane to Dijon for the renowned Lenten preaching of the Bishop of Geneva. The moment Francis de Sales came into the Sainte-Chapelle, Jane, "overcome with joy," recognized the man of her vision at Bourbilly.

A classic biographer has written that above all others Francis de Sales was "the saint of friendship." Friendship was his personal "decor," the "atmosphere of his sanctity" — a great asset in his extensive spiritual direction. Another more recent biographer emphasizes that Francis' friendly, spiritual influence was universal, and not, as is commonly thought, restricted mainly to women. Acknowledging the saint's many "Philothées," he asks: "But who thinks of the Théotimes — so many prelates, abbots, canons, priests, and laymen to whom the holy bishop communicated his flame — to Revol, Ancina, Frémyot, Bérulle, Duval, Gallemant, Favre, Soulfour, Des Hayes, Vincent de Paul. . . ." Because Francis' women friends and penitents kept more of his letters, they have become much better known. Among them are: the Abbess of Montmartre, Angélique Arnauld, Mme. de Charmoisy, Blessed Mme. Acarie, Jacqueline Coste, Mlle. de Bréchard, Sister Simplicienne, Mme. de Gouffiers, "the little Mlle. Françon, the scandalous Mlle. Bellot, the beautiful Mme. Armand," and above all, St. Jane de Chantal. In addition to this convincing witness to Francis' influence with women, his writings testify that he possessed an intimate understanding of woman's psychology, especially with regard to human and divine love. Indeed, his letters are a virtual treatise on feminine psychology. In one part of his masterpiece on the spiritual life he describes a woman's perfect love for her husband to explain how filial fear remains in the soul who perfectly loves God.

A vast amount of Francis de Sales' personal correspondence, the greater portion of which is addressed to Jane de Chantal, is extant today. Both cherished the other's letters, Francis to the extent of carefully annotating hers in the margins, but Jane, having discovered this after his death, burned nearly all of them. From those that remain, however, and from other writings, the main stages of their relationship are clear.

From their first meeting and earliest acquaintance, Jane felt a deep admiration for Francis. "I called him a saint within my heart, and was convinced that that is what he was." Because of her ardent, precipitous nature, Francis wanted to restrain at first any "enthusiastic friendship," but he later admitted that as he listened to her he felt "his soul lodge itself intimately within hers." At the same time he saw clearly how to lead her toward sanctity and had no doubt that God was entrusting her to him. Somewhat later he wrote to her: "Madame, God forces me to speak to you in confidence: His goodness and grace have always granted that whenever I am celebrating Holy Mass, I have no distracting thoughts; but for some time you have always come to my mind, not to distract me, but to attach me more to God. . . ."

Soon Jane decided to fulfill her promise to God and to transfer her vow of obedience from her current director to Francis, whom she was certain God had given her. Francis hesitated, however, testing both her and the proposal for four months. Jane remained persistent. They corresponded over several details, once even discussing St. Teresa's vow of obedience to Gracian, and Francis finally wrote: "I want to speak to you heart to heart." They met at the pilgrimage town of Saint-Claude, half-way between Dijon and Annecy, in late August, 1604. They talked long, discerning the will of God. The next morning, after he had heard her confession, she pronounced her vow to him during Mass, and he promised God: "to direct, help, serve and advance Jeanne-Françoise Frémyot as carefully, faithfully, and saintly as possible in the love of God, accepting and holding her from henceforth as his own, for whom I am responsible before Our Lord." Jane spoke to him of her growing desire to leave the world for the cloister. His reply was that she must now sanctify herself in her present state and not be concerned with what might come later.

Francis returned to Switzerland, from where he shortly afterwards wrote to her:

> My very dear sister, know that since you talked with me about your interior life, God has given me a great love for your spirit. Especially when you vowed yourself to me, it wonderfully bound my soul to cherish yours more and more. This made me write to you that God had given me to you. I did not believe that he could add anything to the affection that I felt in my spirit, especially when praying for you. But now, dear daughter, a certain new quality has arisen, which I am unable to name. Its effect, however, whenever I wish perfection for you in the love of God, is a great interior sweetness. No, I am adding nothing to the truth; I speak before the God of my and your hearts. Every particular affection is different from any other, and that which I have for you has a certain particularity

which is extremely profitable to me. I did not want to say so much about it, but one word draws forth another — and I think that you will take it well. . . .

Since I left Dijon, after we had spoken, I recall in prayer many particular persons who recommended themselves to me, but you nearly always first, or when not first, which is rare, then last so that I might linger. Can anything more be said? But, for the honor of God, tell this to no one whomsoever, for I have said a little too much, although in all truth and purity. I will tell you the rest one day, either in this world or in the other.

Then follow long instructions on the ascetical ordering of her daily life, with, however, the reservation that she is not to be scrupulous. Francis wrote the general rule of her obedience to him in capital letters: "YOU MUST DO EVERYTHING FROM LOVE, AND NOTHING FROM FORCE; YOU MUST LOVE OBEDIENCE MORE THAN YOU FEAR DISOBEDIENCE." His evident concern was to leave her the freedom of spirit that allows authentic obedience.

Francis and Jane saw each other once more six months later for some unknown, urgent reason. She traveled to his family estate at Sales and later wrote of her visit: "Those few days I spent with this man of God were great blessings; my inmost soul felt no other desire than to obey God's will, which I wanted to know solely from the mouth of this holy man He had given me for my direction." Two years passed before they could see each other again.

During this time, Jane managed her home estate, raised her children, and perfected her spiritual life according to Francis' rule of life. Often she entertained the longing for a contemplative vocation. They corresponded regularly, and on two occasions, at least, she sent him gifts. The first was a corporal for the sacrifice of the Mass, and he wrote: "Do you know what I say in spreading it for the consecration? I say, 'This can well be the unfolded heart of the one who has sent it to me. . . .'" Another time she wove him some serge. He sold it for alms to the poor, but wrote: "Who, though, could estimate its true value? For, if I wanted to give alms according to the price at which I value it, I assure you, I would never obtain as much."

Francis' judgment of Jane's human qualities, spiritual development, and desire for a religious vocation corresponded more and more to a hope for a contemplative-active Congregation, that he, as bishop, had entertained for his diocese. What he could only vaguely tell her

90

about earlier had become clarified as a definite plan. Francis called Jane to Sales in May, 1607. Their mutual expectations were high: "These two beings, who in one way or another thought of each other constantly in the terms of their serene friendship immersed in God, had not seen each other for two years." After a few days, and after testing her detachment and docility through a variety of proposals, Francis described for her the Congregation he wished her to found. Jane's reaction was positive: "To this proposal I immediately felt a great interior correspondence accompanied by a sweet satisfaction and light which assured me that it was the will of God. I didn't feel this about the other proposals, although my soul had been entirely submissive." In view, however, of immediate, practical obstacles — her family, estate, and especially her four children — they indefinitely postponed implementation of the decision they had taken.

Not until 1609 could Jane again return to Switzerland. Because of family troubles over the marriage of her eldest daughter, she had asked to visit Francis. "How welcome you will be, my dear daughter," he replied. "Since I have known [of your distress], my soul embraces yours lovingly. Leave on the first good day you can. My mother wants to have you stay at Sales . . . but do not think that I will leave you there alone. Certainly not, for I will be waiting for you as soon as I hear you are coming. . . . Do you know, I am already glad at heart, waiting for your arrival." About their six weeks together we know little, except that Francis introduced her to individuals and groups of people in Annecy who would be important for the future founding of their Congregation there.

At home during the next year, Jane arranged her final affairs. Her father, so attached to her, resignedly consented to her plans. Her eldest daughter, Marie-Aimée, had married; her youngest, Charlotte, had died mysteriously that very winter. Celse, her son, decided to stay at Dijon to finish his studies; Francon would finish her education with the Ursulines. Francis, too, had lost his beloved mother that same winter. Since she had loved Jane, Francis wrote of his mother's last days, revealing at the same time his affection for his spiritual daughter. "Because I am speaking to you, I will tell you a little story — you to whom I have given the place of my mother in my memento [of the living] in the Mass, without removing you from your former place there. I didn't know how else to hold you as firmly as you are held in my heart, for there you are the first and the last." At the end of March, 1610, Jane de Chantal left her family, home, and country for Annecy, where she was welcomed by Francis and a great cortege. On June 6, she and three other protégées of the bishop were able to establish a small, poor monastery, marking the origin of the Congregation of the Visitation.

Francis came regularly to instruct his daughters and to take care of their needs; as a consequence he and Jane saw each other often in the next years. When his episcopal duties called him elsewhere, they corresponded, as they did also when the founding of new houses later took her away. This phase of their friendship lasted twelve years, during which time they shared many worries, joys, and sorrows, including, between 1613-1615, a woman's two-year campaign of calumny. During the latter period of suffering, the two grew closer to each other through mutual support and inspiration.

Their relationship and their correspondence lasted in all eighteen years. A glance at even a few "of innumerable passages" from Francis' letters spanning the period shows that "the friendship he had for Jane surpassed every other affection."[19] The quality of her love, too, becomes apparent.

— I have just now said Mass for you, I always say it for you, my daughter, for you have such a special and particular place in it that it seems to me almost only for you.

— Believe me, my own soul is in no way dearer to me than yours, or so it seems to me. I have only the same desire, the same prayers for both, without division or separation. I am yours: Jesus wants it, and so I am.

— Thus our bond, our chains, which, the more they bind and constrain, the more they give comfort and freedom. . . . Therefore, keep me tightly bound to you and do not worry about knowing anything more than that this bond is contrary to no other, either of vow or of marriage.

— My soul is joined to yours and I cherish you as my own soul!

— She is very sick, this good mother [Jane], and my spirit a little in pain because of her illness. I say 'a little,' but it is really very much. . . .

— I love [you], my very dear soul — which [his soul] you have — without measure, without end, beyond all comparison and above anything anyone is able to say. . . .

— My poor, very dear mother, my life [*ma vie*] (I assure you, I was about to write 'my darling' [*ma mie*] — and that would not have been so bad). . . . The greatness of my heart in your regard remains above all comparison. . . . Lord God, what a consolation it will be to love each other in the full ocean of charity, if [already] these little streams give us so much!

— I always read [your letters] with such eagerness the first time that I receive only a general consolation, [and am] nearly unaware of what I have read.

One of the few extant letters from Jane to Francis was written in 1621. For months she had longed to see him:

Indeed, I am glad and nothing angers me, thanks to God, because I truly want everything that pleases him. . . . But this unity [of will with God] does not prevent all the rest of my soul sometimes feeling an inclination or affection toward you. . . . The incomparable happiness of seeing myself again at your feet and receiving your holy blessing fills my spirit. Incontinent, I am so touched that I am moved to tears, and it seems to me that I would utterly melt should God grant me this mercy. . . .

It seems to me that if one of us should die before I am able to make my confession to you once more, I will be troubled by many qualms of conscience and anxieties.

Her own letters that she destroyed must have expressed her affection even more openly. One from Francis indicates as much. While not disapproving of what she had written to him, he asks her for something he could make public:

You see, my very dear mother, when I visit our daughters, they ask for news of you, and if I could show them your letters, they would be very happy. That is why I ask you for some sheets that I could show them. And as for my niece Bréchard, she well knows that I and you are one, because she saw some pages containing that truth; nevertheless, I would not want to show her these last three letters. . . .

In the last years of their friendship, Francis and Jane often had to go separate ways, he, to the corners of his diocese and beyond; she, to the several houses of their rapidly expanding Congregation. During his absences, he entrusted her to the spiritual care of his own penitent and friend, Vincent de Paul. Francis died on December 28, 1622. He had seen Jane briefly some two weeks before. For nineteen more years, while continuing the direction of their Congregation, Jane worked for the spread of his writings and his canonization.

Upon her death in 1641, her new spiritual father, Vincent de Paul, attested to his certitude concerning Jane's sanctity and revealed, signing the testimony, the sole supernatural vision he had ever had:

> There appeared . . . a small globe as of fire, which rose from the earth into the sky to join itself to another, but larger and more luminous globe. These two, becoming one, rose higher, entered and were lost in another globe infinitely greater and more resplendent than the others. Interiorly, . . . [a voice] said that this little globe was the soul of our worthy mother [Jane de Chantal], the second that of our blessed father [Francis de Sales], and the other, the divine essence.

Tracing even briefly the relationship between Saints Francis de Sales and Jane de Chantal brings into relief not only the developed capacity of two people for fulfilling love toward both men and women, but also the complementing friendship they had for one another. History witnesses to their fruitful collaboration in external events, and their own words reveal both the tenderness and depth of their human love and its role in encouraging their growth toward fullness of Christian love.

CONCLUSIONS

The saintly experience just presented actualizes the scriptural possibility uncovered in chapter one and confirms the psychological assertions and theory of chapter two: celibate, masculine-feminine friendship can be lived in such a way as to promote growth in divine love. From this experience flow also some necessary principles and general characteristics of such relationships.

Nearly all the examples involved men and women in religious life: those of fulfilling love, often members of different religious families; those of complementing love, more often members of the same Order. Two of these last friendships exemplify also the masculine-feminine complementary nature of the religious Order itself. Any selection of individual cases has its limitations, but the choice made in this chapter represents persons of both different eras and of major western European nationalities and cultures. The principal epistolary evidence is drawn equally from two men and two women. In addition to it, the pertinent doctrine of the two women is given not only because of its relevance, but also because the two have so recently been proclaimed the first women Doctors of the universal Church.

Substantially, St. Catherine of Siena and St. Teresa of Avila agree in their teaching about human friendship and charity. They hold that for consecrated men and women with the right spiritual disposition of faith, prudence, and zeal for the other virtues — psychology would term this the "sufficient motive" for self-restraining and sublimating love — human friendship can be a providential means for growth in friendship with God. Such a relationship perdures in heaven, and on earth can be a great help and joy. Fully human in its affection, it is supernaturally oriented. A friendship of this nature elicits mutual enlightenment, encouragement, restraint from sin, and intercessory prayer, and so helps one avoid many spiritual dangers. It inspires self-knowledge, humility, selfless love, and the predominance of Christian love in all relationships. In religious lacking sufficient supernatural orientation, human friendships, under satanic influence, can lead to sensual self-indulgence, loss of vocation, and spiritual death.

Catherine and Teresa not only taught this sound doctrine — they lived it, as did the other men and women cited. All of them exhibited the volitional and emotional maturity characteristic of adequate personalities. All had exceptional capacities for friendships of fulfilling love with the men and women they led closer to God. The four complementing friendships studied reveal further several characteristics common to the men, the women, and their relationship in nature and grace.

Both the men and the women had attained an advanced state of natural and supernatural maturity. They had integrated their human loves and consecrated lives, and so had developed the psychological requirements of primacy of the spiritual, self-knowledge, and self-restraining, sublimated love. They demonstrated this achievement by the clear orientation of their lives to the fullness of Christian love and their acceptance from the divine will of whatever sacrifices this entailed.

In every case, the men were learned in both human and divine knowledge, leaders of their times and milieux, affable to all, and loved by all. They had a particular understanding of women and the ability to direct them to holiness.

The women were likewise in every case intelligent, spirited, avid for spiritual instruction and development in the contemplative life. They were devoted to prayer, penance, and to their apostolate. Three of the four had extraordinary spiritual experiences, prayed for an adequate director, received him in an unusual way from Mary or Christ, and made a private vow of obedience to him.

While always ordered to God, the friendship between these men and women was fully and deeply human, bringing them to experience a spiritual unity of two-in-one love. They were constantly present to one another in mind and heart. Personally or by letter they shared in full trust the intimate details of their human and spiritual lives. They admired each other's qualities and virtues and openly expressed a unique, intense affection for one another. Each was ever anxious for the other's human and supernatural welfare. Both suffered from separation and rejoiced singularly when they were together or could at least receive letters from each other.

Through mutual cooperation and assistance in nature and grace, these friends grew humanly and spiritually and were better able to fulfill their apostolic tasks.

In the order of nature, the man offered advice and encouragement for the woman's internal development and external activity. Often he provided material and diplomatic aid. The woman inspired and encouraged him to fulfill his human potential as an individual and as leader of others.

In the order of grace, the man directed the woman through wise asceticism toward full love of God and neighbor, a program involving balanced spiritual instruction, adept guidance toward self-knowledge and detachment, and the firm setting of goals and means. He urged and prayed for her progress. The woman, by her inspiration and enthusiasm, drew the man along with her to God in an evermore generous striving toward the fulfillment of his personal vocation. She devotedly prayed and sacrificed for his holiness and his work.

Both from the writings and the lives of select, celibate men and women of different epochs and backgrounds, it is clear, then, that mixed friendship of either fulfilling or complementing love was an important means through which they grew toward perfect Christian love. Their personal union with each other helped them become one in love with God and his creation.

4

BECOMING HOLY

"Be holy for I am holy. . . ."

One might think it unfair that the Word require us to be as holy as God. Is he exaggerating? What about our inborn limitations, our weakness, our failures? What about the influence of others that makes our own struggle so difficult? From every point of view, is it not just too much to ask?

But God is Love. This is a scriptural definition of his holiness, his perfection. In becoming holy like God, then, I am to grow toward perfect love. Not alone, though. My effort and God's aid are both needed. For man, the task is impossible; for God, nothing is impossible. The supreme goal of loving perfectly, as God loves me, depends crucially on his pouring perfect love into me, sharing his own love with me. It depends, too, on my opening to the gift, my stretching toward universality, welcoming the pain of expansion to all that God is and has made. That's terrifying enough, but if left to my own resources, unfair and impossible. But the care of a Father's Providence works everything out for me, better than his care for birds or flowers or for the whole, indescribably detailed, utterly majestic universe. What I uniquely need to achieve the "impossible" goal will appear, at chosen moments, in chosen ways.

Yet, neither everyone nor everything that might enter my life's struggle for the goal will help me. Some can do harm. Often I must reject. Always I must weigh, testing the spirits. I must weigh in the

Spirit of Jesus, in light of the pattern of Jesus, and according to my ability now to live Jesus. Does everything fit? If so, the particular person or thing is a help toward my goal. My Father has provided it. Harmony with his plan alone helps me more and more to become holy as God himself is holy.

In trying to achieve this harmony of Christian judgment or give counsel about mixed celibate friendship, the totality of each individual must obviously be taken into account. Such friendship is not for all consecrated celibates, not even for all who meet the psychological requirements. These latter simply qualify for the possibility. A Christian evaluation of several aspects of the person's *actual* growth in his vocation and *actual* integration of masculine-feminine friendship must be made. Anyone giving spiritual counsel about these relationships needs an integral understanding of all the elements at play in order to reach a pastoral judgment as to whether or not they strike harmony in the lives of the individuals seeking guidance.

Numerous reasons call for caution in making a judgment: the realistic dangers of ignorance, temptation, and weakness into which many have fallen; the power of passion and the sexual appetite to befuddle the mind and debilitate the will; the general advice of saints and spiritual writers to flee such budding relationships as lawful, perhaps, but certainly inexpedient because risky, even the height of imprudence. And yet, other saints have ventured into this very friendship and discovered its potential for human development and growth in the love of God and neighbor.

The theologian is therefore called upon to analyze each situation from the vantage point both of Catholic faith and morals and human experience and reason and to apply the norms of prudence fitting to the person and the circumstances. Drawing implications of faith and applying them to life — this is the business of the theologian. In such context, he arrives at a prudential judgment of a means to an end, thereby fulfilling a pastoral function corresponding to the need of the people of God for wisdom to find meaning in their use of science.[1] A priest is as much shepherd as teacher. In guiding his people, he must work, yes, from the background of natural prudence supplied by psychology and enriched by the living example of saints. But in vital faith he must also turn to classical philosophy and theology to learn how mixed celibate love can be a means toward fullness of Christian love wholly compatible with the vow of chastity. Only when he does so can he reach pastoral judgments of supernatural prudence.

From the outset, let it be clear that a dedicated celibate, capable of a masculine-feminine friendship, but who does not in fact enjoy one, should not set out in search of one. Such friendship is not necessary, even for those capable of it. Fundamentally a free gift of Providence, it cannot be humanly forced, much less sought as the answer to some persistent need. Rather, one's attitude should simply be openness to the benevolent love of people of either sex. To manipulate would be to substitute one's own providence for the Lord's. Should an actual friendship with someone of the opposite sex present itself, it should then be assessed intelligently with both natural and supernatural prudence.

GOAL OF CONSECRATED MEN AND WOMEN — FULLNESS OF CHRISTIAN LOVE

Since prudence deals with concrete human actions and circumstances, one of the first concerns in judging whether a consecrated man and woman should cultivate a friendship must be to evaluate the actual depth and stability of the individual vocations. How each understands and lives the life of charity[2] integrated with the life of chastity is crucial.

Charity is the starting point, not only because as the goal of the consecrated life it should guide all other thoughts and choices, but also because so much confusion about it exists today among religious and priests. One prevalent opinion is that charity is love of God, certainly, but *only* through love of neighbor. So runs the argument: God cannot be known or loved directly — only indirectly, as manifested in creation. And among created things, the best opportunity for discovering and loving him is in the neighbor. This view severely limits contact with God and reverses the true order of charity. Christ proclaimed, " 'You must love the Lord your God with all your heart, with all your soul, and with all your mind.' This is the greatest and first commandment. The second resembles it: 'You must love your neighbor as yourself' " (Mt 22:37-9). To follow the reverse order would prove disastrous in any developing friendship between a dedicated man and woman, because their love would inevitably terminate in each other. This prediction flows also from the psychological insights already considered in regard to marriage as the natural goal of complementing love, unless restrained and sublimated for a sufficient motive that includes the primacy of the Ultimate.

Charity must be understood accurately and in its proper order before it can be integrated with chastity and eventually with friendship. A prudent judgment, therefore, requires first this clear grasp of essentials, then the assurance of each friend's commitment to growth toward fullness of charity as a life goal. Only strong, personal adherence to a superior love for God himself will allow a consecrated man and woman to avoid the danger of concentrating principally or exclusively on the love between the two of them.

What kind of love is charity? Discernment is needed to distinguish it as unique among many types of love. For a believer this is not difficult — at least theoretically. Charity is the most excellent of all loves, most different from any other in human experience, and this *precisely* because it is *divine love*, infinitely nobler than the most spiritual human love. It is a participation in infinite Love for infinite Goodness, the Holy Spirit himself, the Person uniting the Father and the Son. Even though man's deepest longings of spirit are for unlimited goodness, beauty, and truth, charity is not a love man can acquire or earn. It comes into his life only as a gift from God. By it he loves what God loves and as God loves — not as he alone would or could love.

The priorities or order of charity result from the very kind of love it is. God, the utterly perfect, lovable being, first and above all loves himself. Secondly, he loves all created things in himself as they reflect to one degree or another his own perfect goodness. Only by charity can man love all things in this way, the divine level of loving. A person, therefore, who does not love God primarily and all else in God has no claim to loving with charity. Should he think differently, other types of love would in fact account for the experience he misinterprets. It is precisely the primary and secondary orientation of divine love that any Christian, especially the consecrated person, must preserve and develop in his life of love and friendship.

Many today seem unable to grasp how such an exalted, literally divine love can exist in a human being. It is quite possible, however. If God so chooses, he can share his own nature with man, raising the life of the human spirit to a divine level by the grace of his sanctifying gift. Together with this fundamental grace, God bestows the gifts of charity, the other infused virtues, the gifts of the Holy Spirit, and the divine indwelling.

But even with all these gifts man cannot directly see God. God is solely and infinitely spirit, while man is limited in his experience of *knowing* both by his natural, bodily way of seeing and by his abstractive, stepwise process of understanding. Nonetheless, by the vision of faith, a Christian has God's assurance of the divine presence within him; there is, then, no obstacle to his *loving* God directly. The human experience of loving is not limited in ways human understanding is. Loving relates the person to the very concreteness of whomever or whatever is loved. And so, no matter what object the mind presents to the will, whether it be known by natural vision or by faith, one can love directly. By faith a believer knows that God loves him, is personally present to him, and has raised him and empowered his will to love his Lord personally and intimately in return. With such faith he can love God directly with the love of charity.

There could be no greater impoverishment of Christian love than to restrict it to the indirect love of God through creatures. Creation surely is one rich, quite tangible avenue of approach to him, but God desires beyond this the direct, spiritual, divine love-response which he has made possible. This is especially true of consecrated celibates who dedicate their entire lives to growing in Christian love.

Without doubt, the secondary object of charity is all creatures. The Christian is to love them with divine love, because this is how God loves them. Though necessarily secondary, his love of neighbor is not simply an inconsequential adornment to his love of God. It is essential, even commanded, as Jesus made utterly clear. Jordan Aumann speaks about human friendship as a very helpful, if not required, preparation for fulfilling this commandment of Christ: "Love of one another is so central to Christian teaching that we could say no man can hope to achieve the universal brotherhood proposed by Christ unless he has first learned to live and experience the generous love of genuine friendship."

These fundamental points about charity, its nature, and basic order must shape the habitual, conscious perspective of the dedicated man and woman who accept the possibility of friendship. The Christian goal they propose is not easily achieved. For genuine charity to become the principal motive of daily activity requires years of ascetical striving in order to gain the purity of motivation and strength of will such an orientation implies.

Because of this primary requirement, prudence would judge many consecrated persons insufficiently developed in Christian love to be capable of favorably incorporating a friendship with the opposite sex into their vocation. If, however, the celibate is rooted in authentic love, there is no reason thus far to declare an actual friendship imprudent.

CONSECRATED CHASTITY
AND THE FULLNESS OF CHRISTIAN LOVE

An adequate theological evaluation must consider the celibate's motive for choosing a life of consecrated chastity and the degree to which he has integrated it into his life of charity. The two are intimately related.[3] In each case it is necessary to know whether the relationship is vital and effective, or whether chastity has been chosen predominately for some human motive such as ignorance, fear, immaturity, or merely as a condition for ordination or admission into religious life.

To begin the evaluation: does the celibate understand precisely the negative side of his vow, the full extent of what he renounces — not only genital sexuality and its pleasures, but a complementing life-companion, parenthood, and the experiences of building a family and home of his own? The concreteness of his renunciation is grasped often only progressively.

At the same time, does the celibate clearly realize that he does not renounce human love of persons of either sex, but only the relationships that lead him toward self-centeredness and the situations which either endanger his vow or give grounds for scandal? Lacordaire, the Friar Preacher who revitalized Catholicism in nineteenth-century France, had many close friends. Understandably he argued for genuine affection in celibate friendships, but also for freedom-giving renunciation in terms of detachment and its effects:

> Detachment . . . is a law of the Gospel and a condition of perfection, but it certainly does not follow that we ought here below to love no reasonable creature except with general charity that is of obligation for everyone. Well ordered affections, that is, subordinate to the law of God and to the love we owe him above ourselves and all things, are in no way an obstacle to sanctity. The lives of saints, and in first place that of our Lord, are full of and are animated with such affections. No one would ever say, I imagine, that our Lord did not love Saint John and Mary Magdalene with tenderness and predilection — and it would be curious if Christianity, founded on the love of God and men, resulted in dryness of soul in regard to everything that is not God. However, there is often passion in friendships, and this is what can make them dangerous and harmful. Passion troubles at the same time our senses and our reason, and too often even leads to evil, to sin. This is why the masters of the spiritual life recommend

detachment, but not lack of affection. Detachment from self, far from diminishing love, maintains and augments it. What ruins love is egotism, not the love of God. Never on earth have there been ardent affections more lasting, more pure, and more tender than those to which the saints gave their hearts — hearts at the same time emptied and filled, emptied of themselves and filled with God!

The correct managing of affections of which Lacordaire writes flows from integrating the renunciations of consecrated chastity with the overriding perspective of charity. The result is reason-guided self-control in both the restraint and the exercise of one's feelings — a spiritual freedom from emotional determinism. While this is an objective of every Christian, it is the habitual achievement of few, even among consecrated Christians.

Any pastoral evaluation should focus principally on the positive side of the vow of chastity, determining the extent to which the celibate has chosen it as a help toward reaching fullness of love. In their decrees on religious life and the formation of priests, the fathers of Vatican II restate the traditional, spiritual advantage of consecrated chastity. It is a renunciation of the values of marriage *for* the kingdom of heaven, both as it is developing here in individuals and in the Church, and as it will be in eternity. Liberating the celibate in a unique way, vowed chastity keeps his human heart from immersing itself in innumerable preoccupations of family and secular life that can easily divide it, permitting it to apply itself totally to the twofold preoccupation of charity. It is important, therefore, to ascertain how much the celibate prizes freedom from the specialized life-involvement of marriage precisely to be better able to develop freedom for universal life-involvement with God and all that God loves.

The foremost part of the double preoccupation of Christian love is prayerful contemplation of God himself through faith and love in order to attain as intimate a union with him as possible in this life. A. M. Perreault speaks of the total and exclusive gift of self to God in love, which only consecrated chastity makes possible:

The sole valid motive for renouncing the joys of marriage to give supreme homage to God is a superior love for God, because one does not speak of consecration to God if marriage is renounced for motives of fear, indifference, egotism, or pride. In fact, it is charity which animates in depth one's consecration of chastity: one renounces the possibilities of human love offered by marriage in order to penetrate more profoundly into the mystery of divine love. Thus, the object directly envisioned by the consecration of chastity is not a creature . . . but an uncreated reality, God himself, eternal Love, to whom the religious desires to bind herself definitely. . . . Because she loves God in such a total manner, she renounces willingly, by this love of God, every other love that would risk absorbing her or dividing her possibilities of loving.

Growth in prayer is a practical index of how well a Christian is reaching the goal of personal union with the Triune God. Freedom to spend all his life in achieving this union is a major value flowing from consecrated chastity.

Of crucial importance, then, in determining whether other features of a celibate's life help or hinder progress toward this goal is the quality of his personal prayer. In evaluating mixed friendship between celibates, it is necessary to ask not merely whether the relationship offers danger to chastity, but also how it influences each friend's life of prayer. If the friendship begins regularly to absorb time for prayer or attention at prayer, the relationship is obviously counterproductive. If, however, the dedication of each friend to prayer encourages greater faithfulness in the other; if their varied approach and experience in prayer mutually enriches each other's prayer, then the friendship is obviously a sound means for growth in the very purpose of their lives. This vital question cannot be asked or answered quickly. Time must elapse in order that permanent trends can be recognized. Here, honest self-evaluation in the practice of daily prayer must be the standard of judgment.

Vatican II stresses a related aspect of consecrated celibacy, that of witnessing *now* to the eschatological union of God with man — a nuptial union without end: "For all Christ's faithful, religious recall that wonderful marriage made by God, which will be fully manifested in the future age, and in which the Church has Christ for her only spouse."

The second preoccupation of charity is to love all else that God loves. Here, too, consecration in chastity helps the priest or religious become totally committed to the divine service of all people in Christ. A celibate's love is freed from commitment to one or a few people and so is opened to all. Not only can he better love the Lord; he can also better love and serve all whom God loves. With greater ease he prays for all and gives himself to the apostolic work that the Lord himself would want to do for them.

Thomas Dubay adds that consecrated virginity brings about not only this human and universal, but a deep and warmly expressed Christian love for others as a matter of course. Immersed foremost in God, the consecrated person experiences progressively, in maturing prayer, that love which alone satisfies the thirst of the human heart. This growing love for God makes him more and more sensitive to goodness and beauty and allows him to respond ever more easily and fully to goodness and beauty wherever he finds it — in himself and in others. Slowly but effectively he acquires more of the mind and heart of God through his prayerful lifestyle and comes to see and love everything as God himself does.

Paradoxically, consecrated chastity could not make these major contributions toward the fullness of Christian love without being supernaturally enlivened by this very love itself. Charity alone permits man voluntarily to select God, the supreme good, as the goal of his life. It alone enables him to harmonize his every action with that end. By extending its own goal to every activity of man's life, Christian love subsumes all within the universal sphere of the love of God. Although its particular goal is the reasonable control of sexuality, chastity, vivified by love, now orders sexuality to the love of God. Like every Christian virtue, chastity becomes a particularization, a concretization of Christian love in a specific area of human life.

Because of his dedication to the fullness of Christian love through the living of perfect chastity, the soul and the body of a consecrated celibate are completely ordered to God instead of partly either to some self-centered or to some natural goal. The very purpose of his consecration is to hasten and heighten the process of sanctifying his entire being. From this perspective we see the superior, spiritual dignity and beauty of the grace of consecrated chastity in comparison with the grace of Christian marriage. Vatican II, then, rightfully expects religious to regard their state of life as an "exceptional gift of grace" which they should gratefully receive, cherish, and guard.

Some religious and priests have succeeded in integrating chastity with the goal of charity in the ways just described. Should it come into their lives, these individuals need not necessarily fear masculine-feminine friendship. Their spiritual orientation and development will be self-preserving, one result of the supernatural prudence they have gained. *Perfectae Caritatis* observes that it will give them "a kind of spiritual instinct" by which they "reject whatever endangers chastity." Moreover, in terms of natural prudence, they possess one essential psychological requirement already considered. Their twofold orientation in Christian love is the "sufficient motive or ideal" necessary for both restraining and sublimating love.

FRIENDSHIP IN GENERAL

Because a consecrated person should know the types of friendship that are compatible with both charity and chastity, a consideration of human friendship is important here.

Aristotle noted eleven essential characteristics of friendship, which St. Thomas Aquinas later adopted, developed, and inserted into the Christian tradition. Telescoping the eleven into three, Aquinas introduced them into moral theology in a way most useful for discerning between generous and selfish forms of friendship and providing an optimal framework for understanding charity.[4]

It should be clear from the beginning that friendship cannot exist between highly dissimilar people. Enough likeness in being and life-style must be there for attraction and appreciation to spring up between two persons. When both become aware of these similarities, love spontaneously begins to exist. This initial love is prerequisite to friendship and is in this sense its foundation. Such a dynamic occurs because everything naturally loves its own being and perfection. And so in the measure that one person resembles another by sharing in the same good qualities, love springs into existence.

To develop into the love of friendship, this beginning attraction must in each person become an unselfish, affective and effective love of the other. Each must consistently wish for and make earnest efforts to procure the genuine good, the true perfection of the other — his health, for example, his education, moral improvement, increase in grace, and union with God. Only in this way does a person love generously with a love that Aristotle and Thomas call "benevolent" and regard as basic to friendship.

Unless motivated by such benevolent love the human heart is prone to self-oriented love, whether wholesome or selfish. Either openly or subtly, it can seek from a relationship predominantly pleasure or utility. It does not, then, really love the other person or seek his true good. Instead it looks mainly or solely for its own satisfaction or profit. Authentic friendship cannot be built on such a foundation. Only benevolent human love is an apt, natural disposition for the graced benevolence of Christian love.

106

The tendency of seeking pleasure or utility is greater at the beginning of a friendship, but can be regulated and tempered. Aumann outlines the proper development:

> The love of friendship begins with the mutual attraction that stimulates the passion of love, the affection for each other, but it passes beyond that to become more and more an expression of the spiritual love which is called volitional. The 'I-thou' relationship merges into a sense of 'us' and then, indeed, the friendship seeks an ideal which transcends the two who are friends.

At the root of such a wholesome evolution is self-knowledge. The celibate must be clear about his motivation, reviewing his own mixture of motives from time to time, striving to eliminate selfishness, reduce self-orientation, and cultivate benevolence as the basis of his friendship. Any other dominant motive would endanger charity and chastity.

To exist, benevolent love need not be mutual: no exchange need occur between two people. A parent with a small child, a teacher with students, a doctor or nurse with patients — all can unselfishly desire and work for the other's true good, not receiving nor expecting benevolent love in return. Such are the affirming, salvific, and various functional loves described by psychologists in chapter two.

Generous love itself is not friendship. Friendship is the relationship between *two* people who reciprocally perceive, appreciate, and return benevolent love. If love is not returned, it is not satisfied. Each friend must *know* that the other loves, not by words only, but as love reveals itself to the full over a period of time. In this way only can real, personal union occur. Aristotle and Thomas call this second, essential requirement for friendship "mutuality."

Mutuality does not compromise the unselfish motivation of benevolent love because its emphasis is not on desire but on knowledge. Benevolent, mutual love preserves a readiness to sacrifice actual reciprocity if necessary for the other's greater good. Such a disposition presupposes strong self-control, great respect for the other person, esteem for his true good, and a love of moral beauty — philosophical terms for the requirements of friendship that psychology calls the loves of restraint and sublimation.

The third and crucial element of true friendship is the friends' actual exchange. Evoking a many-leveled sharing of true goods for their mutual fulfillment and happiness, it can deepen their similarity to the point of unity. St. Thomas calls such sharing a "communication in happiness." Fundamentally, it is an intercommunion of spirits in thoughts, feelings, and choices by which friends achieve unity in the common possession of truth and love. This authentic, human perfection and happiness can be communicated through silent awareness, words, gifts, or activity. Whatever the medium, it brings about an interior union of hearts whereby "friends are one heart and one soul." Loving exchange between them can involve nearly complete self-revelation one to the other, including bad as well as good qualities. The more friends trust each other, the less they withhold or conceal from one another. They come to know intuitively that their friend will both understand and help them with regard to their flaws of character and appreciate and encourage the development of their aptitudes.

Each can come to experience the other as himself so intimately that in his affection and joy he is "filled" with the other and does not want to be separated from him. The height of such communication, and so the height of friendship, is sharing everything to the point of living together. The friendship becomes an intercommunion of life itself: "Nothing is so delightful to friends as to *be* in one another's presence."

Intercommunion can exist on any of several levels, each of which qualifies the friendship. The deepest human level is communication of the natural goods of intelligence and moral values, forging a unity of corresponding depth. Such forms of friendship are what psychology describes as fulfilling love. Complementing love involves a still more complete form of sharing between men and women. If the sharing is wholly complete, the love inspiring it is the complementing friendship of marriage; if exclusive of sexuality, the exchange can lead to the intimate, chaste, masculine-feminine friendship of consecrated celibacy. The exchange between Christians can further include the highest supernatural goods, such as enlightenment in faith, encouragement in hope, and upbuilding in charity. The lives of the saints quoted earlier furnish examples of such intimately natural and supernatural communication.

In the classic thinking of Thomas Aquinas, then, benevolence, mutuality, and communication in true happiness are the three essential features of authentic friendship. Association between celibates which would compromise any one of them would be incompatible with the consecrated person's goal of charity and must be avoided.

Profound reasons explain why true friendship can lead to the mutual, noble improvement of friends. In the first place, the very nature of the love between them is a religious reality. Andrew Greeley judges that this is because of the exchange of selves without reserve: "Friendship is religious behavior in the primordial sense of that word. In the friendship relation we give of *ourselves,* and such an offering of the totality of our being is so primordial and intimate that it touches the very roots of our existence and forces us necessarily to face questions of the ultimate." Charles Heris goes further and explains that the image of God in us can be brought to perfection by such love of others:

> Thus, people in love will love each other in something which goes beyond themselves, something greater than themselves, but something also which they already possess in the depths of their soul, and they need to perfect. It is really the divine which we love in ourselves and in others, but frequently it does not appear in our consciousness until it is revealed by others, and then, in the mutual gift of self, love guides us toward this reality through a common effort.

He concludes that, "love, when lived in its fullness, is genuinely religious in its essence, for the adventure which it represents, pursued in spite of risk and peril, is not and cannot be fully realized except in God."

MASCULINE-FEMININE FRIENDSHIP

Masculine-feminine friendship can be the preeminent form of true friendship. At first sight it may seem that a man and a woman are not similar enough for the basic requirement of friendship. Two men or two women would seem more similar. The reality of complementarity between the sexes, however, shows that two halves of the human whole may be more "alike" than any two incomplete halves of the same sex.

In the course of explaining the principle that likeness is the cause of love, St. Thomas introduces the distinction between actual and potential likeness.[5] Actual likeness between persons arises from the fact that each possesses the same quality. In this respect the affections of the one will tend naturally to the other as being another self for whom he wishes the good he desires for himself. Potential likeness, on the contrary, is rooted in the fact that one person alone actually possesses the quality; the other, by inclination or desire only. The latter perceives it from need, as something he loves for his own good and perfection. In this respect he loves the other in reference to himself. The first type, actual similarity, is the basis for gift-love (benevolence), or authentic friendship. The second, potential likeness, is the basis for need-love (concupiscence), or "friendship" founded upon what one receives from the other in terms of self-perfection, even usefulness or pleasure.

Since men and women are a mixture on all levels of masculinity and femininity, it becomes clear how they can love each other with a mixture of both loves, based respectively on the actual likenesses they share and the mutual need for perfection they offer each other.

In Jungian psychological terms, the *anima* of the man makes him actually similar to his feminine complement in friendship, while the *animus* in the woman makes her actually similar to the man. His masculine nature can develop her *animus* beyond what it is at any given stage: similarly her feminine nature can develop his *anima*. There is, consequently, both an actual and a potential basis of likeness for complementing friendship.

Two men alone perhaps more easily share concepts and reasoning at first; two women more easily sense or feel what is good, beautiful, and true, but since they are not potential to each other as complement, in their exchange each will develop only partially. The woman has the potency to understand a man's insights, however, and can profit from his clarity of knowledge and strength of conviction. He, in turn, can be led deeper into the mysteries of life by her intuition and so profit from her depth of vision and warmth of approach. In this way each can elicit perfection in the other that would otherwise have remained undeveloped.

But the perfection of each, proper to his own sex, can also be strengthened. Gerald Vann observes:

> The two perfect each other through their love; can bring to perfection the qualities proper to each. The man can, through his tender, humble cherishing of her, lead the woman to grow in depth and strength and in her own feminine tenderness; the woman can, through her love and loyalty and absorption in his vocation, lead the man to the perfection of his male qualities; his power and strength purged of brutality and aggressiveness, his ambition purged of ruthlessness, his protectiveness purged of condescension, his concern with the immediate purged of impatience and short-sightedness. And each can teach the other to be deeper, wiser, more human and so in the end more divine.

In this context of masculine-feminine, mutual enrichment through friendship, much is gained by the struggle to pursue the elusive mystery of person, which repeatedly emerges in the relationship. The striving between celibates for personal communion as such over any other attraction between them can result in improving their spiritual lives. They must develop innumerable virtues, such as generosity, self-forgetfulness, and the will to bridge small differences by understanding, compassion, and patience. The lesson of trust in the other to the point of surrender is slowly learned. The self-knowledge, detachment, self-integration, and freedom that this occasions are invaluable. The man and the woman grow to accept sacrifice and sufferings willingly in order to prefer and develop personal love. The effort involves moderating love's desire and controlling external and internal senses and feelings in order to achieve body-spirit equilibrium individually and maintain the integrity of their relationship on all levels. Both are made sensitive to the other's needs, humble in regard to their own, faithful and prudent in their mutual pursuit of moral refinement and the beauty of modesty and virginity. They learn to rely on prayer and grace, to trust in Providence, and to be grateful for divine security and help. They become more an individual man and woman in each other and derive from this experience freshened creativity in their state of life and the fulfillment of its duties.

Heris extends the benefits into the realms of spiritual maternity and paternity:

> Each individual, in different degrees, is made up of a double psychism, at once masculine and feminine. Now if a masculine psychism that the man normally possesses makes him desire woman with a love of concupiscence, it also allows him to exercise a certain protective fatherliness in her regard. On the other hand, the more relative part which femininity has to play in him gives him the power to conduct himself toward woman with a respectful, delicate and even friendly understanding. As for the woman herself, her feminine psychism, if it inclines her to man by her desire, also inspires a truly maternal sentiment in his regard, and so far as she possesses virility, she can treat with him on a plane of equality and fraternal cooperation.

From this discussion it should be clear how a masculine-feminine friendship, presuming its benevolence, can be friendship preeminently: the other essential elements, mutuality and communication, are more complete than in any other relationship. That such complementary fulfillment is the creative intention of God was pointed out in chapter one. Through it each human half learns better how the human spirit as such can know and love. In children, personal fulfillment is partially brought about by parental influence and the social context. In adults, mature masculine-feminine friendship can bring it to completion.

Obviously for fallen mankind, the very power of complementarity offers dangers which are heightened for celibates by the fact that the creative intention is perfected in marriage. Grace, however, does not bypass nature but works through it: the divine redemptive intention does not disregard the divine creative intention of masculine-feminine complementarity. Nor does consecrated celibacy of itself demand psychic disassociation or complete exclusion between the sexes.

As a general norm, Christianity's prudent reserve in this area is nonetheless a wise one. Most men and women cannot avoid the hazards to charity and chastity occasioned by close, unmarried, masculine-feminine association. Yet, the possibility is still open for individuals who, because they have become capable of prudent love, are fundamentally free. In this perspective Vann reflects on the beauty and the terror of the human use of freedom:

> The Pieta is the symbol of God's love. If none of his creatures had free-will, what a neat and tidy place the world would be: all things joining together in an unsullied song of praise to God; no problem of evil, no problem of pain, no problem of hell, no hatred. No hatred; but also no love, no friendship: and it was love and friendship that God wanted most of his creation; it was to make love possible that he gave some of his creatures freedom.
>
> The terrible choice is given. You can put power at the service of love; and then it is creative and beneficent and lovely, as it is in God. Or you can divorce power from love; and then it becomes destructive, evil, ugly.

Any developing friendship between a consecrated man and woman must, therefore, be fundamentally honest and generous on both sides. A one-sided or mutual relationship of utility or pleasure cannot be true friendship.

FRIENDSHIP AND CHARITY

From Jesus himself we know the quality of the relationship he desires to develop with each of us. He declares it in his farewell talk to his apostles at the Last Supper: "I will not now call you servants . . . but my friends" (Jn 15:15). Sooner or later, each Christian given to pondering his faith must search into the content of this declaration of divine friendship and penetrate it as deeply as possible in terms of human experience. Such a reasoned approach to faith will raise the question: how much can a believer trust his merely human powers of mind to grasp the divine meaning of Revelation?

A truth runs through all reality, giving confidence to the believer that his correct insights into the human terms God chooses to speak to men will truly bring out divine meaning: all things, in one degree or another, resemble God, their maker. If we accurately understand any created thing, then, we also learn something of the source it partially reflects. Revelation of the things of God in the language of men supposes this truth. Indeed, Scripture continually makes use of it, for example, when declaring the similarity between man and his maker: "God said: 'Let us make man in our own image, in the likeness of ourselves' " (Gn 1:26). Jesus' favored way of teaching the invisible things of his Father's kingdom was through parables based on the visible things of daily, human life. This process, of course, has limitations. One must avoid taking the medium for the message, but once the earthly features of the parable are clearly taken into account, the thinking believer can truly use his human experience as a medium through which to know something about the infinite God and the things he has revealed. Christians through all ages have used this mental process called analogy, the very heart of theology. Some examples illustrating it will at the same time help integrate human friendship with divine charity.

St. Paul voices the general principle: "Ever since God created the world his everlasting power and deity — however invisible — have been there for the mind to see in the things he has made" (Rm 1:20). Applying this principle, St. Augustine came to understand much about his love of God through his love of creatures. He tells how in his experience of bodily beauty, timing of the seasons, brightness of light, melody of song, fragrance of flowers, ointments and spices, or the embrace of friends, he found more than what his senses enjoyed. In each sense experience, his spirit discovered grounds for knowing God more richly and loving him more deeply.[6]

C. S. Lewis, an admirable Christian thinker of our day, expresses differently this same process:

Nature never taught me that there exists a God of glory and of infinite majesty. I had to learn that in other ways. But nature gave the

113

glory a meaning for me. I still do not know where else I could have found one. I do not see how the 'fear' of God could have ever meant to me anything but the lowest prudential efforts to be safe, if I had never seen certain ominous ravines and unapproachable crags. And if nature had never awakened certain longings in me, huge areas of what I can now mean by the 'love' of God would never, so far as I can see, have existed.

Leo Bond, in his competent, Thomistic study of human and divine friendship, explains how man's use of the principle of analogy aids his understanding of, rather than minimizes, divine truth:

The more man appreciates the fact that between himself and God there exists a true friendship, the better he understands the nature of the love God has for him and the nature of the love he should have for God. He thus acquires a more concrete conception upon which to model his love for God, and this, in turn, is conducive to an intensification of that love. Since it is in accordance with the nature of the human intellect to arrive at a knowledge of things less known through the medium of things better known, it appears that the best means of acquiring a greater appreciation of man's friendship with God would be to examine it in the light of the friendship which he has with his fellowman. A comparison of this kind must not be considered as an attempt to humanize God by reducing Him to the level of a human friend, but rather as an attempt to divinize man by a consideration of the great dignity to which friendship with God elevates him.

Bond is here commenting on a crucial point in the writings of St. Thomas: his explanation of divine charity precisely in terms of friendship, original in the history of Christian thought. Others had approached charity from many points of view, but Thomas culminated centuries of theological development by his innovation, a view he held consistently. In his early *Commentary on the Ethics* of Aristotle he writes: "Charity is friendship between man and God, or the love with which man clings to God as to his friend." He tersely concludes a later work on the *Sentences* of Peter Lombard with the statement: "Charity is friendship with God." His most mature investigation of charity in the *Summa Theologica* comes to the same conclusion: "It is evident that charity really is friendship with God." In our own day, others, too, have richly developed this theme.[7]

114

What is important to realize is that divine love corresponds point by point to human friendship, whose core reality, considered earlier in the chapter, harmonizes with the above theological tradition and is triple in nature: a *mutual* love of *benevolence* based upon a common bond of similarity and expressed through some kind of *communication*.

At first sight it would seem that in man's love for God the prerequisite of fundamental similarity is lacking. Clearly, true human friendship is out of question with mere things, no matter how precious; even with animals, no matter how beloved. Man can develop friendship only with another human being who is personally very much like himself actually and/or potentially. How then can man, so different from God, have a basis for true friendship with him? Genesis does reveal that man is the created image of God, but this resemblance gives him only enough similarity for the natural, human love of admiration and worship of the creator. It does not endow him with the equality required for friendship.

Earlier reflections on the fullness of love as goal of the consecrated person raised the question: how does God enable man to love him with divine love? The answer involved the Catholic teaching on sanctifying grace, the common bond of similarity between God and man, whereby the latter's spirit is elevated to share in the divine nature and life. With this elevation, the infused virtues corresponding to man's natural, spiritual powers, and the gifts of the Holy Spirit are bestowed. Graced in this manner, the Christian is enabled to conform mind and will to God's and respond to his illuminations and inspirations, now no longer in a solely human but also in a divine way. The fundamental gift of grace establishes, then, sufficient likeness or equality between man and God to make possible the communication in mind and heart necessary to friendship. Scripture expresses it in terms of our receiving from God "the spirit of sonship. When we cry, 'Abba! Father!' it is the Spirit himself bearing witness with our spirit that we are children of God" (Rm 8:15-17).

Though this equality is relative, it is quite enough that man be made similar to God by grace. "It is not necessary to say that God is similar to man in order to establish a basis for friendship between them, since friendship, as well as anything else which is predicated of God and man, is predicated only analogously." It is divine, not human friendship that charity establishes.

But is charity between man and God a *benevolent* love? To any person of faith, it is evident that God's love for man is both an affective and effective desire for his true good: "God so loved the world that he gave his only Son, that whoever believes in him should not perish but have eternal life" (Jn 3:16). "Our human fathers were thinking of this short life when they punished us, and could only do what they thought best; but he does it all for our own good, so that we may share his own holiness" (Heb 12:10). God wants good for us on every level, but he especially desires our perfect and complete happiness. In God himself, in his goodness, his happiness known, loved, and enjoyed is our fulfillment.

To perfect our minds with infinite Truth, God allows us to see him obscurely in this life by faith and directly in heaven by vision: "For now we see in a mirror dimly, but then face to face" (1 Co 13:12). To fill our hearts with infinite Love, he provides us with his own love: "The charity of God is poured forth in our hearts by the Holy Spirit who is given us" (Rm 5:5).

God's love does not stop at well-wishing, but effectively procures our happiness. Precisely in view of our individual, eternal fulfillment, for example, his Providence bestows or withholds temporal favor. Furthermore, since God is perfect, his love for us can in no way be self-directed for pleasure or usefulness, or be selfish in any way. The finite can add nothing to the infinite.

Our love for God, too, must be benevolent. We must affectionately desire and rejoice that God's good is his, that he is utterly happy in his fullness. A friend's joy at the other's well-being is to be ours — delight in God's internal perfection or glory. Nor is this all. We are to desire his external good or glory by wanting everything in existence to realize the perfection that God himself wishes for it. In fulfilling his will, everything reflects him as best it can, thus glorifying him. As conscious creatures, we are, then, to render God external glory in thought, desire, and speech. The Psalms are replete with examples of such human praise.

Our love for God must also be active, stimulating us to praise his internal perfection in action: adoring, thanking, begging his favor, making amends. It must further urge us, as it did St. Paul, increasingly to acquire our own natural and supernatural perfection for God's glory, to use resources of nature reasonably, and to help as many others as possible to work toward their perfection.

A selfless love for God does not exclude our desiring him for our own happiness. This desire is compatible with benevolent love if we regard ourselves and our good as subordinate objectives — those of a

116

creature attaining the perfection God wants for it. In this way our desire does not stop with ourselves, with our wanting God for our own happiness only. Rather, it terminates in him, since we wish our happiness also for the sake of his greater glory.

Is love between God and the Christian truly a *mutual* love? St. Thomas notes that God so desires friendship's return of love from us that he makes us able to respond by creating divine love itself in us:

> The proper effect in man of divine love seems to be the fact that he loves God. Indeed, this is the principal thing in the lover's intention: to be loved in turn by the object of his love. To this, then, the lover's main effort inclines, to attract his beloved to the love of himself; unless this occurs, his love must come to naught. So, this fact that he loves God is the result in man . . . of divine love.

Man's return of love in friendship with God begins at the basic minimum of observing his commandments: "You are my friends if you do the things I command you" (Jn 15:14). It extends, as Christ came to show us, to the total conformation of the human will to God's through following his Spirit in every detail of life: "I can do nothing on my own authority; as I hear, I judge; and my judgment is just, because I seek not my own will but the will of him who sent me" (Jn 5:20).

True friendship, finally, demands *communication*. Does such sharing transpire between man and God? What kind of communication characterizes their friendship? God's happiness, we know, stems basically from his knowledge and love of himself. By communicating his happiness to us, he associates us with his self-knowledge and self-love. In the exchange, God considers man and man considers God as another self: both are of one heart, one mind, even one life. Man and God, then, do enjoy the familiar exchange of friendship: "God is faithful, by whom you are called into the fellowship of his Son, Jesus Christ our Lord" (1 Co 1:9). In this life, even at his best, man dialogues imperfectly with God through the medium of sanctifying grace, whereby he is capable of intimate acts of faith, hope, and love in prayer. His communication becomes perfect in heaven: "Our conversation is in heaven" (Ph 3:20). We know that when he shall appear we shall be like to him because we shall see him as he is" (1 Jn 3:2).

Yet, even in this life of faith and bodily limitations, our intimacy with God through charity can far exceed what is possible in the best of human friendships. By grace God lives *within us*, and we *within him* by faith and love: "Whoever confesses that Jesus is the Son of God, God abides in him, and he in God. So we know and believe the love God has for us. God is love and he who abides in love abides in God, and God abides in him" (1 Jn 4:15-16). "May they all be one, Father, may they be one in us, as you are in me and I am in you, . . . that they may be one as we are one. With me in them and you in me, may they be so completely one that the world will realize that it was you who sent me and that I have loved them as much as you loved me" (Jn 17:21, 23).

Friends' intimate living together, at least in thought and desire, involves a two-sided communication. God tells us through the sacred Word, the teaching Church, and the interior promptings of his Spirit who he is, what are his traits, what he is interested in, what pleases or displeases him, and what he thinks and wills in our regard, even to the very details of our lives.

> Faith is, in a sense, a conversation with God, for though we do not actually hear God speaking to us, we can know with the certitude of faith what He would say to us in some given circumstance if He were to speak to us personally. For instance, when we perform some genuinely good work, supposing that we are in the state of grace, we can by faith be as sure that God is pleased and that He will reward us as if He appeared to us personally and said, 'This is very pleasing to Me and I will reward you.'

The most intimate communication between God and man in this life takes place in the activity of prayer. Many Fathers of the Church define prayer in terms of personal communication. Gregory Nazianzus, for example, says: "Prayer is a conversation and a dialogue with God"; St. John Chrysostom, "Prayer is a speaking to God"; St. Augustine, "Prayer is a turning of the mind to God through pious and humble affection." Citing St. Catherine of Siena and St. Teresa of Avila, Roberto Moretti regards prayer as the best means of cultivating friendship with God. Relationship with him can develop through all the degrees of prayer, from the simplest to the full operation of the contemplative gifts of the Holy Spirit: understanding, to grasp the truths of faith; knowledge, to judge created things rightly; wisdom, to esteem divine things correctly; counsel, to apply these judgments to concrete actions. Bond develops this point:

It is evident then that through the operation of these four gifts the human intellect receives participations of the divine truth from the intellect of God and that, therefore, God can truly be said to communicate with man through the gifts, which operate especially during prayer.

We have seen how the mutual communication required as a basis of friendship between man and man is realized with regard to God and men; first, the communication established by natural knowledge of God and knowledge of the natural law impressed upon man in creation; secondly, the more perfect communication established by the supernatural knowledge of God through faith, and lastly, by the most perfect communication possible in this life, which is that of prayer, especially the prayer of infused contemplation.

Justifiably, St. Thomas concludes: "Charity signifies not only the love of God, but also a certain friendship for Him, which indeed, over and above love, adds a mutual return of affection with some mutual communication." All the elements essential to friendship are there: the analogy of human friendship to divine charity between man and God therefore holds. Charity is friendship for God.

Nor does the existence of human friendship necessarily jeopardize man's intimate relationship with God. In fact, numerous spiritual writers point to a harmonious influence between human friendship and charity.

Vann thinks, for example, that human friendships need not mean loving God less; they can even be reason for loving him more:

> When God brings a human love to a soul who before loved only himself it is not a rejection of her [the soul's] love but the exact contrary: he is giving her more to love him with. He may well be asking something harder, more complicated, of her: he is certainly not asking something smaller. Every love you have — of nature, of art, of men, of wisdom — is an added way of loving and worshipping him, an additional gift to offer him.[8]

One aspect of authentic friendship is that it leads friends to seek their perfection, not in themselves, but in a higher ideal outside themselves. It can inspire cooperative effort in art, in politics, in humanitarian projects. It can heighten Christian friends' search after God and exercise their charity toward this ideal. Aumann writes: "It is of the very nature of genuine friendship to lift both parties to something beyond themselves and that is why such a friendship can aid greatly in the development and fulfillment of the person and can also serve marvelously as a vehicle for that supernatural love which is charity."

Charity can well be intensified by Christian friendship. In comparing the Christian love of friends and enemies, H. D. Noble expounds St. Thomas' mind on the point:

We love our friends supernaturally by loving them as God loves them, in that ideal which God himself proposes in loving them. We must desire for them the good which God in his infinite goodness wishes and destines for them.

If we truly love them, nothing will dishearten us in this work of love. We will help toward their sanctification, we will pray for them, we will give them advice and good example.

Saint Thomas is so convinced of the value of supernatural friendship that he advances an apparent paradox: 'It is of more merit to love a friend than an enemy.'

The radical distinction between supernatural and natural merit helps clarify this paradox. Our supernatural charity for our friends is, in fact and by right, more intense, and, consequently, more meritorious than our charity for our enemies.

Clearly, our friendship disposes us for a more intense charity. A friend who loves us is more lovable than an enemy who hates us. He is close to our heart; he is bound to us; he is thus open to our every affection. An enemy, to whom we render a passing service, does not elicit this devotion or mark of attention by friendship toward us. He does not love us; he is unjust in our regard; we are rather incited to hate him. But . . . we go to his help 'for the love of God.' Whereas a friend, who loves us and toward whom the joy of our friendship tends, always kind and attentive — how could we not love him with an enveloping charity whose fervor is measured by that of our very friendship? Our human reasons for love can only corroborate our motives of charity, and in consequence, stimulate and quicken our friendly devotion. Saint Thomas, to illustrate this point, compares a fire that burns more ardently if burnable material is near than if it is at a distance. We have more warmth of charity in our dealings towards friends than in some trifling services rendered occasionally to enemies.

Charity itself, according to Heris, tends to develop friendship between capable Christians:

> When charity is directed to persons capable of returning love, it takes on the form of friendship, the highest possible friendship which unites lover and beloved in God. We have seen that in true friendship the friends love each other in something greater than themselves, in an ideal which they pursue by mutually sharing the endowments they possess. Charity inevitably prompts us to such friendships with our fellow men. All who live the divine life of grace already possess God and tend toward eternal beatitude which will remove the veil which hides him from vision. And if charity prompts us to love all God's creatures, even more so it will turn us toward our brothers in love. This love will inspire us to aid each other in our spiritual ascent. There is no higher friendship than this.

God, in his charity for us, will providently introduce friendship into our lives. C. S. Lewis notes that one motive is thereby to reveal himself more thoroughly to us:

> But for a Christian, there are, strictly speaking, no chances. A secret Master of the Ceremonies has been at work. Christ, who said to the disciples 'You have not chosen me, but I have chosen you,' can truly say to every group of Christian friends 'You have not chosen one another but I have chosen you for one another.' The Friendship is not a reward for our discrimination and good taste in finding one another out. It is the instrument by which God reveals to each the beauties of all the others. They are no greater than the beauties of a thousand other men; by Friendship God opens our eyes to them. They are, like all beauties, derived from Him, and then, in a good Friendship, increased by Him through the Friendship itself, so that it is His instrument for creating as well as for revealing.

Charles Freible affirms that human love and friendship can ultimately develop appreciation of the most intimate, divine mysteries:

> When you come to examine it closely, this is a most extraordinary statement. 'May they all be one. Father, may they be one in us, as you are in me and I am in you, . . . that they may be one as we are one.' [Jn 17:20-3.] Our Lord is saying that He wants men to be so united that their union will actually resemble that of the Trinity itself. We could never have thought it unless our Lord had said it!

121

What sort of unity do we find in the Trinity? It is a union of persons so close, so intimate that these persons interpenetrate and fuse with one another to form one single being. Yet in this complete fusion of the Persons of the Trinity, the uniqueness of their personalities is not lost. They do not cease to be three unique Persons even though they constitute the one God. . . . What is it in the Trinity that does this? It is love! Love personified, the Holy Spirit, the living, dynamic bond between Father and Son.

From a theological point of view, then, not only is charity precisely divine friendship, but human friendships can both result from it and aid its growth in many ways. Saints, too, have discovered that in their providential friendships they had more to offer God; these loving relationships stimulated them to admire and to seek him more earnestly.

CELIBATE MASCULINE-FEMININE FRIENDSHIP AND CHRISTIAN LOVE

If human friendship in general is capable of the closest integration with divine love, is that preeminent form, masculine-feminine friendship equally so? Is there not in this relationship a serious rival to the total love of God required of persons consecrated to him? Can a man and a woman who are friends also have the unrestricted friendship for God indispensable to total dedication to him in love? Vann sees no inevitable difficulty. He speaks meaningfully to those who think that the two loves necessarily compete:

The difficulty arises from the fact that you put the love of God and the love of man on a level, as though they were the same kind of love; but they are not. If a woman, happily married to a man she loves, finds her life invaded by a new love, perhaps of an intensity she had hitherto not dreamt of, she may well feel this sense of tension, of unfaithfulness, because the two loves, however different in intensity, are still essentially the same kind of love: not only the will but the emotions and senses are essentially engaged. But the love of God is essentially only in the will, though the other levels of the personality may incidentally be involved at times. That is why the test of whether you love God is not whether you feel very loving but whether you do his will. . . .

If then your emotions are elsewhere engaged, why should you take this to be inevitably a betrayal or a diminishing of your love of God?

If your senses rejoice in colour or harmony or the sun's warmth on your body, do you love God the less? If great painting makes you catch your breath, if great music brings you near to ecstasy, if great poetry makes you cry, do you love God any the less? But, you retort, all these are quite different: the love of a human being is much more *dangerous*. So we return to the cult of safety.

More dangerous, yes: it is easy for some temperaments to become so absorbed in music or literature as to neglect their duties. But danger is not the same as disaster: danger is a matter of degree, and a purely individual matter varying with each human being. If you love both a human being and music, are you to say you must reject the human love because that is more dangerous but you may keep the love of music because though dangerous it is less so? Or are you to outlaw everything? . . . If, in other words, you grow more and more free from egoism and greed and rapacity, then you have less and less cause for fear: you can find a better motive in all that you do than the cult of safety.[9]

This distinction between kinds of love is important. So also is the fact that when it is not a question of conjugal friendship, it is even possible for one person to love two human friends faithfully without competition, if he knows that neither will make conflicting demands on him and if both are secure in his faithfulness. Should he have this sort of spiritual love, by the very fact of distinct objects his two loves are distinct, even though they be the same kind of love. In a similar way, it is possible for one person to love both God and man without breach of faithfulness to either. Should he love both even with the same love of charity, there is no conflict, since authentic charity has distinct primary and secondary objects.

Two human friends who love each other in charity can be aware that the supernatural bond of grace they share is the same bond that unites each with God. Indeed, instead of causing conflict, this common bond of charity is the ultimate basis for the integration of their two loves.

Presuming that a given man and woman are free from competition between themselves and their divine friend, the question now arises: can their human relationship be for both of them a positive aid to the development of charity? As pointed out in chapter two, psychologists see the best developed fulfilling love as the minimal type of personal love required for human friendship. They describe it as a mutual, generous communication of something of the self. Obviously, since such a human love exhibits the three essential characteristics of charity, it can serve as a created reflection of divine love. And complementing love, involving a more complete sharing of the self, is an even clearer likeness, resembling still more faithfully God's overflowing communication of his nature and happiness. Here is the solid basis for claiming that either type of mixed celibate friendship, fulfilling or complementing, can be helpful for both persons' growth in charity.

In the first place, the masculine-feminine friendship closely represents the friendship between divinity and humanity. Both are relationships of *relative equality*. Although sanctifying grace enables Christians to share in the divine nature, it does not make them wholly equal to God. Neither is there total equality between a man and a woman. Interdependency flows from their very complementarity. Both are human beings, perhaps similar enough even to be "two halves of a whole," but this very fact of complementarity makes it clear that they are not equal in every way to each other. From this truth several consequences follow.

Since sexuality pervades a person's entire being, a man and a woman will experience love — both human and divine — differently and think of it differently, too. Owing to their temperament and background, some individuals can understand to a degree the other sex's approach to life, even without much close association. They can analyze the other from rather distant observation and formulate theories of masculinity or femininity, but without closer experience their abstract knowledge is insufficient for concrete living based on masculine-feminine differences. To love God not abstractly but concretely, it might be helpful, for instance, for a man to know how a woman loves and for a woman to know how a man loves. Friendship is not the only source of this insight; it can come from many contributing causes. Nevertheless, actual friendship can be extremely helpful by providing experience that will vicariously enrich each friend's understanding of God's love. Augustine Rock pinpoints two requirements if vicarious experience is to be drawn from a person's understanding through association with others or from literature and history. "To appreciate vicarious experience one must have a definite store of personal experience both horizontally and vertically (both in extent and in depth); one can appreciate another's experience and assimilate it to oneself only to the extent or to the depth that has already been opened within oneself." Through friendship's intimate communication in thoughts, words, desires, and mutual service, a man and woman can see more deeply into God's approach to human beings and their response to him.

A woman can more fully understand God's love for her if she evaluates it from more than a feminine point of view. How enlightening for her to realize the differences between masculine and feminine love! Through mixed friendship she can better appreciate "masculine" aspects of divine love: its rectitude, firmness, protectiveness, providence, etc. On the other hand, from his friendship with a woman, a man can more gratefully accept the "feminine" aspects of God's love: the mystery of it, its gentleness, mercy, self-giving to the point of sacrifice.

A man cannot be exclusively masculine toward God in his spiritual life. From knowing a woman, he can better grasp the necessary attitudes of receptivity and sensitive response that every soul should have before God. Vann develops this truth:

> The soul is feminine to God. An activist world is a world which thinks it can be masculine to reality without first being feminine. It cannot. Gender is a much wider term than sex: whether human beings are male or female they have to learn the same essential lesson: that they must be feminine before they can hope with success to be masculine: they must be contemplative before they can hope to be wisely and graciously active: they must receive before they attempt to give. The great scientists know this, who humbly sit at the feet of reality before they attempt to use the resources of reality; the great philosophers know it, who will not attempt to imprison reality with all its mysteries into a neat and finite system; the poets and artists and makers of music know it, who give the world only what they have heard or seen; the wise men know it, who when they have made as best they can their explanation of reality, realize humbly that their best is merely 'as so much straw.' . . .

> The soul is feminine to God. In all the testimonies of the mystics it is God who purifies, the soul which is purified, for we are not 'sufficient to think anything of ourselves as of ourselves, but our sufficiency is from God.' There is of course all the labour, the arduous struggle, of asceticism: without that primary 'active purification' there could never be the 'passive purification' which is God's ultimate drawing of the personality into union with himself.

By the same token, a woman may not be so one-sided in her response to God that she treats him as she would one of her feminine

125

friends. The need of either sex consciously to know, appreciate, and become somewhat of the other is unconsciously helped by the processes of nature itself. M. J. Andre describes this phenomenon:

> All sex desires its plenitude. . . .
>
> But before it is finally achieved this intersexual plenitude is sought in the varied alternations from one sex to another in the same individual. Feminine and masculine sexuality succeed each other in every person. So it is that masculine puberty regularly admits of a period of feminine dominance. The adolescent boy looks very much like the 'boy with a woman's limbs' (Lucretius), with his soft skin, his silken hair, the delicate mould of the jaw, his fragility, his high-pitched voice. When the evolution is complete, and he is headed toward the equilibrium of his own proper sex, the young man will stand out unequivocally in his predominately masculine sexuality.
>
> In the man, femininity has been a brief stage of transition. The state of feminine predominance is, of course, much more lasting in the woman. In her, the cycle of femininity does not run its full course until after the menopause. Then appear the signs of virile involution; it is the weakening of inhibitions on the secondary sex. In becoming more masculine at that time, the woman is only obeying biological injunctions. In our day, psychologists observe that it is precisely at this time in a woman's life that there is more evidence of her need to give orders, to find social activity outside the confines of the family.

Both men and women experience similar need for the plenitude of complementarity, even in coming to know God. Natural human knowledge of God derives from either intellectual reasoning or symbolic intuition. The former is typically masculine, whereby something of God is known through the highest analogies stripped intellectually of their earthly limitations; the latter, typically feminine, whereby the goodness of God is richly but vaguely experienced through the symbols of creation. Grace elevates natural human knowledge through the infused intellectual virtues and the corresponding gifts of the Holy Spirit. The richer the knowledge, the fuller the response of love. And so if an individual were capable — at least to some enriched extent — of both human modes of knowing God, the more complete could be his response to God through the grace of charity.

Pre-modern conditions of civilization tended to give people a better opportunity to develop unconsciously a psychic, bi-sexual completeness. The living context of family, culture, and agrarian lifestyle

126

was usually more natural than today's. In it the feminine element was well represented in daily experience. But because men have since over-developed the "masculine" aspects of civilization, such as science, technology, industry, etc., we have inherited an ordinary life experience in which the masculine far outweighs the feminine. Western civilization has become too masculine to be healthy. This malaise is currently reflected in the alarming number of people who suffer from the inability adequately to know and love one another or God.

And yet, any ennobling love experience can teach man the workings, or "laws," of love. Once he knows what lover-beloved interrelationships are, he is well disposed for the love of God. Even a simple friendship with someone of the same sex can activate this capacity, furnishing, at least, experiential insight into God's desire to love us as friend. But a friendship between the sexes can most fully develop both persons' dual potentiality for reciprocal, loving relations with God. It can optimally teach both the man and the woman what it is to love God with a love blending the typically masculine and active with the characteristically feminine and receptive, moving them at the same time to sensitive (womanly) receptivity of God's aggressive (man-like) love. Mixed friendship furnishes experiential insight into God's proposal to love us not only as friend to friend, but precisely as bridegroom to bride.

Happily married people have direct experience to open them to this spousal relationship with God, although they find difficulty in giving themselves wholly to it because of the many preoccupations of married life. Spared these preoccupations, celibate men and women friends both know vicariously something of the married model of love and have direct experience of the model that is specifically theirs.

That celibates absorb as much as possible from the model of marriage is important. Up to the present, marriage has largely been used to understand God's love for mankind — probably because most men will relate to God through married love. But this model has always held rich meaning for religious and priests, also. From the beginning, the Church's relationship with Christ has consistently been regarded as a nuptial reality. Jesus called himself the bridegroom. St. Paul reiterates this truth by describing Christ's relationship with mankind in terms of married love. During the patristic period, friendship with God was often referred to under the symbolism of conjugal love. The writings of Origen and St. Gregory of Nyssa are good examples. This concept received fresh impetus from twelfth-century Cistercian spiritu-

127

ality of pure love, especially the preaching of St. Bernard on the Song of Songs. He was the first in theological history to treat the mystical life synthetically and fully around the central image of spousal love. Later, mystics almost universally described the higher stages of prayer in nuptial language. They speak, for example, of the beginning of unitive contemplation as "an engagement" between the soul and God, a period of "transforming union" leading to the "consummation of love" and the permanent life-union of "marriage." John of the Cross, after contemplating the mystery of the Incarnation, affirmed that God the Father had provided a spouse for his Son by creating the angels and men. Writing about her experience of spiritual marriage with Christ, St. Maria Maddalena de' Pazzi exemplifies the western Church's view of the spiritual goal of consecrated virgins:

> I saw how Jesus united with His bride in closest embrace. He laid His head over the head of His bride, His eyes upon her eyes, His mouth upon her mouth, His feet upon her feet, all His members upon hers so that His bride became one with Him and wanted all her Bridegroom wanted, saw all that her Bridegroom saw, and savoured all that her Bridegroom savoured. And God wants nothing but that the soul unite with Him in such wise, and that He may be utterly united with her.

In a similar spirit, Lacordaire searches for the most suitable human image to describe the love between Christ and his Church, a relationship that should exist between Christ and each Christian:

> We do not love God other than we love men, and the tenderness of the saints, as divine as it is, is not in its nature other than human tenderness. It is necessary, then, to find among the nuances of our diverse affections, the one which best expresses the love of Jesus Christ for his Church and the love of the Church for Jesus Christ — which implies the love that each of us should have for one another.
>
> One could think, having reflected on the infinite difference between God and us, that the most exact rapport between his and our sentiments would be paternal tenderness on his part and filial piety on ours. Or, if one wished to accord more equality because of the willing humiliation of Christ in the flesh of Adam, one could think that friendship would be the true name for our reciprocal life. But, while the affection of a father puts too much distance between us, that of a friend puts too much familiarity. We need a relationship

that maintains the sovereign authority of Christ and the thought of our weakness, and which surpasses in sweetness, in effusiveness, in ecstasy both friendship and paternal love. You will think of the conjugal bond, that unspeakable metaphor which, since the *Canticle of Canticles* in the Old Testament has answered both the ardor of the saints and the flaming love of Christ. Thus, as a young woman, so beautiful in her virginity, overcome with the happiness her virtue contains, brings an immortal promise to her engagement, so a soul, touched by God, brings to Christ who purifies her the submission of a spouse, a submission tempered by the tenderness of both, a fertile bond which will give sons to both and will culminate their joy in posterity.

Those who have never felt the breath from on high pass over their hearts and who laugh at our engagement with Christ and at our wedding ring all colored with his blood — we pardon them without hurt. Being ignorant of the reality, how could they understand the language? To you who have tasted in your sincere youth the first fruits of divine love, I speak a language that is not strange to you.

In our own day, Vatican II emphasizes the Pauline image of Christ's nuptial relationship to his Church, a view still integral to the Roman Church's conception of the spirituality of its priesthood. The priest is to " 'lead the faithful to the nuptials with the sole Spouse and to present them to Christ as a chaste virgin' — a spiritual mission which only a celibate priesthood can fulfill."

How frequently, too, in the Common of Virgins of the revised Roman *Liturgy of the Hours* is Christ referred to as bridegroom and spouse of his bride, the consecrated virgin!

Mixed celibate friendship can enrich charity in another dimension: the parental aspect of the apostolate. The more a person grasps both spiritual paternity and maternity, the fuller is his avenue of approach to these facets of God. "In both man and woman the paternal-maternal brings them closer to God . . . who, in the Trinity, is at once Father and Mother." Married people have direct experience of parenthood, but the priest in Christ's name must also reflect this divine breadth of perfection. J. D. Corcoran shows that he must be at once father and mother to the divine life in the faithful:

This is the role of the priest: to exercise paternity in Christ. . . . But the priest represents God both as father and as mother. Saint Augustine says that God can be called mother as well as father. The

129

fullness of parenthood is found in God although divided among men. But in the priest the fullness of divine parenthood demands a fatherly and a motherly function, a fatherly and a motherly mode of thinking and concern for the people of God, that is distinctive and proper to the priest. Saint Paul writes in the same vein: 'My dear children, with whom I am in labor again, until Christ is formed in you' (Ga 4:19). Isaiah says 'As nurslings you shall be carried in her arms and fondled in her lap; as a mother comforts her son, so will I comfort you' (Is 66:12; 13). Again Saint Paul says: 'Although as apostles we could have demanded much of you, while in your midst we acted as if a mother were cherishing her children' (1 Th 2:7). And our Lord himself says: 'How often I would have gathered thy children together, as a hen gathers her young under her wings, and thou wouldst not' (Mt 23:37).

In his study of the cooperation between nature and grace, Andre uses the concept of complementarity to stress the priest's obligation to develop both sides of his psyche. He concludes that a priest, whose vocation is "paternal and maternal," is bound to strive for the "inner equilibrium willed by the Creator" through integrating his femininity with his masculinity, instead of neglecting or repressing it for some mistaken motive. In possession of the intuitive, compassionate side of his psyche as well as the precise, logical side, he will be happier due to his own fullness and "better able to be all things to all men." As result of such insights and apostolic dispositions, the fruitfulness of Christian love cannot but increase in the lives of priests and religious.

Lastly, a prudential assessment of any mixed celibate friendship cannot neglect one aspect of apostolic action — the man's and woman's immediate, social context of life and work in community. Is their relationship a help or hindrance in this area of fraternal charity? Does it withdraw them physically or psychically from the brothers and sisters given them by Christ, or does it increase their understanding and appreciation, their compassion and service toward those with whom they live? The lives of the saints quoted reveal the answer: for them, friendship was a stimulus to an extended, enriched fraternal charity.

Considerations thus far presented in this ongoing prudential evaluation permit the conclusion that a celibate masculine-feminine friendship can be a source of personal benefit in the development of charity. It can give individual friends an enriched, natural basis for becoming supernaturally the beloved bride of Christ and God's minister of paternity, maternity, and fraternity.

MASCULINE-FEMININE FRIENDSHIP AND CONSECRATED CHASTITY

But what about the integration of masculine-feminine friendship and consecrated chastity? Can the two mix? Leo Cardinal Suenens points up the necessity of returning chastity to its place of vital importance in personal development:

> ... The very word 'chastity' has an almost archaic ring about it today; people hestitate to use it, so discredited is it. Yet this virtue has an indispensable role to play, today as yesterday. It is nothing but self-mastery, which must govern the sexual instinct to put it in the service of true love and integrate it, in its place, in the development of the human person.[10]

Of yet greater necessity is the integration of chastity in a mixed celibate friendship. In theory, there is no problem: perfect consecrated chastity is a concretization of charity just shown to be wholly compatible with masculine-feminine friendship. In practice, however, there are two possible areas of difficulty.

The first threatens the benevolence essential to authentic friendship. Generosity can easily be jeopardized in a relationship between a man and a woman by either the natural or the selfish desire for sensual satisfaction, which directly threatens their friendship and at least indirectly their virtue and vow of chastity. Since this danger is so real, some attention here must be given to the subjects of physical and sensate loves. The second area of possible difficulty involves marital love as such. While mixed celibate love and married love share much in common, they also differ in critical ways. Without a clear awareness of these differences, a relationship of celibate love can assume characteristics of married love beyond the two friends' powers of recognition and control. A comparison of the two kinds of love will uncover how the consecrated man and woman can avoid unconsciously developing something of the "spirit of marriage."

First, a word about the mixture of motives operative in human loving: C. S. Lewis cautions that even loves we think most generous and harmonized with charity need a good deal of ascetical training.

> Our loves do not make their claim to divinity until the claim becomes plausible. It does not become plausible until there is in them

a real resemblance to God, to Love Himself. Let us here make no mistake. Our Gift-loves are really God-like; and among our Gift-loves those are most God-like which are most boundless and unwearied in giving. . . . Their joy, their energy, their patience, their readiness to forgive, their desire for the good of the beloved — all this is a real and all but adorable image of the Divine life. . . . We may say, quite truly and in an intelligible sense, that those who love greatly are 'near' to God. But of course it is 'nearness by likeness.' It will not of itself produce 'nearness of approach.' The likeness has been given us. It has no necessary connection with that slow and painful approach which must be our own (though by no means our unaided) task. Meanwhile, however, the likeness is a splendour. That is why we may mistake Like for Same. We may give our human loves the unconditional allegiance which we owe only to God. Then they become gods: then they become demons.

We experience generous "gift-love" (benevolent) and self-centered "need-love" (concupiscible) together in friendship. The latter is certainly not "selfish" or immoral in itself and carries no threat, as generous love does, of posing as perfect and divine from the outset. Need-loves, Lewis notes, "do not set up to be gods. They are not near enough (by likeness) to God to attempt that." He then makes the important point that never in actual life do we isolate the one type of love from the other. They precede and succeed one another and perhaps never exist alone for more than an instant.

The living fact of mixed motivation must be kept in mind in considering celibate love in relation to the bodily, emotional, and spiritual levels of the human being. As part of the explicit object of their vow of chastity, genital sexuality is excluded between consecrated persons. Implied in this exclusion is any intention or action preparatory to either genital sexuality or the spirit of conjugal love. Here it should be emphasized that the test of prudent experience and clear self-understanding over a period of time is necessary to avoid rationalization. Emotional and sexual drives heighten the tendency to rationalize, particularly during early stages of love. It is easy to judge motives wholly benevolent, need-loves at least wholly reasonable, circumspection wholly prudent. But to rationalize rather than to reason clearly is to risk the sudden explosion of sexual instinct when least expected.

Consider, for example, the times and places of the friends' meetings. Common sense and prudent reason judge late hours and lonely places to be circumstances fostering romantic feelings and stimulating the sexual drive. People given to rationalization, however, judge themselves exceptional in this regard and permit themselves time and place settings favoring emotional and sexual reactions they do not intend but which can overwhelm them.

Informed Christians know that their maturity can never become self-sufficient. They realize that God does not intend that grace perfectly restore man's internal order of spirit over body as in the state of original innocence. It is always possible for the reasonable limits and balance of bodily, emotional, and spiritual loves to become upset, should changing external or internal circumstances direct too much attention and desire to the first two, which, of their very nature, are need-loves. An unreasonable amount of need-love in one's motivation makes that love selfish. Even mature adults must be vigilant in order to keep their motivation generous.

Mindful of these prudent cautions, celibates may find enjoyment on all three levels: bodily, emotional, and spiritual — generous love seeking the true good of both persons. Need-love, too, is open to them in reasonable measure. In fact, psychological evidence already cited points to the necessity of both gift-loves and need-loves in the formative stages of childhood and adolescence, if adult love capabilities are to be properly developed. In the fulfilling and complementing friendships of those adults, mature in self-knowledge and control, both gift-loves and need-loves have their rightful place.

Throughout history physical and sensate loves have been poorly understood in relationship to total consecration to God. A balanced view should neither overemphasize the dangers nor minimize the benefits.

Too often, even in the recent past, the negative side of the vow of chastity has been overstressed. True, the positive side of the vow for growth in charity was also emphasized, but all too frequently religious or priestly candidates tended as much toward "non-sexuality" as toward continence and chastity. Such malformation inhibits mature, virtuous control. Rock describes the disastrous results that can make apparent chastity a facade for selfishness and so a thorough obstacle to authentic charity. When sexuality on all levels is suppressed in the young candidate, many other aspects of his human nature, normally not considered sexual, are suppressed with it, e.g., most of his capacity for genuine concern for others. In its place, when society's demands are perceived, a system of seeming concern is devised, the contrived compassion sometimes appearing more attractive than other people's spontaneous reaction to human difficulties and sufferings. Such "ideal" religious or seminarians have a strong instinct for pleasing those who can do them good. They are often bright and talented and have no difficulty adhering to principles they set for themselves. They never arouse opposition, are impeccably neat and proper, and make fine scholastic records. They have no difficulty praying, because prayer for them *is* ritual — the correct words and rubrical behavior at the proper time. They are incapable of symbolizing themselves and their relationship with God *in* ritual. They are on pleasant terms of acquaintance with everyone, but are unable to develop deep friendships. For them, the outward expressions of friendliness are friendship. Here also in the human realm they are incapable of giving themselves to another or of receiving another through symbols. In this sense they are incapable of love. Yet they exhibit a formidable, seemingly invincible chastity. Rock completes his thought:

> Of course, the virtue of chastity is no trouble to them at all. They do not have the virtue because they have no need of it; the matter of the virtue is not part of them. It is not part of an angel either, but angels were made to achieve without it what man can only achieve in a far less perfect way through it. Just as an angel needs no senses or brain to know, so also he does not need the sexual element, the matter which the virtue of chastity controls, to love. But man does.

Making oneself a eunuch for the sake of Christ should be understood correctly. The negative side of consecrated chastity must not amount to annihilation.

Great profit can come to priests and religious from a successful attempt to discover the proper balance between sexuality, love, and charity. They must "avoid the two extremes of love without sex (at least in a wide sense) and sex without love," because all human activities, including the spiritual, require energy for vigor and creativity from the body, even the sex glands:

> We ought not to believe that the state of virginity implies a radical incapacity for physical love. This would mean reserving virginity for incomplete and feeble persons. The truth is quite the opposite: there can be no virtuous virginity without love, and human affection, in its most sublime manifestations, makes use of the humble physiological substratum of the human composite without which it would have

134

neither this ardor nor this power which we discover in truly great souls. The sex glands, as Doctor Carrel tells us, do not merely incline us to the act which perpetuates the human species; they also intensify our physiological, mental and spiritual activities.

In this context it follows that consecrated celibates need not, even should not avoid every aspect of human sexuality. Freible's view of sexual love explains further: "Sexual love being the . . . loving synthesis of masculine and feminine, is not essentially passion and genital expression. It is rather the personal union in oneness-of-being achieved by a man and a woman, an interpenetration and constant exchange of thoughts, dreams, affections, and prayers. In other words, it is essentially a union of the spiritual centers of man and woman and different from the genital expression of that union." He concludes: "If consecrated celibates seem to live uninspired existences, knowing little or nothing of this love and its vivifying, unifying effect, it could well be due to a distorted or too narrow view of the place and value of sexual love in their celibate lives."

For celibates both the dangers and the advantages of human love between the sexes are considerable. The obvious, principal danger is genital desire and activity, but this danger is not equally threatening to everyone. Physiologically and psychologically, each person reacts differently to the many objects and situations which can stimulate the genital appetite. Certainly, most celibates must avoid direct exposure to the stimuli considered provocative by common opinion. Each must avoid those things which he personally finds directly stimulating or indirectly so through memory and imagination. Many celibates, lacking a well-developed virtue of chastity, find that they can remain faithful to their vow only by strict avoidance of even remotely threatening situations. For those with a more strongly developed virtue of chastity, self-knowledge will determine which situations are within their ability to exercise self-restraining, sublimating love. To satisfy the minimal demands of prudence in a given friendship, the celibate man and woman must first determine whether they are consistently without proximate threat of sin against their vow. Then in their ongoing experience, they must refuse to allow whatever elements of self-seeking they might discover to become a major element in their motivation. They must always be principally motivated by benevolence, so that when they recognize any self-indulgence, they are willing to sacrifice it through the disciplined training of self-restraining, sublimating love. If thereafter the tendency to self-indulgence arises less often, they will know that their virtue of chastity is developing, not weakening. Prudence would not ban their friendship as necessarily dangerous. Heris writes of the growth that can take place:

> From the very fact that a man has dedicated his virginity to God, he has not for all that attained the perfection of love. The first step, the essential one, is virginity of the flesh. Virginity of the heart and mind can be acquired to perfection only over a long time. It requires a severe self-renunciation, a painful withdrawal from the possession of creatures. On these conditions, such a love of friendship, even if it partakes of sense love and human love, does not go counter to virginal love. The virgin soul is a soul who has renounced creatures, but for all that she has not been weaned, nor should she be, from their love.

Without sufficient experience it is easy to confuse physical and sensate loves; in reality they are distinct levels of bodily appetite. St. Thomas correctly regards the attraction which draws a man and woman to each other for physical union and generation as different from the affective sympathy which inclines them to love each other on the sense level, independently of genital sexuality. We might term the former love *physical;* it has sexual intercourse and all actions preparatory to intercourse with its accompanying pleasures as immediate, direct objects and expressions. We can call the second, *sensate love* and understand that its object is the whole of the other person, known from his external, sensible qualities. Sense awareness of another's external grace or beauty, for instance, can cause a pleasure keenly felt. This is sensate love. It exists for the same basic reason that every kind of love does: the beloved object fits the lover's appetite perfectly, bringing fulfillment and joy on that particular level.

Sensate love can give rise to either physical or spiritual love. In its own right it engenders a desire for closer unity, a more total possession of the beloved. This is good and natural, but only a need-love on the bodily level of feelings — a person's self-directed, emotional enjoyment of another. Because it is close to physical love, it will eventually and naturally lead to it. This is not to say, however, that sensate love is identical with physical love. Since the soul is more involved in the former, it even touches on the confines of the spiritual, and so is of nobler quality than physical love. Yet because it occurs on the plane of sense experience, it creates a harmony between people at the bodily level and, consequently, a predisposition to physical love. In this way, even though genital union is not the direct object of sensate love, it can easily result from it.

Every human person is a single creature of body and spirit, and so both sides of his nature influence each other in every experience. Man's spirit decidedly has its claims. When, for example, a person's genital appetite urges him to prefer physical satisfaction to any other value in a relationship, his spirit can still see values beyond those of physical love and can choose love for the other as person in preference to physical enjoyment. Heris forecasts selfish or generous results of sensate love on the basis of whether or not each friend loves principally the *person* of the other and his true good. To achieve a benevolent result from sensate love of another, the mind and will must be trained to interract correctly in such experiences. The mind can see through externals to the personhood of another. Then, even under the influence of sensible pleasure from those externals, the will must freely decide its preference: continued sense enjoyment of the beloved, or in the case of conflict, the beloved's higher good. A willingness developed into active ability to sacrifice one's own sensate enjoyment is the love of restraint serving the benevolent love of friendship.

The above discussion presupposes that the sensate enjoyment in question is good for both celibate friends. This would not be so in the case of temptation to sexual pleasure deriving from sensate love. Perreault has made a lucid and practical study of the interaction of the physical, sensate, and spiritual levels of human psychology in the experience of sexual temptation, meriting closer consideration. He outlines first the natural lines of communication among the three levels:

> This group of functions [sensation, resultant emotion, and resultant physical action] which constitute sensibility undergoes in its own way the influence of sexuality, receiving from it a particular 'coloration.' The spontaneous action of the sexual organs can be perceived by sensation and evaluated as a source of satisfaction. A feeling or emotion is aroused, and normally tends to provoke certain bodily movements in order to maintain or intensify this satisfaction. This can be recognized as the psychological mechanism of all temptations against chastity. However, it must be noted that in itself this mechanism is neither bad nor good morally, but completely indifferent. It will become bad or good only by the use the person makes of it according to the moral rules of conduct. One must thus avoid speaking at this purely physiological or psychological level of 'impure' sensa-

137

tions or images, because sexuality and its effects on sensibility in themselves are not impure. Nothing that has been created by God is impure. But the conscious and voluntary conduct that follows this natural action of sexuality will be pure or impure.

After noting that our spirit has no direct influence on the sexual appetite, Perreault indicates how it can control sexual stimulations at least indirectly:

> Because sensibility comprises the functions of sensible knowledge and love, it can receive the direct influence of the spirit which will communicate to it the directives of the intelligence and the inclinations of the will. There is thus communication between spirit and sensibility because, functioning in terms of knowledge and love, both 'speak the same language,' so to say.

> On the other hand, sensibility has bodily organs in order to exercise its functions of knowledge and love — for example, vision, a function of knowledge, cannot occur without eyes, the organs which serve this function. These organs of sensibility, like all organs, are subject to the general conditions of the organism — for example, the tongue, organ of the sense of taste, is affected by a general state of fever, so much so, that the taste of food is changed for someone suffering from fever. The organs of sensibility are thus subject to the influence of sexuality in the measure that it acts on the whole organism, imposing upon it certain physical conditions. Sensibility, due to the organic nature of its functions, is in communication with sexuality, and again one could say that sensibility and sexuality 'speak the same language' because they have in common the fact of using organs to function. . . .

> The sensibility is the natural intermediary between spirit and sexuality because it 'speaks the language' of both. Hence, it can receive the influence of the spirit by its functions of knowledge and love, and can then regularize the action of sexuality on the rest of the organism. . . .

> If the sensibility were left alone, it would follow the inclinations provoked in it by the action of sexuality. This is what happens in the animal. But in the human person, the spirit watches and acts on the sensibility in order to regulate its perceptions, inclinations and movements which are provoked by sexuality. It is thus by the intermediary of the sensibility that the spirit can control sexuality. . . .

To achieve the integration of the personality, it is absolutely necessary that the sensibility remain 'permeable' both to sexuality and to the spirit, in order to permit the spirit to control the influence of sexuality on the sensibility. It is only thanks to this permeability of the sensibility that one can achieve equilibrium of the personality. Consequently, one sees the importance of a sane education of the sensibility. . . .

When the sensibility registers, by its sensations, images, emotions, etc., the action of sexuality, the first thing to do is to identify clearly these impressions for what they are. . . . Then the situation is clear; one knows where he is and what he must do. The spirit can next intervene in all lucidity and firmness to regulate the movements aroused in the sensibility. In the case of a person who has consecrated his chastity to God, his spirit knows that on one side the sensibility is assailed by some temptation against chastity, and that on the other side, it must fight this temptation. The spirit therefore opposes a clear refusal to the suggestions of sexuality. It calls forth wholesome images from sense knowledge destined to distract the imagination or the memory from the sexually colored images. It suggests bodily activities that will even more thoroughly remove the sensibility from the influence of sexuality. It provokes feelings, movements of sensible love, in regard to the good of the whole person, and not only toward the good of the inferior part. Thus, little by little, the spirit gathers the energies of the sensibility and withdraws them from the influence of sexuality. Deprived of the resonances of sensibility, sexuality itself little by little becomes calm, and finally the person enjoys a general peace, the fruit of real struggle. This peace is also the fruit of the openness of the sensibility to the spirit from which it received the desired virtuous orientations.

This useful, detailed analysis of restraining love has value not for one or a few isolated instances only. Used repeatedly, the procedure can develop control in general and bring about moral maturity. Consider a person troubled at some point in his life by advertising's constant use of sexual allurement, or someone tempted by memories from his past. From their experience of turmoil both persons may feel that they will never be able to achieve mastery over these stimuli. Regular use of the above strategy, however, in cooperation with grace, will progressively clarify their understanding of temptation and will radicate and strengthen their ability to cope with it successfully. Time and repeated effort are the key, even if there is intermittent failure. In any case, rather than deny the sexual nature of repeated temptations or repress them from some distorted motive,

> the only solution is always to have the courage and the simplicity to recognize, when it is the case, the sexual character of certain sensations, images, emotions, etc., and not become more upset than one would from contractions that told of a hungry stomach. So far, one has only felt (not consented). One must then have recourse to the reasonable and perfectly conscious motives that the spirit can invoke to refuse consent to these modifications of the sensibility under the action of sexuality. The spirit finds the sensibility open to its action, it communicates its motives of acting, its proper spiritual energy, and hence furnishes the sensibility the desired strength to neutralize progressively the influence of sexuality and to reestablish peace. In this way, the spirit acquires ever increasing control over the sensibility, which will obey it more and more easily and which will feel less and less the contrary influence of sexuality.

Whether to avoid moral evil to oneself or the other, awareness of the distinction of physical, sensate, and spiritual loves and the mind's and will's control and direction of them in view of a virtuous goal allows one to develop and act in mature, benevolent love. Here psychologists and theologians are of one mind.

Albert Plé's study of emotional love for women in the lives of priests recognizes these same values, but goes one step further. After expressing sublimation in Thomistic terms, he integrates it with sensate love, chastity and charity. He begins by noting that a priest, like all men, suffers the divisive effects of original sin in his spirit's control of sex and emotion, but unlike most men, he suffers in addition the physical and emotional voids which marriage naturally fills. This intensifies his struggle to integrate sexuality and emotions with his vow of chastity and goal of perfect charity. Grace will not wholly compensate for either sin's effects or his celibate void. If he attempts to eliminate the problem by repression — a type of "forced emotional fasting" — he may become neurotic. Grace and the correct control by reason and will, however, result in restraint and sublimation.

> This is possible, as Freud himself recognized, but it presupposes that a very special training be effective, which does not command by interdict and suppression, but by the hold of charity upon the affective life. The government of the passions, to use the analogy of Aristotle and Saint Thomas [Aristotle, *Politics,* I, 3; Saint Thomas,

Summa Theol., I, q. 83, a. 3, ad 2; I-II, q. 56, a. 4, ad 3; q. 58, a. 2c], must not have as its model the police regime of a tyrannical government, but that of a democracy whereby the government has no intention of reducing the minority to silence and inaction, but of negotiating with it and persuading it to work for the common good of the country according to the views of the majority. It should and may only have recourse to police force in extreme and exceptional cases. . . .

To put the same without analogy in the very terms of Saint Thomas, we would say that it is an imperfect government of the passions when they undergo violence and are subjected to a state of passivity. Their government is good when it becomes second nature to the passions to participate spontaneously and actively in the loves of intelligent affectivity — when the passions become intelligent. [*In III Sent.*, D. 23, 1, 1c.]

Such reasonable dominion over emotion not only quells possible rebellion and uses its very force for the goals of reason, but it results also in special "joys of spirit," which "are essentially the joys of charity . . . lived even until the level of sensibility." Only through this control and its happy result can a priest successfully cultivate friendship with women. Only such a man is mature enough in nature and grace.

Reliable moralists and spiritual writers have always been aware of these truths, even though they express them differently. Hubert Van Zeller, for example, speaks of the essential key of restraining love in friendship:

There must be strict austerity about friendship. . . . Sacrifice and not satisfaction is the expression of love, and the willingness to sacrifice the satisfaction of expressing affection is one of the highest and hardest forms the sacrifice can take. Friends should be prepared to forego [when necessary] the gratification of either giving or demanding evidence.

Heris describes the goal of this asceticism and warns against pessimism in a healthy approach:

The human senses are certainly inclined to savor these joys for themselves, to make them its [sic] possession. Hence the necessity of a certain asceticism in the use of things that are pleasurable to our senses. But this asceticism must not be an absolute negation of every

141

sense pleasure, as if it were evil in itself. 'Virginity,' says Saint Thomas, 'does not refuse every sense pleasure, but only sexual pleasure, and this in accordance with the dictates of right reason.' [*Summa Theol.*, II-II, q. 152, a. 2, ad 2].

Lucien-Marie, O.C.D., in his introduction to the works of St. John of the Cross, makes a similar remark with regard to this saint. Despite his apparent rigor, he says, which could make one see a certain pessimism in the Mystical Doctor, there is no question of destroying every vestige of our sense of being. There is no question of annihilating every physical possibility of sensation. He means only to suppress every voluntary self-seeking in sense activity. What the saint does not want is for anyone to be too fond of, or to lose his heart to, or to fall in love with, seeing, hearing, feeling, touching, etc. He does not claim to destroy even the smallest part of our being — for our person has been created by God and is good in itself — nor any external things — 'which are good in themselves' — but only voluntary attachment, which easily becomes ill-regulated seeking after pleasure.

Such mastery of self is rare among people, even among dedicated celibates. It is normally acquired only as result of a long, healthy asceticism motivated by striving for ever more perfect Christian love. But a consecrated person should not become sterile psychically because of his ascetical efforts. Rather, he should learn to incorporate a rich sensate life into his development in charity.

C. S. Lewis sees how the experience of eros (understood here as equivalent to sensate love) can yield its own insight into charity:

Eros, honored so far as love of God and charity to our fellows will allow, may become for us a means of Approach. His total commitment is a paradigm or example, built into our natures, of the love we ought to exercise towards God and Man. As nature, for the nature-lover, gives a content to the word *glory*, so this gives a content to the word *Charity*. It is as if Christ said to us through Eros, 'Thus — just like this — with this prodigality — not counting the cost — you are to love me and the least of my brethren.'

Jordan Aumann observes: "It is important not only to join eros and sex, lest man become merely an animal — and less than an animal — but to understand that eros can be a marvelous creative force in the field of aesthetics, social life and even in religious experience."

Noble asks whether or not human affections compromise a consecrated person's single-hearted love for God:

> Can God tolerate other affections? This question is posed in many forms, especially by those who aim at spiritual progress and are in pursuit of the perfection of supernatural charity.

> Are our legitimate affections compatible with the love we owe God? Can they live at ease with charity and even benefit and serve it?

> Indeed, all [good things] that we love beyond God we should love, because in doing so we accomplish the will of God who approves of us to love. . . . Charity for God certainly cannot help but approve and adopt our filial affection for our parents, our gratitude for our benefactors, our attachments to virtuous friendship. These are very noble human sentiments which God ratifies. . . .

> Filial piety, gratitude, and friendship are moral virtues. Without strain they become 'infused' supernatural virtues when grace stimulates them from the depths of the soul and when charity assumes them by ordering them to its goal, which is to love God. As this same charity commands us to be good sons and to be grateful to benefactors, it also commands us to be, for our friends, very good friends.

> Charity obliges us to love, in God, whatever we already love for legitimate human motives. Supernatural love joins itself to natural love in order to ennoble it — it does not suppress it, and in no way eliminates its *raison d'être*.

Heris recalls that development in charity may be not only a happy result of affectionate friendship between celibates, but is equally a requirement for it:

> Thus, intimate friendships can spring up between persons consecrated by virginity. The sense level is not excluded, but it is only the stay and support of their spiritual union. . . . It is here, obviously more than in any other love, that two people need to love themselves in something greater than themselves, loving each other in God and joining together in him to unite with each other. Charity can thus develop to the fullest of its power and draw from human tenderness the expressions of its brotherly love.

From the foregoing discussion it is clear that because sensate love easily leads to sexual love, prudence counsels many celibates against close association with the opposite sex. The hazard is serious. Consecrated celibates who have such friendships must be vigilant to keep the level of their emotional exchange free from that which is selfish, imprudent, or, of course, strictly sexual. At every developmental stage of the relationship each person must follow appropriate, general moral guidelines until sufficient experience has taught him enough about himself to be able to judge which situations result in temptation against chastity and which do not. These guidelines will alter with time, according as he neglects his virtue of chastity or develops it by wise natural and supernatural means.

In chaste relationships with friends of the opposite sex, sensate love becomes morally reprehensible in imprudent circumstances or if indulged in through self-seeking. It is morally acceptable if either given benevolently or received from a friend's benevolent love. This implies that each in his own conscience must clearly distinguish between need-loves which circumstances, grace, and his own moral development allow him to fulfill without a selfish spirit and those which he is tempted selfishly to fulfill by compromising either his true good or that of the other. To preserve benevolence, each friend must always be able to say that the *person* of the other, not any romantic or emotional aspect of the relationship, is his principal reason, among many perhaps, for loving the friend.

Some consideration should be given here to so-called romantic, sensate love, quite distinct from the love between consecrated persons just described. Indeed, how misleading and dangerous it would be to think that the romantic love morally proper for engaged couples is also good for priests and religious in mixed friendships!

The consecrated person is challenged to achieve enough mastery of sensate love both to avoid domination by the romantic tendency and to attain freedom to use the media of sense expression for personal, Christian love. The difficulty of this challenge is without question severe. Think only of the sense of touch, the most basic and extensive of the senses, present in all parts of the human body. It can confuse objective judgment and resist free control. Highly emotional expressions of personal love become more powerful if given or received through touch rather than looks or sound. And when the exchange is between men and women, the difficulty is magnified, because the sense of touch is closely allied with genital sensation and physical love. Misjudgment is likely for most people in experiences of embracing, kissing, or other common, tactile expressions of romantic love between men and women. Owing to the effects of original and personal sin, the human spirit's control of the senses is not integral. Even the noblest intentions of expressing personal love can turn, especially through touch, into experiences of romantic love, then into temptations to physical love. Since engaged men and women are free to develop their relationship toward its natural conclusion in marriage, chaste but romantic sensate expressions of love are fitting between them. Consecrated men and women are not free to contemplate marriage; any expressions of personal love between them must be not only chaste but non-romantic as well.

Christian tradition has always perceived these truths. The Lord has urged all — but celibates with greater intensity — to a spirituality of preferring spiritual and eternal values over sensate satisfaction. Christian freedom from the unbalanced demands of sensate love is acquired only through persistent, graced restraint and sublimation, radicating a control against which the appeals of physical and romantic love are usually no longer a threat. The celibate then experiences the superior joys of spiritual activity, which in turn help to fix his preference even more firmly.

With this freedom, the celibate possesses beautiful, human ways of expressing Christian love and moving people's hearts. Through looks, voice, or touch he can show sympathy, compassion, affirmation, or affection in his ministry, and people will not misunderstand his intentions. On the contrary, they will experience him as an integrated, free apostle, rooted in Christ, who acts through him.

A social dimension of sensate love between consecrated men and women demands attention also. Celibates must restrain not only what could offer them danger, but what common estimation judges to be a dangerous example for the ordinary person. St. Paul both practiced and counseled self-restraint in order to avoid scandalizing the weaker brethren. External expressions of love, wholly virtuous for the individuals involved, may cause the average person either to misjudge them as romantic or unchaste between celibates, or to follow suit and enter naively into occasions of temptation to himself. By their consecrated chastity religious and priests give public, eschatological witness to total love for Christ and his kingdom. They may not express friendship in ways perhaps appropriate for the two friends, yet in ways which provoke lay persons, fellow religious, or priests to question the witness value of total consecration. In the lives of the saintly celibates considered in chapter three, there is no evidence of inappropriate expressions of sensate love. Their apostolic years abound, nevertheless, with instances of warm, emotional, sensate manifestations of Christian love. Acting consistently with discernment and prudence, they did not perplex the common man's sense of propriety nor induce him by example into ways beyond ordinary control. Rather they drew universal admiration as living examples of integrated human and divine love.

Admittedly, western society does not help celibates in their struggle for free, personal love. Quite the opposite, the "playboy" and "playgirl" atmosphere that permeates western communication media constantly emphasizes the romantic and erotic dimensions of masculine-feminine, sensate love. Open exposure to it can stimulate genital love, and when this becomes one's habitual experience, it can constitute an almost insuperable barrier to maturing in personal love. Unless they are deeply prayerful persons, it seems probable that two celibates in love with each other spiritually will, today, end up in genital activity. Yet, for prayerful Christians who do not follow the immoralizing lead of their society, God's preventative grace is available to confirm their own prudent resistance; his other graces will be given to support and fructify their efforts to develop in chaste, personal love. They must consistently ask for and learn to rely on grace to assist their attempts at self-restraining, sublimating love. If grace and nature work hand in hand so that from day to day the changing proportion of both friends' motivations comes more and more to favor generosity over self-seeking, then their masculine-feminine friendship is doing service to their virtue and vow of chastity and their goal of perfection in charity.

Because sensate and physical loves are such a part of married love and can engender desire for it, two celibate friends of the opposite sex must also avoid acquiring the "spirit" of marriage. Even though in their relationship they have excluded physical expressions of sexuality and have developed that control of emotion and touch which avoids romantic love, nature may seek its fulfillment on higher levels between them. If they are undiscerning, they may unconsciously come to think that they are in a state where these levels of complementarity can become complete. In other words, celibate men and women may have to face the problem of a possible "dry marriage" without the physical use of sexuality. How can they keep their friendship distinct in their minds and hearts from the spiritual complementarity of married love? The distinction is subtle: marriage is not only for genital and emotional satisfaction and the bearing and rearing of children. Marriage is also friendship:

> It is primarily the highest form of friendship that can exist between two human persons who are able to complement each other in every way. . . .

> This union has a perfection that no other friendship can have because it is a *full* relationship of two persons who are equals. The love between a mother and her child always has a protective element involved in its perfection. Lesser friendships, no matter how enduring, always have an element of restraint, some boundaries that cannot be passed over.[11]

St. Thomas Aquinas is of similar opinion: "There obviously exists the greatest friendship between man and wife; they are united not only in the conjugal act which, even among animals, can produce a sweet and tender friendship; they are joined even more in their common sharing in the whole of family life." But marriage is a special kind of friendship. Through the centuries Catholic tradition has distilled its basic nature, characteristics, and benefits. A brief look at these will help focus on what the spirit of conjugal friendship necessarily includes.

Christian marriage is a natural and divine union of man and woman for the purpose of pursuing a common goal and leading the same, intimate, family life. It entails the union of bodies by the act of intercourse and the union of souls by human love and charity. Its characteristics are unity, which restricts the relationship to this one man, this one woman; and indissolubility, calling for the permanency of the union until the death of either party. Chief among the benefits of marriage are: bearing and rearing children, the right to sexual intercourse, the sacrament and its unique graces, and fidelity — or the "company" of marital love, involving the constant giving of the one to the other in the service of the conjugal union. The love which joins a Christian husband and wife is sacred, since through the sacrament it becomes the symbol of the union of Christ with his Church. Among others, this transcendent dimension is a profound reason for indissolubility.

Today much needed theological work is being done in the area of Christian marriage. Past experience and thought have furnished a wealth of insight with which to carry on this work. Peter Ketter, in his study of how Christianity has benefited women, summarizes the synthetic connection among these traditional aspects. He sees five pillars

147

essential to the support of the "edifice" of true Christian marraige. Oneness of the marriage bond (monogamy) ensures that wives do not have to share the love of a husband with jealous, rival wives. Purity of married love fosters personal and interpersonal harmony within the marriage and strengthens it against inroads from without. Indissolubility removes anxiety about the permanence of the marital relationship. These three features surround motherhood with a special security and dignity. But the benefit of surpassing worth that Christ has given to womankind through Christian marriage is the holiness offered each partner through the sacramental consecration of their relationship.

In our own day, the late Paul VI gave an integral description of Christian marriage in his encyclical on human life:

> It is a wise institution of the Creator to realize in humanity his design of love. By means of the reciprocal gift of self, proper and exclusive to themselves, spouses tend to a communion of their being in view of a mutual personal perfection, to collaborate with God in the generation and education of new lives. For those baptized, moreover, matrimony has the dignity of being a sacramental sign of grace, in so far as it represents the union of Christ and the Church.

These Catholic statements offer a basis for comparing the love that is conjugal friendship with that which is celibate.

In the first place, marriage partners belong to each other by possession. It is their will and the permanent will of God that they give themselves to each other in every possible dimension. This giving includes all but the inner being of the person that is incapable of being communicated to another, and the individual, transcendent allegiance each owes to God personally. The tendency to such extensive self-giving and possession of another is imprinted in human nature itself. Edith Stein speaks for women: "to surrender oneself in love to another, to belong wholly to another and to possess that other wholly, is the deepest longing of the female heart. This covers that simultaneous focus on the personal and on the concrete which we regard as specifically feminine." The physical act of married love symbolizes this wonderfully. Each partner's gift of body in its essential, life-giving powers expresses love without reserve. It is an instrument of the fusion of persons, a sign of total, reciprocal abandon, whereby two become one in body and soul. In the case of celibates, their mutual love (whose limits have been indicated) cannot mean mutual possession. Their love is, rather, a gift which they enjoy conditionally, upon God's will, since they have given themselves up instead to total possession by God. Their renunciation of the act of marriage as part of the specific object of their vow conveys this very meaning:

> In itself, sexuality has nothing to do with the love of God, but the gift of love made to another person by the use of sexuality in marriage prevents the *exclusive* gift (of self) to God that can be made in a greater love through the consecration of chastity. Indeed, the very meaning of the spiritual marriage between the consecrated person and God requires exclusiveness, the absence of sharing of intimacy with all but God.

Married partners alone enjoy love and all that it entails, not only by generous self-giving, but also by right (1 Co. 7:3-5) — by contract ratified by God. No other friendship includes this right; celibates, then, can have no such claim upon each other's love. Their love is reciprocally given and accepted freely.

Married love is further an interdependent way of life for spouses, the daily living of a common destiny in all life's details. Celibates live fundamentally independent lives, not directed by the well-being of a destiny for two, but by the demands of Christ and the Church in the service they are given to perform for the people of God.

A married man and woman can look forward to the joys of being not only husband and wife in love, but also father and mother; they are the architects of home and family life. In cooperation with God, they shape from birth until maturity new lives that have been given to their love and care. Celibates cannot know personal fulfillment as husband or wife. Theirs can be that of true complementing love only, an experience less extensive, of course, than that of married love. Nor can they have a home or family together. But all aspects of parenthood need not be excluded. They can beget and care for new life in Christ through common prayer and at times common ministry. In spiritual and human dimensions apart from marriage, a religious sister can truly be "helpmate" to a friend in his priesthood. In shared apostolic effort, the two can experience the spiritual paternity and maternity that in Christ is an expected result of their individual vocations. Rock compares married and celibate parenthood in the case of priests:

> Certainly human love is necessary to any man if he would be fully human. Human love does not need marriage to reach its highest per-

fection, but it is in marriage and through marriage that it is frequently to be found. The mutual attractions that brought man and wife together are nature's impulse toward love. The sexual union is able to overcome threats to the development of that love, and the children they love together as their own promote unselfishness and deepen their love. This is not, however, to say that marriage is the exclusive domain of human love.

Celibacy is indifferent in itself. It is good or bad depending upon why it is embraced. If it is undertaken for selfish reasons it is evil. If, on the other hand, it is undertaken for generous reasons it is undertaken precisely to promote human love. Again to quote Ida Görres:

"Priestly celibacy represents the marriage of Christ with the Church. Thus the priest *lives* a marriage, not in the narrow space of his individual self but on the spiritual level of Christ's marriage with the Church. The essence of marriage is not excluded from his experience; he is not denied all human relations to live solely for a 'cause.' Fidelity, gentleness, patience, responsibility, spiritual fatherhood, love are the qualities he must build in himself. Not from mere chance do most people call him 'Father.' " ["A Laywoman's View of Priestly Celibacy." *Theology Digest*, St. Louis, Spring 1966, pp. 57-8.]

A strict interdependence also exists between married people in their working toward salvation. By vocation the husband and wife are to find their personal salvation through each other, through the mutual carrying out of the duties of their married state. This is not true between celibate friends. Each must individually work out his salvation by fulfilling with Christ's help the duties of his vocation. There is place, of course, for the free and generous interdependence of charity, for mutual prayer, encouragement, and inspiration, for example, but this arises, not from their individual consecration, but from their friendship.

Conjugal love is exclusive to the married partners; this specific love may not be given to others. By contrast, the love between celibates cannot be founded on physical union and its consequences. It is primarily the spiritual love of charity, a love which cannot be restricted to two or to a family. Rather, it opens celibates' hearts to the world. Such love cannot be exclusive, except in its unique depth. There can be only one complementing love in their lives — that between themselves — but it is different solely in degree from the fulfilling love they must

150

be prepared to extend in Christ's name to innumerable people. Conjugal love, however, is different not necessarily in degree, but in kind. From its specific difference it is strictly exclusive.

The exclusiveness and permanence of married love are dependent not only upon the hearts and wills of husband and wife, but also upon the will of God: "What God has united, man must not divide" (Mt 19:6). The sacrament gives unlimited stability to withstand any human weakness that may emerge in time or through changing situations. This security larger than themselves is a basis for total self-revelation, for giving themselves wholly to each other for the entire unknown future of their lives. Indissolubility also occasions a lesser security: provision for temporal needs, promoting serene individual and family life. Celibates, however, are united in friendship only by the bond of their own free wills. Time may prove this bond stable enough for sufficient self-revelation and communication to develop noble forms of fulfilling or even complementing love. Yet without total security, complete self-revelation and self-giving are inappropriate. The prudent reserves with regard to physical and sensate loves discussed earlier are required, therefore, not only by their consecrated celibacy, but also by the very absence of the marriage bond.

By becoming aware of their conjugal love, married people are able to understand Christian love more deeply. Their developing relationship as husband and wife can illumine their grasp and enrich their appreciation of God's relationship with humanity. They can know uniquely something of the intimate exchanges of Christ and his Church. The sacramental grace of matrimony urges them toward this end (Ep 5:21-33). Celibates do not live this model of charity, nor do they have the aid of its specific grace. Yet their friendship can bring them to a like understanding of God's intimate love without many of the distractions to this supernatural relationship that beset the married from within and without.

Marriage is a rich model proposed by Christ for man's coming to know the Trinity and its divine love for him. Recognizing this, R. F. Trevett explains how marriage and virginity challenge each other to realize that which is proper to each. The married can reveal the fruitfulness of love to the priest or religious, whose "life has its temptations, nonetheless crude and obvious than those which face the married. He may become sterile in his love for Christ. His is the temptation of the pharisee, to glory in good works. He too must bear fruit in the lives of others as do the married in the lives of their children." On the other hand, virginity can inspire the married with the spiritual meaning of their state.

> They [consecrated virgins] reveal to the married the essence of their own marital union. That essence is itself truly virginal. Christ has assumed into his mystical body the processes of generation, but these and the sacrament which consecrates them will pass away into the world to come. Only love, pure and out-going to the Father, the Son, and the Spirit, and to all the members of the mystical body, will remain for ever and ever. Already in this life, this pure love is the ideal of the married, who are to strive after it in their relations to one another, to their children and to all other men and women. Already in this life, the consecrated virgins, by their renunciation of the joys and sorrows of married life, show — in so far as their lives correspond with the high ideal to which they are wedded — the utter unselfishness of love, the virginal heart too of marriage, which our fallen though redeemed nature finds so hard to see at the very centre of our married life.

Trevett can therefore conclude that, "Religious and the married, each in their own degree of oblation, of self-sacrifice, foreshadow that great day of final revelation and everlasting glory."

Other authors develop this comparison beautifully. Perreault writes:

> Because, in Christian marriage, the man and the woman unite themselves indissolubly one to another, this sacrament merits to symbolize the incomparably more intimate union of Christ with all humanity gathered into the Church. This gathering of all into one Body inseparably united to Christ constitutes, indeed, the goal toward which the whole work of redemption tends. It is by belonging to the Church that each redeemed person enters into this mysterious union with Christ. But beyond this common vocation, the virginal soul who consecrates herself to God realizes this definitive union with Christ in a wholly personal way. For it is by her whole being, including the flesh, that the consecrated person unites herself to Christ as to whom she wants to belong, to the exclusion of every other union implying the intimacy permitted by the fusion of bodies in Christian marriage. As we saw, the abandon of one's whole self, realized by the gift of one's body in marriage, establishes the spouse in an intimacy capable of releasing the most profound energies of one's personality. The virginal person who vows herself to God renounces precisely this intimacy, and not by indifference, fear or disgust for the goods of mar-

152

riage, but because of love for Him to whom she intends to consecrate her energies in an absolutely unconditional way.

Stanislao Gatto puts this explicitly in terms of charity:

> In this light, thanks to their reciprocal, vital compenetration, Christian matrimony appears permeated with a *'virginal spirit,'* just as the virginal state appears permeated with *'spousal love.'* This is not a play on words. The essential and immutable in every form and state of Christian life is charity, that is love: love is unitive (spousal) and, therefore, must be pure (virginal).

The foregoing comparison between celibate and married love shows that each state of life has advantages and disadvantages with regard to growth in charity. God intends married love — complete union in body and spirit — as the primary, natural expression of his loving relationship with men. Consequently, the love between married Christians can reveal much about charity to them, even though since the fall of mankind it no longer provides a trouble-free experience through which to grow toward the fullness of Christian love. So much in married life distracts from full concentration on this supreme goal, the disturbances ranging from difficulties in building harmony sexually, emotionally, and spiritually to the never-ending flow of temporal preoccupations. A life of consecrated chastity avoids these distractions to giving oneself wholly to growth in charity. It must be admitted, though, that as some attempt to live celibacy, the human ability to love — as man or woman — remains partially undeveloped. Here chaste, mixed celibate friendship can help: it both avoids the distractions inherent in marriage and allows the man and woman full psychic and spiritual development in human love. The lives of the saints earlier referred to demonstrate further that this last situation favors the realization in this life of the divine offer of mystical marriage.

It should be noted that features which some consider exclusive to marriage, although they have in fact nothing specifically to do with it, may evolve between celibate friends. They may, for example, attain a deep, personal intimacy, a complementarity that many married people never actually develop — and this with no intrusion into the realm of marriage. Complementing love, as has been shown, is clearly not a feature exclusive to married love.

What practical standard of judgment can be drawn from this theoretical comparison to help celibate friends remain totally faithful to

Christ in their ongoing experience, avoiding the undesired development of conjugal love? A necessary experiential test is whether each celibate friend senses himself fundamentally *free and independent* of the other, rather than *possessed and possessing* as in marriage. If so, their love of friendship and the implied, virtuous giving of themselves to each other can evolve even to an intimate sense of two in one, a oneness-of-being far closer than most married people experience, with no betrayal of their dedication to Christ. Their mutual trust in opening to each other can be agent for both human growth and purification of motives, if the two are constantly aware that their giving and receiving occur not at will, nor by right, but only by gift. And this gift must never oppose the demands — the possession and rights — which stem from their separate, total gift to God and his to each of them.

Within the limits of virtue and their vows, then, the love which celibate friends have for one another measures how much they freely give and receive. By permanent right, married partners give not only according to the measure of their love, but, within the limits of virtue, everything of themselves besides. They literally *belong* to each other until death and should joyously sense possessing and being possessed. Consecrated celibates literally *belong* to God until death. Two such friends may have no sense of mutually possessing and being possessed. Rather, they must joyously sense freedom and independence from each other. Theirs must be the abiding experience of having given that freedom to God. They should sense both possessing him and being possessed by him. To this God has called them: to give themselves to him totally, on all levels, in order more easily and effectively to maintain a single-hearted dedication to spiritual marriage with him. This does not mean that the Lord will not provide for consecrated people to love others also with divine and human love. He wants it, in fact, even commands it, but only with human love in harmony with total consecration to him. In this spirit, quite distinct from that of marriage, consecrated persons may love as man and woman, thereby rendering manly and womanly perfection to God. Heris concurs in this judgment:

> Now, the virgin soul can indeed feel itself drawn by love to another soul; but since there cannot ever be any giving and possession of bodies and sense experience at the basis of this love, it follows that many limitations are imposed upon this exchange of souls. What is more, the virgin soul, more than others, needs to have an exact sense of God's rights in the spiritual domain. Since she has given herself

entirely to God, she could never become the property of a creature. And since she cannot go out to God except by renouncing the goods of this world, she no longer has the right to possess a soul through love. Thus, if a soul offers itself to her or consents to her friendship, she must receive it as a sacred trust confided to her by God himself, a trust over which she has no property rights, but which she must treat with extreme care, giving it the best that is in her. We can always give our spiritual treasures without impoverishing ourselves and doing any wrong to God; in this respect there is no danger at all.

This possibility has not been widely recognized. From early centuries, a current of thought among Christians has looked upon all masculine-feminine intimacy outside of marriage with suspicion. The cleavage between spirit and body resulting from original sin came to be considered so great that little virtuous control of sexuality was expected. Marriage was viewed mainly as giving relief to the sexual appetite. Celibates were given one counsel: flight from the opposite sex. This opinion, of course, was never the official doctrine of Christianity. The Church always recognized the possibility of reasonable continence through grace and the virtue of chastity. Rather, it was a popular teaching that became quite universal.

Throughout history experience has taught individuals that God can and does reveal his love to people, either directly or indirectly. In persons who dedicate themselves to him as priests or religious and have been adequately disposed by a fortunate human background, his gift of the Holy Spirit may freely and directly expand itself within their souls. This is often the experience of men and women living a strictly cloistered life. In others less advantageously disposed at the human level, but who similarly dedicate themselves to him, God may use the medium of human love to develop their hearts. Without compromising their consecration to him, God allows many a saintly priest and religious to open in love to a person of the opposite sex. Having learned how to love humanly, they are able better to love God and neighbor in charity.

God will certainly never inspire priests and religious with two, mutually exclusive vocations. If they begin to experience a love proper to marriage, they will know that it originates from their side, emanating from self-deception, over-attraction to the goods of marriage, or a self-seeking compensation prompted by some dissatisfaction with their vocation. If they are confused, they must seek instruction; if tempted, they must apply wise asceticism. If neither strategy is effective, or if their problem stems from a dissatisfaction with their vocation caused by negligence in it, they must avoid the threatening relationship, pray, and work for the renewal of their vocation. On the other hand, if the intentions of both friends are pure and clarity continues; if they suffer no serious temptations and in any ascetic struggle maintain a realistic trust in the light and strength of grace; if they remain willing and able to learn from experience, their friendship can be wholly compatible with their consecration to Christ.

Aumann synthesizes this prudential evaluation of masculine-feminine friendship and consecrated chastity, observing: "Celibacy, therefore, requires total abstinence from physical sexuality; it requires also a kind of 'psychic abstinence' as regards the expressions and manifestations of emotional love and psychic sexuality; it requires a spiritual sublimation of genetic sexuality or the desire for parenthood."

CONCLUSION

This chapter purposes to evaluate theologically and pastorally the scriptural, psychological, and experiential evidence given in the first three chapters by attempting, with the aid of classical philosophy and theology, to integrate masculine-feminine friendship and the life of consecrated celibates. The endeavor involved a theoretical exposition of charity, chastity, and friendship, together with a prudential assessment of their compatibility in the lives of dedicated men and women. Nor were the dangers and benefits inherent in such an integration overlooked. Carefully weighed, both were found to be considerable. Those capable of avoiding the dangers seem undeniably few. Hence the conclusion: intimate friendships between consecrated men and women cannot be recommended generally, because rare indeed are the persons who can sufficiently avoid the dangers so as to enjoy the benefits.

Prudence does not demand that such friendships be totally banned, however. In each case, a practical judgment must be based upon the two individuals involved.[12] They might indeed be capable of developing, with the aid of wise counsel and grace, a chaste relationship, enriching every aspect of their lives of Christian love. They might even be capable of a foretaste of glory, where human relationships are most intimate because of their rectitude. St. Francis de Sales recognized this possibility:

The more exquisite the virtues are, which shall be the matter of your communications, the more perfect shall your friendship also be. If this communication be in the sciences, the friendship is very commendable; but still more so, if it be in the moral virtues: in prudence, discretion, fortitude and justice. But should your reciprocal communications relate to charity, devotion and Christian perfection, good God, how precious will this friendship be! It will be excellent, because it comes from God; excellent, because it tends to God; excellent, because its very bond is God; excellent, because it shall last eternally in God. Oh how good it is to love on earth as they love in heaven; to learn to cherish each other in this world, as we shall do eternally in the next!

The ultimate theological and pastoral evaluation of friendship between consecrated celibates is one of prudence. Rock points out: "There can be much mutual love in the priest's life or in the life of the religious. Sometimes there is some danger involved in it, but there are situations in which a certain amount of danger is the price of life." And if it is, despite the hazard, the final judgment cannot be an inflexible morality of safety. Vann concurs that prudence is the last judge:

Be prudent. There is one very important question which helps to a prudential judgment: Does this love, whatever it is, make me less faithful and devoted to my *vocation?* Does it take my mind and heart away from my work, my family, my prayers, the good I can do and ought to do in the world? If so, there is indeed something wrong. But it need not be so: and if you find on the contrary that through it your work is enriched, your prayer deepened, your family life made more gay and tender, your work for men more wise and sympathetic and gentle, then you have nothing to do but to thank God: there is nothing more to be said.

Conclusions

UNTO ETERNAL LIFE

The New Dawn of Christ bursts into the fullness of eternal life, into the vision, as St. John describes it, of the only true God as He is. St. Paul prefers the phrase "face to face": knowing God as he knows me, directly, intimately, fully. The more, then, that I know the one true God from what he has made, the better I can know him through what he has revealed, the better live toward eternal life now and open myself to its plenitude hereafter. Authentic masculine-feminine intimacy, as the foregoing chapters attest, can provide an enriched opportunity for *knowing* more profoundly the Living God of creation and redemption.

The *heart,* too, is mightily involved in eternal life, for "love endures forever," and "God is love and anyone who lives in love lives in God, and God in him. . . ." The more, then, that I learn how in this life to love persons for their true good, the better I am fitted for eternal life. Clearly, authentic masculine-feminine love can expand hearts to the full potential of human nature and to the universality of Christ's grace.

But St. Paul was realistic. Our present human condition complicates the beauty of this simple picture. "They will have their troubles . . . in their married life, and I should like to spare you that. . . ." Paul knew that the more one is free from these "troubles," the more he can attend to the one thing necessary: "all he need worry about is pleasing the Lord." Authentic *celibate love* can provide now, unto eternal life, both masculine-feminine enrichment of mind and heart and the precious freedom "to give . . . undivided attention to the Lord."

159

This book confronts a pressing issue, one that has divided many priests and religious in mind and heart and has lead some to tragic decision. It seeks a balanced approach, examining first God's Word, then man's in contemporary science, historical testimony, and classical philosophy and theology. It explores both positive and negative considerations concerning masculine-feminine friendship between celibates consecrated to the pursuit of the fullness of Christian love. Such a subject lends itself, of course, to several possible approaches, but the one followed allows the drawing of two general conclusions by way of review and the formulation of some practical guidelines.

The first conclusion emerging from the study represents a basic agreement among the disciplines and sources: this friendship is a possible and, given certain requirements, desirable means for growth in charity. Textual evidence supporting this conclusion includes the treatment of characteristics, benefits, and requirements of masculine-feminine friendship, relationships to charity occurring throughout.

A second general conclusion focuses on prudence. The school of psychology followed throughout this work points to the necessity of natural prudence for a successful, celibate, masculine-feminine friendship. The theological evaluation of chapter four validates this judgment and incorporates it in a conclusion emphasizing the necessity of supernatural prudence. The saints further strengthen the conclusion by exemplifying in their lives of friendship a personal integration of natural and supernatural prudence.

To aid in judging prudentially the quality of friendship between consecrated men and women, a number of practical norms drawn from the text are presented here. Such guidelines can help in an overall assessment of any given relationship or in the isolation and resolution of particular difficulties.

1. As an indispensable natural condition, both the man and the woman must be fundamentally mature persons emotionally and volitionally. (chapter two)

2. The primary supernatural condition requires that the human friendship be integrated into authentic Christian love. It must be correctly ordered to loving God in first place and the self and neighbor with divine love. The relationship should, moreover, contribute in both breadth and depth to a greater love of God and lead to increasing love of and service to others, especially those with whom one lives. Deep prayer should find in the relationship stimulation and enrich-

ment. In every aspect, the friendship must be made obedient to God's will. Friends must not seek to force circumstances in order either to initiate a friendship or to further the enjoyment of an existing one; rather, they should discern and accept the actual circumstances of Providence and work creatively with them. Finally, the relationship should be raised continually to the supernatural level, specifically to the goal of growth toward fullness of Christian love. (chapter four)

3. As a result of the friendship, both the man and the woman should increasingly appreciate the role of consecrated chastity in the fulfillment of their individual vocations; also the many ways in which the vowed life fosters growth in deep prayer. Each must be aware of and able to avoid the natural possessiveness of married love; each must consciously grow in single-hearted adherence to God. (chapter four)

4. In times of struggle to preserve benevolence and perfect chastity in their relationship, both friends must intensify their realistic reliance on prayer and grace for light and strength to supplement their own self-knowledge, self-restraint, and efforts at sublimation. The result must be a continually increasing generosity in all aspects of their exchange. Particularly in their experience of need-love and gift-love on the physical and sensate levels, imprudent circumstances must be avoided, selfishness willingly sacrificed, excessive emotional or tactile expressions of affection restrained and sublimated, and anything of genital sexuality completely excluded. These precautions must be accompanied by an ever greater clarification and purification of motives. For both friends, the true natural and supernatural good of the other must become the overriding interest and concern. (chapters two, three, and four)

5. The two friends' communication or exchange should be one of appreciation and cooperative assistance as man and woman, in order that by complementary enlightenment and encouragement their personalities may be enriched and developed beyond their original, basic maturity. Their mutual help should furnish strength and comfort in the trials of life and stimulate both to greater creativeness and devotedness in the fulfillment of their individual duties. (chapters two, three, and four)

6. Finally, the relationship should be fundamentally characterized by happiness and joy. (chapters one, two, three, and four)

Honesty is the key to evaluating a friendship according to these norms; rationalization, the enemy. Unavoidable emotional involvement, especially in the early stages of a masculine-feminine relationship, can be so strong that objectivity in self-evaluation becomes well-nigh impossible. To attain an unprejudiced judgment, it is important for celibate friends to seek reliable counsel early in their relationship and throughout its development to maturity.

At any point along the way the above norms can be confronted globally by asking one question: does the friendship help or hinder the natural and supernatural dimensions of both friends' vocations? If it is fostering growth humanly and spiritually, enabling each to carry out his apostolic role better, then the friendship is prudent and good.

Consecrated men and women friends who can honestly answer this last question in the affirmative will agree that "love is the meaning of life." They will not be confused in their understanding of this saying, however, as many are today. In possession of natural and supernatural discernment and prudence, such friends will sort out and deal with the complexity of elements such a truth includes. They have learned to grow in authentic, human maturity and friendship and in ever more perfect chastity. They have come to see as central to Christianity God's presenting himself as lover and spouse to mankind collectively and to each human person individually. They know that the Church and each Christian are to respond as beloved bride. To accept and to live the divine proposal they realize how helpful it is to have the analogical experience of either Christian marriage or mixed celibate friendship. Both experiences lend vitality to a developing personal union with the Indwelling God through prayer. And yet, these friends would not say that those to whom Providence has not given the call of marriage or the grace of such friendship cannot live fulfilled, human lives and grow toward perfect love. They know that God is drawing every person uniquely to himself and that both human and divine love develop in many ways. But they also know that because of their friendship, they themselves are better able to live lives of manly and womanly celibate love, lives consecrated through chastity to the fullness of Christian love — now . . . unto eternal life.

Notes and References

PREFACE

1. I appreciate some of the psychological understanding and summaries, particularly those of the dynamics at play in several human relationships including friendship, in the popular book, *The Sexual Celibate*, by Donald Georgen (New York: Seabury Press, 1974). I find, however, that the author frequently steps aside from and outside of his declared purpose, "to discuss celibacy in the context of the theology and psychology of sexuality." I find further, that his final conclusions are considerably more moderate than his chapter discussions. In my judgment Goergen is sincerely searching, but is seriously confused about theology, the interpretation of Scripture, and several critical areas of faith and morals in Catholic Tradition. He tends to find reliable statements of truth more in his own evolving experience than in principles of permanent insight. And so his book seems to counsel integrating sexuality and spirituality more as one intuits and feels his way along, than as one lives and strives, perhaps struggling, toward integration of all his experience according to norms of faith. Goergen expresses the hope that his "book will contribute something simply by opening up intelligent discussion." It has stimulated me to respond in the public forum.

When I refer to Goergen's theological deficiencies, I do so from a comparison of the thought processes throughout his book with the common Catholic view of theology, as evidenced, for example, in the statement of Paul VI to Catholic Bishops, December 8, 1970: ". . . We have a duty to recall, with the Council, that true theology rests upon the written word of God, together with sacred tradition, as its perpetual foundation. . . . However necessary may be the function of theologians, it is not to the learned that God has confided the duty of authentically interpreting the Faith of the Church. . . ." See also *Dei Verbum*, the *Dogmatic Constitution on Divine Revelation* of Vatican II, No. 10; Paul VI's address of October 1, 1966, on the "Theology of the Second Vatican Council"; the *Declaration in Defense of the Catholic Doctrine on the Church Against Certain Errors of the Present Day*, issued by the Sacred Congregation for the Doctrine of the Faith on June 24, 1973, No. 2, 3 and Conclusion; the lucid treatment of the nature, functions and components of theology in *The Theological Formation of Future Priests*, by the Sacred Congregation for Catholic Education (Rome: Vatican Polyglot Press, 1976), especially pages 9-26; and theses 3.3., 3.4, 4, 5.2, 6.2, 7.2, 8.1, 8.2, 10 and 11 with commentary of the *Theses on the Relationship Between the Ecclesiastical Magisterium and Theology*, by the International Theological Commission (Washington, D.C.: U.S.C.C. Publications Office, 1977).

INTRODUCTION

1. Leo Cardinal Suenens, Archbishop of Malines-Brussels, Pastoral Letter "Christian Love and Sexuality Today," published in the English edition of *L'Osservatore Romano*, September 23, 1976.

2. An article by Donald J. Keefe, "Sacramental Sexuality and the Ordination of Women" *(Communio,* Fall, 1978, pp. 228-251), compares Catholic and non-Catholic assessments of masculine-feminine polarity in relation to God and his people, Christian marriage and sacramental priesthood.

To avoid misunderstanding of this book's view of masculine-feminine polarity, it should be stated that any linguistic use of masculine terms for humankind are intended solely in a generic sense.

3. Cf. Paul Philippe, O.P., *Le Rôle de l'amitié dans la vie chrétienne selon St. Thomas d'Aquin* (Rome: Angelicum, 1938), and Baudoin de la Trinité, O.C.D., *Nature de l'amitié selon Saint Thomas d'Aquin* (Rome: Collegium Internationale O.C.D., 1960).

4. A fine recent example is *Friendship in the Lord*, by Paul Hinnebusch, O.P. (paperback from Notre Dame's Ave Maria Press, 1974). In his small book Hinnebusch is concerned with integrating human friendship, especially between consecrated men and women, with their spiritual goal of contemplative union with God. He does this more through personal witness than through psychological or theological reflection. After beautifully presenting its many values, he concludes that such friendship is one of the Lord's greatest works, because it is the perfection of the Trinitarian image in mankind.

CHAPTER 1

1. Biblical theologies of "friendship" as it relates to divine love are rare, and those I have encountered, incomplete. I intend in this chapter to investigate this specific theme in general and in its married and mixed, celibate forms. For a more complete biblical teaching on divine love as such, one can profitably consult many available treatments, such as entries under "Love," Xavier Léon-Dufour (Ed.), in *The Dictionary of Biblical Theology* (New York: Seabury Press, 1973), pp. 322-7; and in *The Encyclopedic Dictionary of the Bible* (New York: McGraw-Hill Book Co., Inc., 1963), cols. 1377-1385. The most thorough biblical theology of divine love is the three volume *Agape in the New Testament* by Ceslaus Spicq, O.P. (St. Louis: Herder Book Co., 1963); cf. also his short *Charity and Liberty in the New Testament* (New York: Alba House, 1965).

2. Cf. 13:20; 15:17; 17:17; 18:24

3. Xavier Léon-Dufour (Ed.), *Dictionary of Biblical Theology,* article entitled "Friend" by Claude Wiéner, p. 191.

4. Philip Roets, C.SS.R., "Scriptural Teaching on Sexuality," Augustine Rock, O.P. (Ed.), *Sex, Love & the Life of the Spirit* (Chicago: Priory Press, 1966), pp. 93-94.

5. Cf. Léon-Dufour, *loc. cit.*; and Jn 19:26.

6. Rv 21:3. Cf. note "d" in Revelation, Chapter 21, *The Jerusalem Bible* (Garden City, New York: Doubleday, 1966), p. 449. It relates this messianic vision to several Old Textament texts we have considered as their fulfillment. Cf. also Rv 21:10-22:5 and Rv 22:16-17 with note "f" in Revelation, Chapter 22, *ibid.*, p. 451; and Rv 19:7-9 with note "a", Chapter 19, *ibid.*, p. 447. In confirmation of the conclusion to this section, cf. the Declaration *Inter Insigniores* of the Sacred Congregation for the Doctrine of the Faith, pp. 12-13; the official commentary on the Declaration, p. 43; and Raimondo Spiazzi, O.P., "The Advancement of Women according to the Church," pp. 57-58 — all cited from *The Order of Priesthood* (Huntington, Indiana: Our Sunday Visitor, Inc., 1978).

7. Cf. Eugene H. Maly, "Commentary on Genesis," *The Jerome Biblical Commentary* (Englewood Cliffs, New Jersey: Prentice-Hall, Inc., 1968), pp. 11-12; also the Declaration *Inter Insigniores*, p. 14, and Hans Urs Von Balthasar, "The Uninterrupted Tradition of the Church," p. 81, both from *The Order of Priesthood.*

References until footnote 8:

"way of a man . . .": Pr 30:18-19. Cf. J. Terence Forestell, C.S.B., "Commentary on Proverbs," *The Jerome Biblical Commentary,* p. 505.

On scholarly interpretations of the Song of Songs: cf. "Introduction to the Song of Songs," *The Jerusalem Bible,* p. 991; and the entry "Canticle of Canticles," *Encyclopedic Dictionary of the Bible,* cols. 315, 317; cf. A Robert,

P.S.S. and R. Tournay, O.P., *Le Cantique des Cantiques* (Paris: J. Gabalda et Cie Editeurs, 1963), pp. 413-416. An example of differing scholarly interpretations on this point can be seen by comparing the Introductions to the Song of Songs in the original edition of *The Jerusalem Bible*, which I am following, with that of the 1973 French edition, *La Bible de Jerusalem* (Paris: Les Editions du Cerf). The latter favors the literal interpretation, that the Song is about the nobility, goodness, and holiness of marriage.

On linguistic arguments from the Song: cf. Paul M. Conner, O.P., *Friendship Between Consecrated Men and Women and the Growth of Charity* (Rome: Teresianum, 1972), pp. 17-23.

On the Jewish custom of supporting rabbis: cf. William Barclay, *The Gospel of Luke* (Edinburgh: Saint Andrew Press, 1974), pp. 95-96.

8. Cf. Philip Roets, C.SS.R., *op. cit.*, pp. 143, 5.

CHAPTER 2

1. Lucius F. Cervantes, S.J., Ph. D., *And God Made Man and Woman* (Chicago: Henry Regnery Co., 1959), p. 269.

2. John L. Evoy, S.J., and Maureen O'Keefe, S.S.N.D., *The Man and the Woman (Psychology of Human Love)* (New York: Sheed and Ward, 1968), pp. 20, 60, 92.

3. Ignace Lepp, *The Psychology of Loving* (New York: Mentor-Omega, 1963), p. 41.

4. Jordan Aumann, O.P., *Sex, Love and the Christian Life* (Rome: Angelicum-pro manuscripto, 1970), p. 36.

5. Cf. Conrad W. Baars, M.D., "Psychology of Love and Sexuality," Part One of: Augustine Rock, O.P. (Ed.), *Sex, Love & The Life of the Spirit* (Chicago: The Priory Press, 1966), p. 56; and A. A. Terruwe, M.D., "Human Growth in the Priesthood," a conference given at and published by the International Documentation on the Contemporary Church Center, Rome, October 7, 1971. Cf. also A. A. Terruwe, M.D., *The Abode of Love* (St. Meinrad, Indiana: Abbey Press, 1970), p. 42.

6. Ignace Lepp, *The Ways of Friendship* (New York: Macmillan, 1966), p. 21.

References until footnote 7:

"The ordinary man . . .": *ibid.*, p. 114.

"in acting with . . .": *ibid.*, p. 119.

"In friendship . . .": *ibid.*, p. 121: cf. pp. 52-53. A sociologist makes the same claim:

"Self-revelation is both the indispensable core of personality expansion and the essential gift-giving of friendship. We become fuller, richer, warmer, more humane beings, precisely to the extent that we are able to enter into friendship relationships.": Andrew M. Greeley, *The Friendship Game* (New York: Doubleday, 1970), p. 44.

"Its imperfections . . .": Lepp, *ibid.*, p. 127.

"One does not protect . . .": "Sexuality and the Modern World: A Symposium," *Cross Currents*, Vol. XIV, No. 2, Spring, 1964. pp. 255-257, *passim.*

On functional love: cf. Baars, *op. cit.*, pp. 73-4.

7. Karl Stern, *The Flight from Woman* (New York: Farrar, Straus and Giroux, 1965), pp. 24, 285, 292. Cf. also: Dr. Eleanor Bertine, *Jung's Contribution to Our Time* (New York: G. P. Putnum's Sons, 1967), p. 137; Gerald Vann, O.P., *The Water and the Fire* (London: Collins, St. James' Place, 1953), pp. 16-18; Lepp, *op. cit.*, p. 24; and Baars, *op. cit.*, pp. 7-14.

References until footnote 8:

Man and woman must love as man and woman; cf. Baars, *op. cit.*, pp. 6-7.

"Love is authentic . . .": Lepp, *The Psychology of Loving*, p. 26.

For a study of deficient love experiece in early family life: cf. Cervantes, *op. cit.*, pp. 218-224 and Baars, *op. cit.*, pp. 6-7.

On "male" or "man" and "female" or "woman": cf. Evoy and O'Keefe, *op. cit.*, p. 51.

On "this man" and "this woman": cf. *ibid.*, p. 62.

On rareness of persons capable of love: cf. Lepp, *op. cit.*, p. 15.

"In complementing love, . . .": Evoy and O'Keefe, *op, cit.*, p. 95.

"Love enables . . .": Terruwe, *The Abode of Love*, p. 49; cf. pp. 62, 66-67, 86.

"Friendship between . . .": Lepp, *op. cit.*, p. 207. Cf. Terruwe, "Human Growth in the Priesthood," p. 15; also *The Abode of Love*, pp. 101-103.

"It belongs . . .": Terruwe, *The Abode of Love*, pp. 94-95; cf. Baars, *op. cit.*, p. 74.

On similarity of life commitment: cf. Evoy and O'Keefe, *op. cit.*, p. 132.

On mutual enrichment: cf. Lepp, *op. cit.*, pp. 208-9; Greeley, *op. cit.*, pp. 79-84; and Terruwe, op. cit., p. 108.

8. Cf. Terruwe, "Human Growth in the Priesthood," pp. 3-15. For a fuller treatment of affirming love see the volume which has become classic, *Loving and Curing the Neurotic*, by Anna Terruwe, M.D., and Conrad W. Baars, M.D. (New Rochelle, New York: Arlington House, 1972); also its revised shortened version, *Healing the Unaffirmed* (New York: Alba House, 1976). Dr. Baars has written a small volume on affirming love, *Born Only Once* (Chicago: Franciscan Herald Press, 1975).

References until footnote 9:

"two-way interpersonal relationship . . .": Evoy and O'Keefe, *op. cit.*, p. 84; cf. p. 92.

"Friendship is the term . . .": *ibid.*, pp. 84-85.

On salvific love: cf. *ibid.*, p. 83.

"An adequate person . . .": *ibid.,* pp. 86-87.

On premature erotic experience: cf. *ibid.*, pp. 91-92.

"*Complementing love* comprises . . .": *ibid.*, p. 95.

"in immediate possession . . .": *ibid.*, pp. 134-135.

On growth through severe challenge: cf. *ibid.*, p. 132.

"The man and the woman . . .": *ibid.*, pp. 138-139; cf. also pp. 136-137, 140.

"It is psychologically . . .": *ibid.*, p. 141.

"This exclusiveness . . .": *ibid.*, p. 107; cf. p. 142.

"each . . . increasingly understands . . .": *ibid.*, p. 108; cf. p. 141.

9. Lepp, *op. cit.*, p. 195. Cf. *The Ways of Friendship*, p. 49.

References until footnote 10:

"When a woman . . .": Lepp, *The Psychology of Loving*, pp. 209-210.

"Psychoanalysis calls . . .": *ibid.*, p. 211; cf. William F. Kraft, "Celibate Genitality," *Review For Religious*, V.36, July, 1977, pp. 600-612.

"permissible for the man . . .": *ibid.*, p. 212.

"It is simply . . .": *ibid.*, p. 213.

On sublimation in mature men and women: cf. *ibid.*, pp. 73-74.

"I personally know . . .": *ibid.*, p. 208.

"so-called higher values . . .": Lepp, *op. cit.*, p. 210; Terruwe, *The Abode of Love*, pp. 101-103.

"Won't its exercise . . .": Terruwe, *The Abode of Love*, p. 58.

On reason's control of feelings: cf. *ibid.*, p. 52.

"Self-restraint does not . . .": *ibid.*, p. 54.

On maturing in self-restraint: cf. *ibid.*, p. 58.

"When a person . . .": *ibid.*, pp. 53-54.

"because of the exclusiveness . . .": Evoy and O'Keefe, *op. cit.*, p. 142. Cf. also Lepp, *The Ways of Friendship*, p. 29.

On the joy of self-restraint: cf. Terruwe, *op. cit.*, p. 109.

"A priest who . . .": Baars, "The Psychology of Love and Sexuality," in Rock, *op. cit.*, p. 75. Dr. Baars has published a helpful monograph on this topic, *A Priest for All Seasons: Masculine and Celibate* (Chicago: Franciscan Herald Press, 1972); cf. Terruwe, *op. cit.*, p. 107.

"Whether one or . . .": Baars, "The Psychology of Love and Sexuality," in Rock, *op. cit.*, pp. 67-68.

"As determined by the rules . . ." and "Viewed in this light . . .": *ibid.*, pp. 64-66. Concerning what seminary educators can offer to foster healthy psychosexual development in young men preparing for celibate lives, cf. Dr. Philip D. Cristantiello, "Psychosexual Maturity in Celibate Development," *Review for Religious*, v. 37, No. 5, September, 1978, pp. 645-663.

10. Cf. *ibid.*, p. 27.

References until footnote 11:

On men and women and contemplative life: cf. Terruwe, *op. cit.*, pp. 28-29.

On the "faces" of God: cf. Cervantes, *op. cit.*, pp. 249-250.

"For some Christians . . .": Evoy and O'Keefe, *op. cit.*, pp. 108-109.

"In effect, . . .": *ibid.*, pp. 109-110.

Concerning complementing love's influence on fulfilling love for God: cf. *ibid.*, p. 111.

On the witness value of full Christian love: cf. Terruwe, *op. cit.*, pp. 98-99.

"Only a depth psychologist . . .": Lepp, *The Psychology of Loving*, p. 217; cf. p. 220.

11. The explicit intention of this chapter was to present psychological data consonant with the biblical model of celibate masculine-feminine friendship in relation to charity. As this evidence developed, however, it constituted

a strong defense of the human value of religious celibate life as such. By showing psychologically that the human ideal of interpersonal love and union is possible for celibates who are capable of it, the empirical humane sciences have rendered positive witness to a way of life which today has been widely and unjustly discredited.

CHAPTER 3

1. There have been fulfilling and complementing friendships between saintly men and women in every period of Christian history. For readers interested in enlarging the present study, the following partial list of well known cases, together with a lead reference, is offered: St. John Chrysostom and the Deaconess Olympias, cf. *Lettres à Olympias, Collection Sources chrétiennes*, No. 13 (Paris: Le Cerf, 1947); St. Jerome and both Eustochium and Paula, cf. his letters in the biographies of Jean Steinmann, *Saint Jérôme* (Paris: Le Cerf, 1957) and Yvonne Chauffin, *Saint Jérôme* (Paris: France-Empire, 1961); St. Cuthbert and several religious women, cf. the excellent article by G. Vansteenberghe, "l'Amitié," in the *Dictionnaire de Spiritualité*, T. 1 (Paris: Beauchesne, 1937), col. 527; St. Boniface and Leofgyth, Abbess of Minister, cf. *The Letters of St. Boniface*, translated by Ephraim Emerton (New York: Columbia Press, 1940) and F. M. Stenton, *Anglo-Saxon England* (Oxford: Clarendon Press, 1947), pp. 172-3; Raymond Lulle and the Abbess of Eadburg, cf. Count Montalembert, *Les Moines d'Occident*, T. V (Paris: 1863), pp. 340-344; Peter of Dacia, O.P., and Christine of Stommeln, cf. Wm. Hinnebusch, O.P., *The History of the Dominican Order*, Vol. 2 (New York: Alba House, 1973), pp. 294-297; Francis of Assisi and St. Clare, but especially "Fratello" Jacqueline de Settesoli, cf. Ella Boet-Duffil, *l'Amitié cette Accusée* (Paris: Editions du Centurion, 1968), pp. 107-112, and P. Edouard d'Alençon, *Frère Jacqueline* (Paris, 1899); St. Vincent de Paul and Louise de Marillac, cf. Pierre Coste, *Saint Vincent de Paul, correspondance, entretiens, documents* (Gabalda: 1922); Lacordaire and Mme. Swetchine, cf. Michel Guy, *Le Coeur humain de Lacordaire* (Mame: 1962) and correspondence; St. Theresa of Lisieux and a missionary seminarist and priest, cf. *Story of a Soul, Autobiography* (Garden City, New York: Doubleday, 1957) and correspondence; and several cases of recent years, for example, John G. Arintero, O.P., and Mother Mary Magdalene, C.P., cf. *Toward the Heights of Union With God.* Correspondence translated by Jordan Aumann, O.P. (Erlanger, Kentucky: Passionist Nuns, 1972), and Andrew Maginnis, S.J. and Sr. Catherine Mary Reese, S.S.J., cf. *A Priest to a Nun*, correspondence edited by Maisie Ward (New York: Sheed and Ward, 1972).

2. Cf. Bede Jarrett, O.P., *Life of St. Dominic* (New York: Image Books, 1964), p. 49, where he refers to Douais, *Documents de l'Inquisition*, Paris, 1900; cf. Jarrett, *op. cit.*, pp. 56-58; 36-37.

References until footnote 3:

"the first warred . . .": *Annales*, London, 1845, p. 182; cf. *Cartulaire de St. Dominique*, Paris, 1893, V. 1, pp. 243-256, 415.

On St. Dominic's amiable character: cf. Jarrett, *op. cit.*, pp. 56-57, 93, 105, 128-129, 136-137, 149-151.

3. Jarrett, *op. cit.*, pp. 122, 130.

References until footnote 4:

"He sought always . . .": Jarrett, *op cit.*, p. 130.

"quick sympathy . . .": M. Assumpta O'Hanlon, O.P., *St. Dominic, Servant but Friend* (St. Louis, Mo.: B. Herder Book Co., 1954), p. 111; cf. also Jarrett, *op. cit.*, p. 122.

"God's greatest gift . . .": Jarrett, *op. cit.*, p. 122; also O'Hanlon, *op. cit.*, Chapter 1, pp. 1-9.

"public knowledge . . .": cf. M. H. Vicaire, O.P., *Saint Dominique, La Vie apostolique* (Paris: Les Editions du Cerf, 1965), pp. 81-82.

"Everyone was drawn . . ." cf. M. H. Vicaire, O.P., "L'esprit de saint Dominique et son intention dans la fondation des prêchers," *Vie Dominicaine*, No. 4 (Juillet-Aout, 1971), p. 296.

"had reason to . . .": quoted in O'Hanlon, *op. cit.*, p. 175; cf. Jarrett, *op. cit.*, pp. 65, 105, 113-123, 128, 136.

"Brother Dominic . . .": cf. O'Hanlon, *op. cit.*, p. 57; also Vicaire, *Saint Dominique, La vie apostolique*, p. 212.

"after he had . . .": William A. Hinnebusch, O.P., *Dominican Spirituality, Principles and Practice* (Washington, D.C.: The Thomist Press, 1965), p. 27; cf. Jarrett, *op. cit.*, p. 130.

"exhorted them . . .": cf. M. H. Vicaire, O.P., *Histoire de saint Dominique* (Paris: Ed. du Cerf, 1957), V. II, pp. 278-279; also O'Hanlon, *op. cit.*, p. 140.

"They became . . .": quoted in O'Hanlon, *op. cit.*, p. 76; cf. Jarrett, *op. cit.*, pp. 58, 65, 82, 103, 130.

". . . bound to us": cf. Vicaire, *Saint Dominique, La vie apostolique*, p. 90, and Jarrett, *op. cit.*, pp. 69, 129, 147-149; cf. Vicaire, *Histoire de saint Dominique*, V. II, p. 294, for St. Dominic's maturation toward universal friendship.

4. Jarrett, *op. cit.*, pp. 31-32; 147; cf. Vicaire, *op. cit.*, p. 351.

References until footnote 5:

"Willelma, the wife": Jarrett, *op. cit.*, p. 32; cf. Vicaire, *op. cit.*, p. 351.

"Another young woman . . .": Jarrett, *op. cit.*, pp. 32-33.

"She had known . . .": Hinnebusch, *op. cit.*, pp. 25-26.

"had never got him . . .", "Though she saw . . .", "so there was little . . .", "Another young woman . . .": Jarrett, *op. cit.*, p. 32, *passim*.

"She knew that . . .": cf. Vicaire, *Saint Dominique, La Vie Apostolique*, p. 81.

"the solicitude . . .": Hinnebusch, *op. cit.*, p. 26.

"an intimate friendship . . .": cf. Vicaire, *Histoire de saint Dominique*, V. I, pp. 288-289; cf. Jarrett, *op. cit.*, pp. 36-37.

"we [also] see him . . .": Hinnebusch, *op. cit.*, p. 27.

On Sisters Jacobina and Lucy: cf. Vicaire, *Saint Dominique, La vie apostolique*, pp. 120-121.

"another occasion . . .", "attached to . . .": cf. Vicaire, *Histoire de saint Dominique*, V. II, p. 161.

On Sister Benedicta: cf. Vicaire, *Histoire de saint Dominique*, V. I, pp. 247-249; V. II, pp. 118, 167-168, 288-289.

"Through God's grace . . .", "Brother, I think . . .": cf. M. H. Vicaire, O.P., *Saint Dominique et ses frères, évangile ou croisade?* (Paris: Ed. du Cerf, 1967), p. 124; Vicaire, *Saint Dominique, La vie apostolique*, p. 38; cf. also O'Hanlon, *op. cit.*, pp. 172-173.

"When men began . . .": Richard T. A. Murphy, O.P., *The Timeless Dominic* (St. Louis, Mo.: B. Herder Book Co., 1967), p. 45.

5. cf. Jarrett, *op. cit.*, pp. 42-53.

References until footnote 6:

"women who had lapsed . . .", "loyalty, fortitude . . .", "an auxiliary of women . . .": cf. O'Hanlon, *op. cit*., pp. 51-52, 55.

"employment of converted . . .": O'Hanlon, *op. cit.*, p. 55; cf. Jarrett, *op. cit.*, pp. 37-38.

"certain authority": O'Hanlon, *op. cit.*, p. 57; cf. Jarrett, *op. cit.*, p. 43.

"It is clear . . .": Jarrett, *op. cit.*, p. 44; cf. O'Hanlon, *op. cit.*, p. 57.

"They were, and are . . .": O'Hanlon, *op. cit.*, p. 57.

"wisely and patiently . . .": cf. Jarrett, *op. cit.*, pp. 45-46.

"In St. Dominic's scheme . . .": Gerald Vann, O.P., *To Heaven With Diana!* (New York: Pantheon Books, 1960), pp. 12-13; cf. Hinnebusch, *op. cit.*, p. 96.

"The nuns of Madrid . . .": O'Hanlon, *op. cit.*, p. 144; cf. Jarrett, *op. cit.*, pp. 49-53.

"meant in effect . . .": Vann, *op. cit.*, p. 28.

"Following the example, . . .": O'Hanlon, *op. cit.*, pp. 57-58. The last phrase is quoted from a sermon of Vincent McNabb, O.P.

6. Marguerite Aron, *Saint Dominic's Successor, The Life of Blessed Jordan of Saxony* (London: Blackfriars Pub., 1955), p. 4. The author seems unaware of earlier correspondence mentioned in the first note of this chapter. Perhaps she is using hyperbole, however, to emphasize the intimacy and completeness of Jordan's correspondence. Cf. also Vann, *op. cit.*, p. 6; and O'Hanlon, *op. cit.*, pp. 139-140.

References until footnote 7:

"Jordan most nearly . . .", "tempered with . . .", "charm and tact . . .": Jarrett, *op. cit.*, p. 122.

On Jordan's molding the Order of Preachers: cf. Aron, *op. cit.*, pp. 180, 185-186.

"More perhaps . . .": *ibid.*, p. 78.

"a ready and flaming preacher . . .": Jarrett, *op. cit.*, p. 122.

"The most intimate pages . . .": Aron, *op. cit.*, p. 139; cf. p. 201, and Vann, *op. cit.*, p. 101.

"There is one . . .": Vann, *op. cit.*, p. 15; cf. pp. 16-17.

"Beloved of God and man . . .", "so kind and gentle . . .", "personal friend . . .": *ibid.*, p. 15.

"Wherefore I have wept . . .": *ibid.*, p. 87.

"the Queen . . .", "talked with me . . .": *ibid.*, p. 92.

"Father Jordan knew . . .", "a certain Marie . . ." and on Lutgarde and Marie: cf. Aron, *op. cit.*, pp. 105-107.

"Greet for me . . .": Vann, *op. cit.*, p. 131.

"throw a brief . . .": Aron, *op. cit.*, p. 107.

7. Vann, *op. cit.*, p. 10; cf. Hyacinth M. Cormier, O.P., *Life of Blessed Diana and her Associates, Blesseds Cecilia and Amata* (Rome, 1892)

References until footnote 8:

"an active spirit . . .": O'Hanlon, *op. cit.*, pp. 138-139.

"like Dominic . . .": Aron, *op. cit.*, p. 81.

On Jordan's restraint of Diana for austerities: cf. Vann, *op. cit.*, pp. 83, 86, 103, 107, 116.

"heart of the community . . .": Vann, *op. cit.*, p. 21.

"an old friend . . .": *ibid.*, pp. 77, 81.

"The brothers . . .": *ibid.*, p. 66.

"I, brother Henry . . .": *ibid.*, p. 83; cf. p. 82.

8. Aron, *op. cit.*, p. 192.

References until footnote 9:

"she could not but . . .", "was able to inspire . . .", "she could not but . . .": *ibid.*, p. 78.

"were obviously written . . .", "there is born . . .": *ibid.*, p. 192, *passim*.

"Always there is . . .": Vann, *op. cit.*, p. 54; cf. Norbert George, O.P., *Blessed Diana and Blessed Jordan of the Order of Preachers* (Somerset, Ohio: The Rosary Press, 1933), p. xi.

"Brother Jordan . . .": Vann, *op. cit.*, p. 87; Aron, *op. cit.*, p. 193; cf. Vann, *op. cit.*, p. 97.

"they were never . . .": Vann, *op. cit.*, p. 18.

"With Diana . . .": cf. Dominique-Antonin Mortier, O.P., *Histoire des Maîtres Généraux de l'Ordre des Frères Prêcheurs* (Paris: A. Picard et Fils, 1903), V. 1, pp. 167-168.

9. Vann, *op. cit.*, p. 102.

References until footnote 10:

"Yet, though I do not . . .": *ibid.*, p. 128.

"Beloved, since I cannot . . .": *ibid.*, p. 138.

"I do not requite . . .": *ibid.*, p. 84.

"You are so deeply . . .": *ibid.*, p. 104.

"There is another word . . .": *ibid.*, p. 112.

"Yet whatever we . . .": *ibid.*; pp. 138-139.

"Let it not be . . .": *ibid.*, p. 108.

"When I have . . .": *ibid.*, p. 121.

"The longer we . . .": *ibid.*, p. 136.

"As I wish . . .": *ibid.*, p. 130.

"Your poor foot . . .": *ibid.*, pp. 135-136.

10. Cf. Aron, *op. cit.*, p. 92.

References until footnote 11:

"Brother Jordan . . .": Vann, *op. cit.*, p. 69.

"But if the Lord . . .": *ibid.*, p. 92.

"My Beloved, . . .": *ibid.*, pp. 109-110.

"Soon, if the Lord . . .": *ibid.*, p. 118.

"She had done . . .": *ibid.*, p. 49; cf. Aron, *op. cit.*, p. 193.

"is the holy reservoir . . .": Aron, *op. cit.*, p. 92; cf. Vann, *op. cit.*, p. 104.

"wished to help . . .": Aron, *op. cit.*, p. 81.

"it was that power . . .": Vann, *op. cit.*, p. 39.

"Dearest Sister, . . .": Vann, *op. cit.*, pp. 63-64.

"the pure doctrine . . .": Aron, *op. cit.*, p. 81.

"should be ever . . .": Vann, *op. cit.*, pp. 39-40.

"these things we must bear . . .": Vann, *op. cit.*, p. 139; cf. pp. 39-40.

"There is never . . .": *ibid.*, p. 53.

"Tenacity, endurance, . . .": Aron, *op. cit.*, pp. 192-193.

11. Cf. Johannes Joergensen, *Sainte Catherine de Sienne* (Paris: Ed. Gabriel Beauchesne, 1929), p. 187, *passim;* cf. also Algar Thorold (Transl.), *The Dialogue of Saint Catherine of Siena* (Rockford, Illinois: Tan Books and Publishers, Inc., 1974), pp. 110-111.

References until footnote 12:

On dangers of human friendship: cf. *Il Messaggio di Santa Caterina da Siena, Dottore della Chiesa — Tutto il Pensiero della Vergine Senese esposto con le sue parole ridotte a forma moderna* (A cura di un missionario vicenziano) (Rome: Ediz. Vincenziane, 1970), pp. 262-265, 303, 383-384, 402, 797-798.

12. Cf. Arrigo Levasti, *My Servant, Catherine* (London: Blackfriars Pub., 1954), p. 65. Cf. also Sigrid Undset, *Catherine of Siena* (New York: Sheed & Ward, 1954), pp. 16, 115, 170.

References until footnote 13:

On Catherine's *bella brigata:* cf. Joergensen, *op. cit.*, p. 188; Undset, *op. cit.*, pp. 74, 99-100.

"dictated from memory . . .": Josephine Butler, *Catherine of Siena* (London: Horace Marshall & Son, 1894), pp. 107-108, cf. pp. 81, 325.

On Catherine's women friends: cf. Joergensen, *op. cit.*, p. 188; and Undset, *op cit.*, pp. 60, 145.

On Catherine's men friends: cf. Joergensen, *op. cit.*, p. 406; and Undset, *op. cit.*, pp. 60, 106, 128-134.

"He became . . .": Butler, *op. cit.*, p. 101.

On Catherine and William Fleete: cf. Levasti, *op. cit.*, pp. 151, 153.

"The friendship between . . .", "Thus began . . .", "her intuition and tact . . .": ibid., p. 64, *passim.*

" 'When I made . . .' ": Joergensen, *op. cit.*, p. 96.

"Till the last years . . .": Butler, *op. cit.*, p. 112.

On Fra Simone: cf. Levasti, *op. cit.*, p. 108.

"consulted me about . . .": Butler, *op. cit.*, p. 118; cf. Undset, *op. cit.*, pp. 175-176.

"How ever shall we . . .": Levasti, *op. cit.*, p. 272.

13. Cf. Undset, *op. cit.*, p. 146; and Levasti, *op. cit.*, p. 134.

References until footnote 14:

"had given you . . .": cf. Hyacinth M. Cormier, O.P., *Blessed Raymond of Capua* (Boston: Marlier, Callahan & Co., 1900), p. 25.

"strengthened by . . .": Levasti, *op. cit.*, p. 139.

"they had spent . . .": Joergensen, *op. cit.*, p. 399; cf. Undset, *op. cit.*, pp. 26, 55.

"acquired a profound . . .": Levasti, *op. cit.*, p. 134.

"It seems that . . .": cf. Letter 119 quoted in Joergensen, *op. cit.*, p. 405; and p. 404 *passim.*

On Catherine's and Raymond's love: cf. Levasti, *op. cit.*, p. 325; also pp. 139, 324.

"My dear Father . . .": Butler, *op. cit.*, pp. 289-290; cf. Undset, *op. cit.*, pp. 253-254, 256, 262.

" 'Pardon me . . .' ": Butler, *op, cit.*, p. 296.

On Catherine's pseudonym for Raymond: cf. Letter 273 in Joergensen, *op. cit.*, p. 382; also p. 404.

" 'Amid these torments . . .' ": Levasti, *op, cit.*, p. 389.

On Catherine's and Raymond's last meeting, cf. Cormier, *op. cit.*, p. 58; Undset, *op. cit.*, pp. 248-250; and Joergensen, *op. cit.*, pp. 500-501.

On Catherine's and Raymond's common undertakings: cf. Cormier, *op. cit.*, pp. 37-39; Joergensen, *op. cit.*, pp. 270, 348-349, 405; Undset, *op. cit.*, pp. 147, 150-155, 229; Levasti, *op. cit.*, pp. 134, 139, 318.

"her spiritual director . . .": Levasti, *op, cit.*, p. 140, *passim.*

On Catherine's and Raymond's mutual help in grace: cf. Levasti, *op. cit.*, pp. 134, 139; Joergensen, *op. cit.*, pp. 477, 500; Cormier, *op. cit.*, p. 135; Butler, *op. cit.*, pp. 131, 331; and Undset, *op. cit.*, pp. 93, 187, 281, 286-287.

"omitted nothing . . .": Cormier, *op. cit.*, p. 128.

"I beseech you . . .": Letter 102 cited in Cormier, *op. cit.*, p. 134.

" 'official' life . . .": Levasti, *op. cit.*, p. 134; cf. Cormier, *op. cit.*, p. 135; Undset, *op. cit.*, pp. 93, 187, 286-287; and Butler, *op. cit.*, pp. 131, 331.

14. Cf. Allison E. Peers, *The Complete Works of Saint Teresa of Jesus*

(London: Sheed and Ward, 1946), V. I, p. 357 (*Spiritual Relations*, 42), and Peers, *op. cit.*, V, II, pp. 364-377 (*Conceptions*, Chap. 2).

References until footnote 15:

"For the kiss . . .": Peers, *op. cit.*, V. II, p. 363.

"It is clear . . .": *ibid.*, p. 72 (*Way of Perfection*, Chap. 18).

"What better sign . . .": *ibid.*, p. 71 (*Way*, Chap. 17).

"For this reason . . .": Peers, *op. cit.*, V. I, p. 46, *passim* (*Life*, Chap. 7).

On Teresa's three-fold distinction of affections: cf. Peers, *op. cit.*, V. II, pp. 31-32, *passim* (*Way*, Chap. 7).

"It is strange . . .": *ibid.*, pp. 30-31 (*Way*, Chap. 7); cf. Peers, *op. cit.*, V. I, p. 235 (*Life*, Chap. 34).

"O God my Lord, . . .": Peers, *op. cit.*, V. II, p. 31, *passim* (*Way*, Chap. 7).

"true friend . . .", "Where you had . . .", "It is sometimes good . . .": *ibid.*, p. 41 (*Way*, Chap. 9), *passim.*.

"When you make . . .": *ibid.*, pp. 33-34, *passim* (*Way*, Chap. 7).

"never have I . . .": Peers, *op. cit.*, V. I, p. 155 (*Life*, Chap. 24).

15. On Teresa's many friendships: cf. Peers, *ibid.*, p. 99 (*Life*, Chap. 16); p. 303 (Introduction to *Sp. Rel.*) and pp. xliii, 320 (Note 9) and pp. 322-323 (*Sp. Rel.*, 4); p. 365 (*Sp. Rel.*, 63); cf. Peers, *op. cit.*, V. III, p. 15 (*Foundations*, 3); also p. 64 (*Foundations*, 13); and Allison Peers, *The Letters of Saint Teresa of Jesus* (London: Burns, Oates & Washbourne Ltd., 1951), V. I, p. 175 (Letter 72).

"allusions to her friends . . .": Peers, *The Complete Works*, V. I, p. 303.

16. Peers, *op. cit.*, V. III, p. 122, *passim* (*Foundations*, Chap. 24).

References until footnote 17:

"on His right hand . . .": Peers, *op. cit.*, V. I, p. 354 (*Sp. Rel.*, 39).

"I did not reflect . . .", "promised, in fact . . .": *ibid.*, pp. 355-356, *passim* (*Sp. Rel.*, 40); cf. *ibid.*, p. 357 (*Sp. Rel.*, 41); and p. 356 (*Sp. Rel.*, 40).

"I must tell you . . .": Peers, *Letters*, V. I, p. 175 (Letter 72).

On Gratian's direction of Teresa's personal affairs: cf. Peers, *Complete Works*, V. II, p. 345 (Intro. to *Conceptions*); and V. II, p. 188 (Intro. to *The Interior Castle*); also V. III, p. 239 (*Method for Visitation*).

"for such was . . .": Peers, *op. cit.*, V. II, p. 194, *passim* (Introduction to *The Interior Castle*).

"How well I remember . . .": Peers, *Letters*, V. II, p. 693 (Letter 295).

"Now do you . . .": *ibid.*, p. 838 (Letter 366).

"He was a man . . .": Peers, *The Complete Works*, V. III, p. 117 (*Foundations*, Chap. 23).

On Teresa's and Gratian's use of pseudonyms: cf. Peers, *Letters*, V. I, p. 4 (Introduction); also V. II, p. 619 (Letter 256).

"He has not . . .": *ibid.*, p. 670 (Letter 282).

"He is so saintly . . .": *ibid.*, p. 800 (Letter 346).

"I have the saintly . . .": *ibid.*, p. 587 (Letter 239).

"pleasant manner, . . .": Peers, *Complete Works*, V. III, p. 118 (*Foundations*, Chap. 23).

"The greatest caution . . .": Peers, *Letters*, V. I, pp. 316-317 (Letter 122).

"his great desire . . .": cf. Peers, *Complete Works*, V. III, p. 118 (*Foundations*, Chap. 23).

"young . . . and good-looking . . .": cf. *ibid.*, p. 138 (*Foundations*, Chap. 26).

"It may seem . . .," "other things . . .", "I have certainly restrained . . .": *ibid.*, pp. 120-121, *passim* (*Foundations*, Chap. 24).

"She loved me, . . .": Peers, *Letters*, V. I, p. 20 (Introduction).

On Gratian's preserving Teresa's autographed vow and letters: cf. Peers, *op. cit.*, V. II, p. 977 (Footnote); and V. I, p. 20 (Introduction).

" 'He is my true son: . . .' ": Peers, *Complete Works*, V. I, p. 357 (*Sp. Rel.*, 43).

"I was making . . .": *ibid.*, pp. 361-362 (*Sp. Rel.*, 55).

"I thought . . .", "The experience lasted . . .": *ibid.*, p. 358, *passim* (*Sp. Rel.*, 44).

On Teresa's fear for Gratian: cf. Allison E. Peers, *Handbook to the Life and Times of St. Teresa and St. John of the Cross* (London: Burns & Oates, 1954), pp. 35-36.

" 'O woman . . .' ": cf. Peers, *Complete Works*, V. I, pp. 364-365. (*Sp. Rel.*, 60).

"It could not . . .', "Tell him to . . .", " 'What dost thou ask . . .' ": *ibid.*, p. 364, *passim* (*Sp. Rel.*, 59).

17. "As concerns . . .": Peers, *Letters*, V. I, p. 194 (Letter 78a).

References until footnote 18:

"I have been . . .": *ibid.*, p. 285 (Letter 111).

"For many reasons . . .": *ibid.*, pp. 345-346 (Letter 134).

"O, Jesus, . . .": *ibid.*, p. 368 (Letter 147).

"I must explain . . .": Peers, *op. cit.*, V. II, p. 811 (Letter 350).

"I am worried . . .": Peers, *op. cit.*, V. I, p. 202 (Letter 81).

"My great comfort . . .": *ibid.*, p. 322 (Letter 124).

"Oh, how Angela . . .": *ibid.*, p. 358 (Letter 141).

"Oh, my Father, . . .": *ibid.*, p. 367 (Letter 145).

"When he . . .": Peers, *op. cit.*, V. II, p. 568 (Letter 231).

"I must tell you . . .": *ibid.*, p. 591 (Letter 242).

"The life . . .": *ibid.*, p. 977 (Letter 437b).

"That was a great . . .": Peers, *Complete Works*, V. I, p. 363, (*Sp. Rel.*, 58).

"When I reflect . . .": Peers, *Letters*, V. I, p. 240 (Letter 95).

"I . . . should like . . .": *ibid.*, p. 297 (Letter 117).

"I am extremely . . .": Peers, *op. cit.*, V. II, p. 531 (Letter 215).

"I can see . . .": *ibid.*, p. 582 (Letter 237).

"Oh, how much . . .": *ibid.*, p. 661 (Letter 278).

"Angela's mind . . .": *ibid.*, p. 683 (Letter 290).

"Oh, how tired . . .": *ibid.*, p. 841 (Letter 366).

"I am really feeling . . .": *ibid.*, p. 867 (Letter 380).

"Laurentia finds herself . . .": Peers, *op. cit.*, V. I, p. 199 (Letter 79).

"So Angela . . .": *ibid.*, p. 255 (Letter 104).

"In reality . . .": *ibid.*, p. 331 (Letter 128).

"I shall never . . .": *ibid.*, p. 372 (Letter 147).

"May God preserve you . . .": *ibid.*, pp. 400-401 (Letter 160).

"God keep you . . .": Peers, *op. cit.*, V. II, p. 716 (Letter 306).

"Oh, my Father, . . .": *ibid.*, p. 970 (Letter 434).

18. Cf. Maurice Henry-Coüannier, *Saint François de Sales et ses Amitiés* (Paris: Per Orbem, 1922), pp. 188, 190.

References until footnote 19:

"to give me a man . . .": cf. *ibid.*, p. 191.

"There is the man . . .": cf. *ibid.*, p. 192, and p. 196.

"the saint of friendship . . .": cf. *ibid.*, pp. xiii-xiv.

"But who thinks . . .": cf. Etienne-Marie Lajeunie, *St. François de Sales* (Paris: Ed. du Seuil, 1962), p. 75.

On Francis' understanding of woman's psychology: cf. E. LeCounturier, *Lettres de direction et spiritualité de François de Sales* (Lyon: Ed. Vitte, 1951); and St. François de Sales, *Traité de l'amour de Dieu.* (Paris: J. Gabalda et Fils, 1928), V. II, pp. 348-350. The authority Maurice Henry-Coüannier (*op. cit.*, p. 356) says that in writing this work in 1614, Francis had Jane de Chantal specifically in mind and souls which resembled or wanted to resemble her.

On Francis' and Jane's personal correspondence: cf. Henry-Coüannier, *op. cit.*, pp. 203-204.

"I called him . . .": *ibid.*, p. 198.

"his soul lodge itself . . .": cf. *ibid.*, p. 200; also p. 195.

"Madame, . . .": cf. *ibid.*, p. 201.

"I want to speak . . .": cf. St. François de Sales, *Oeuvres de Saint François de Sales* (Edition complète) (Annecy: Nierat, 1892-1919), V. XII, pp. 283-284.

"to direct, help, serve . . .": cf. *Sainte Jeanne-Françoise Frémyot de Chantal — Sa vie et ses oeuvres* (Paris: Plon, 1874), V. I, p. 224.

"My very dear sister, . . .": cf. St. François de Sales, *op. cit.*, V. XII, pp. 354-358, *passim.*

"Those few days . . .": cf. Henry-Coüannier, *op. cit.*, p. 215.

"Do you know . . .": cf. *ibid.*, p. 228.

"Who, though, . . .": cf. St. François de Sales, *op. cit.,* V. XIII, p. 185.

"These two beings, . . .": cf. Henry-Coüannier, *op. cit.,* p. 236.

"To this proposal . . .": cf. *ibid.,* p. 237.

"How welcome . . .": cf. St. François de Sales, *op. cit.,* V. XIV, p. 128.

"Because I am speaking . . .": cf. *ibid.,* p. 261.

On Francis' and Jane's shared sufferings: cf. Henry-Coüannier, *op. cit.,* pp. 325-337.

19. Cf. *ibid.,* p. 452.

Final references:

"I have just now . . .": cf. St. François de Sales, *op. cit.,* V. XIII, p. 300.

"Believe me, . . .": cf. *ibid.,* p. 305.

"Thus our bond, . . .": cf. St. François de Sales, *op. cit.,* V. XII, p. 285.

"My soul is joined . . .": cf. St. François de Sales, *op. cit.,* V. XV, p. 151.

"She is very sick, . . .": cf. *ibid.,* p. 168.

"I love [you], . . .": cf. St. François de Sales, *op. cit.,* V. XVI, p. 337.

"My poor, . . .": cf. St. François de Sales, *op. cit.,* V. XIII, p. 84.

"I always read . . .": cf. St. François de Sales, *op. cit.,* V. XVIII, p. 47.

"Indeed, I am glad . . .": cf. Henry-Coüannier, *op. cit.,* p. 451.

"You see, . . .": cf. St. François de Sales, *op. cit.,* V. XIII, p. 365.

"There appeared . . .": cf. Henry-Coüannier, *op. cit.,* pp. 466-467.

CHAPTER 4

1. Cf. Jordan Aumann, O.P., and Antonio Royo, O.P., *The Theology of Christian Perfection* (Dubuque, Iowa: The Priory Press, 1962), pp. 428-431 on the virtue of prudence; and cf. Francisco P. Muniz, O.P., *The Work of Theology* (Washington, D.C.: The Thomist Press, 1953), pp. 20-29 on theology as wisdom as well as science in the mind of St. Thomas. Cf. also the entry "Theology" in Louis Bouyer, C.O., *Dictionary of Theology* (New York: Desclee, 1965), pp. 441-442.

2. To avoid misunderstanding, we have been careful up to this point to use the expressions "Christian love" or "divine love" in place of the theological term "charity," and "fulness of (Christian) love" in place of "perfection of charity." Since we are considering the unique reality of Christian love itself, the proper terms will henceforth be used interchangeably with others.

References until footnote 3:

In regard to Mt 22:37-39, cf. the conclusions of Jean Guitton in "Arianism and its Relevance Today," in the English edition of *L'Osservatore Romano*, October 7, 1976, p. 9.

On charity, gift of participated divine love: cf. St. Thomas Aquinas, *Summa Theologica*, II-II, q. 24, a. 2c; q. 23, a. 2 ad 1.

Concerning effects of sanctifying grace on the human spirit: cf. 2 P 1: 3-7; *Summa Theol.*, I-II, q. 110, aa. 1, 3; Aumann, *op. cit.*, pp. 49-50; and Thomas Dubay, S.M., *God Dwells Within Us* (Denville, N.J.: Dimension Books, 1971) for a highly readable, scriptural and theological treatment of the Trinitarian indwelling.

On the limitations of human knowledge: cf. *Summa Theol.*, II-II, q. 1, a. 4; q. 27, a. 4.

On the human will's ability to love God directly, cf. *Summa Theol.*, II-II, q. 27, a. 4c.; I, q. 82, a. 3; and I-II, q. 10, a. 1; cf. Archbishop Paul Philippe, O.P., Secretary of the Sacred Congregation of Religious, *The Ends of the Religious Life According to Saint Thomas Aquinas* (Athens — Rome: Fraternity of the Blessed Virgin Mary, 1962), pp. 25-6.

On the secondary object of charity: cf. *Summa Theol.*, II-II, q. 25, a. 1c. Cf. I-II, q. 66, a. 6, and Paul Philippe, *op. cit.*, pp. 26-27.

"Love of one another . . .": Jordan Aumann, O.P., *Sex, Love and the Christian Life* (Rome: Angelicum — pro manuscripto, 1970), p. 39.

3. Cf. Ferdinand Valentine, O.P., *The Apostolate of Chastity* (Westminster, Maryland: Newman Press, 1964), especially pp. 82-88. Other competent treatments of chastity and charity are by M.-J. Le Guillou, O.P., "Virginity and the Theological Virtues," in the collection on *Chastity* (Westminster, Maryland: Newman Press, 1963), pp. 116-127, and Albert Plé, O.P.'s masterful study, *Chastity and the Affective Life* (New York: Herder and Herder, 1966).

References until footnote 4:

On the renunciation of vowed chastity: cf. *Summa Theol.*, II-II, q. 152, a. 1.

"Detachment . . .": cf. Lacordaire, *Jesus-Christ* (Paris: Les Editions du Cerf, 1960), p. 72.

On the spiritual advantages of consecrated chastity: cf. *Optatum Totius*, No. 10, and *Perfectae Caritatis*, No. 12, Austin Flannery, O.P., (Ed.), *Vatican Council II, The Conciliar and Post Conciliar Documents* (Northport, New York: Costello Publishing Co., 1975), pp. 715-716, 617-618.

On freedom to love through vowed chastity: cf. Paul Philippe, *op. cit.*, pp. 21-24, 36-42.

On the foremost preoccupation of charity: cf. Charles V. Heris, O.P., *Spirituality of Love* (St. Louis: B. Herder Book Co., 1965), p. 213; cf. Paul Philippe, *op. cit.*, pp. 29-30.

"The sole valid motive . . .": cf. A.M. Perreault, O.P., *Aspects Psychologiques de la Chastité Consacrée* (Rome: Angelicum — pro manuscripto, 1963), p. 22.

"For all Christ's faithful . . .": *Perfectae Caritatis*, No. 12, in Flannery, *op. cit.*, p. 617.

Concerning charity's wholesome effect on human love: cf. the talk "Virginal Love and Friendship" given by Thomas Dubay, S.M., at Queen of the Holy Rosary College, Mission San Jose, California, March 6, 1977. Father Dubay has checked this thought and in a letter to the author has verified its accuracy.

On vowed chastity as an exceptional grace: cf. *Perfectae Caritatis*, No. 12, in Flannery, *op. cit.*, p. 617. Cf. *Optatum Totius*, No. 10, *ibid.*, p. 715 for the Council's judgment of the "greater excellence of virginity consecrated to Christ" in the lives of priests to the grace of Christian marriage.

On the "spiritual instinct" of authentic chastity: cf. Flannery, *op. cit.*, p. 617.

4. Cf. *Summa Theol.*, II-II, q. 23, a. 1; *Book III, Summa Contra Gentes*, Ch. 95, 5; Ch. 96, 5, 7; *III Sent.* D. 27, qq. 1, 2; D. 32, q. 1; and *Book VIII* of Aristotle's *Nichomachean Ethics*.

References until footnote 5:

On the fundamental similarity required for friendship: cf. *Summa Theol.*, I-II q. 27, a. 3c; *III Summa C.G.*, Ch. 151, 5: Aristotle, *VIII N. Ethics*, 8, 5.

On benevolent love required for friendship: cf. *Summa Theol.*, II-II, q. 23, a. 1c; *In VIII Eth.*, 1. 2, n. 1561; *In IX Eth.*, 1. 5, n. 1825.

"The love of friendship . . .": Aumann, *op. cit.*, p. 39.

On the mutuality of friendship: cf. *Summa Theol.*, II-II, q. 23, a. 1c. Also *III Sent.*, D. 27, q. 2, a. 1.

On the actual exchange required for friendship: cf. *Summa Theol.*, II-II,

182

q. 23, a. lc; *In IX Ethics,* 4, 5; *III Summa C.G.,* Ch. 158; *III Sent.,* D. 32, q. 1, a. 3 ad 3m; and *In Jo.,* C. 15, 1. 3, n. 3.

On the height of exchange between friends: cf. *III Sent.* d. 27, q. 2, a. 1; a. 2; a. 2 ad 4m.

"Nothing is so delightful . . ."; Aristotle, *VIII N. Ethics,* 5, 3.

"Friendship is . . .": Andrew M. Greeley, *The Friendship Game* (New York: Doubleday, 1970), p. 17.

"Thus, people in love . . .": Heris, *op. cit.,* p. 83.

"love, when lived . . .": *ibid.,* p. 88.

5. Cf. *Summa Theol.,* I-II, q. 27, a. lc. It should be noted that both "benevolent" and "concupiscible" loves are natural and good in themselves, although benevolent love is more noble. Only by a proper proportion of the two can an individual attain his perfection. In moral terms, an "unselfish" proportion is compatible with true friendship, whereas a "selfish" proportion is not. This proportion will be governed by the quality of his primary love for self — as we shall see in the next section on masculine-feminine friendship and consecrated chastity.

References until footnote 6:

"The two perfect each other . . .": Gerald Vann, O.P., *The Water and the Fire* (London: Collins, St. James' Place, 1953), p. 126.

"Each individual, . . .": Heris, *op. cit.,* p. 224.

"The Pieta . . .": Gerald Vann, O.P., *The Seven Swords* (London: Collins, St. James' Place, 1950), p. 67.

On Christ's use of "Beloved" in Jn 15:15: the Greek "Beloved" is even stronger than the usual English translation of "friends." Cf. *The Jerome Biblical Commentary* (Englewood Cliffs, New Jersey: Prentice-Hall, 1968), p. 455.

6. Cf. H.A. Reinhold (Ed.), *The Soul Afire* (New York: Meridian Books, Inc., 1960), p. 232.

References until footnote 7:

"Nature never taught . . .": C.S. Lewis, *The Four Loves* (New York: Harcourt, Brace and World, 1960), p. 37.

"The more man . . .": Leo M. Bond, O.P., "A Comparison Between Human and Divine Friendship," *The Thomist,* No. 3, 1941, p. 56.

Cf. *Dictionnaire de Spiritualité,* T. II (Paris: Beauchesne, 1953), cols. 523-594 for the historical development of the theological conception of charity up through the time of St. Thomas.

On Aquinas' view of charity as friendship: cf. Jerome Wilms, O.P., *Divine Friendship* (Dubuque, Iowa: The Priory Press, 1958), pp. 22-26; *In IX Ethics,* 4; *III Sents.,* D. 27, q. 2, a. 1; and *Summa Theol.,* II-II, q. 23, a.1.

7. There are several studies which treat this subject specifically, e.g. the excellent article by Fr. Vansteenburghe, "l'Amitié," in the *Dictionnaire de*

Spiritualité, T. I (Paris: Beauchesne, 1937), cols. 500-29; Paul Philippe, O.P., *Le rôle de l'amitié dans la vie Chrétienne selon St. Thomas d'Aquin* (Rome: Angelicum — published doctoral thesis, 1938); Baudoin de la Trinité, O.C.D., *Nature de l'amitié selon St. Thomas d'Aquin* (Rome: Teresianum — published extract of doctoral thesis, 1960); V.M. Capdevila, *El amor natural en au relacion con la caritas seqún la doctrina de S. Thomás* (Rome: Gregorianum — published doctoral thesis, 1964).

References until footnote 8:

Cf. Bond, *op. cit.,* pp. 57-62, 69 for a theological discussion of man's need of sanctifying grace in order to become a friend of God.

"It is not necessary . . .": *ibid.,* p. 57.

On God's providence and temporal favor: cf. *Summa Theol.,* II-II, q. 83, a. 6, ad 4.

On desiring God for our own perfection: cf. *ibid.,* I-II, q. 65, a. 5, ad 1; and Bond, *op. cit.,* pp. 80-85; also Wilms, *op. cit.,* pp. 42-46.

"The proper effect . . .": *III Summa C. G.,* Ch. 151, 2.

"Faith is, . . .": Bond, *op. cit.,* p. 74; pp. 73-77 give a good treatment of conversation with God in faith and prayer. Cf. also A. Tanquerey, S.S., *The Spiritual Life* (Westminster, Maryland: Newman Press, 1930), pp. 50-51.

On the Fathers' definitions of prayer: cf. Migne, *Patrologia Graeca,* XLIV, c. 1125; LIII, c. 280; and *Patrologia Latina,* XXXIX, c. 1887.

On Catherine's and Teresa's view of prayer and friendship with God: cf. Roberto Moretti, O.C.D., *La Preghièra* (Rome: Teresianum — pro manuscripto, 1969), p. 34.

On the gifts of the Holy Spirit and prayer: cf. *Summa Theol.,* II-II, q. 8, a. 6.

"It is evident . . .": Bond, *op. cit.,* p. 77.

"Charity signifies . . .": *Summa Theol.,* I-II, q. 65, a. 5; cf. Bond, *op. cit.,* p. 94; and Tanquerey, *op. cit.,* pp. 577-578 for a description of some qualities of the friendship between man and God.

8. Gerald Vann, O.P., *To Heaven with Diana!* (New York: Pantheon Books, 1960), p. 57.

References until footnote 9:

"It is of . . .": Aumann, *op. cit.,* pp. 39-40.

"We love our friends . . .": cf. H.D. Noble, O.P., *l'Amitié* (Paris: Lethielleux, 1941), pp. 68-73, *passim.*

When charity . . .": Heris, *op. cit.,* p. 157.

"But for a Christian, . . .": C.S. Lewis, *op. cit.,* p. 126.

"When you come . . .": Charles W. Freible, S.J., "Teilhard, Love and Celibacy," *Review for Religious,* No. 3, 1967, p. 284.

9. Vann, *op. cit.,* pp. 55-56.

References until footnote 10:

On the relative equality of men and women: cf. Hans Urs Von Balthasar, "The Uninterrupted Tradition of the Church," pp. 81-82, from *The Order of Priesthood* (Huntington, Indiana: Our Sunday Visitor, Inc., 1978).

"To appreciate . . .": Augustine Rock, O.P., "The Problems of Contemporary Priests," in Augustine Rock, O.P., (Ed.), *Impact of Renewal on Priests and Religious* (Chicago: The Priory Press, 1968), p. 144.

"The soul is feminine . . .": Gerald Vann, O.P., *The Water and the Fire*, pp. 29-32, *passim;* p. 88.

"All sex desires . . .": M.J. Andre, *Equilibrium, Fidelity to Nature and Grace* (St. Louis: B. Herder Co., 1968), p. 104.

On the nuptial relationship between the Church and Christ: cf. J. M. Perrin, O.P., "Recherche de la sainteté, la direction spirituelle," *La Vie Spirituelle,* juillet, 1967, p. 33; and Gustave Martelet, S.J., "The Mystery of the Covenant and its Connection with the Nature of the Ministerial Priesthood," pp. 108-109, from *The Order of Priesthood, op. cit.*

On the writings of Origen and St. Gregory of Nyssa: cf. Ermanno Ancilli, O.C.D., *Annotazioni per la Storia della Spiritualità Medievale* (Roma: Teresianum — pro manuscripto, 1969), pp. 15-17.

On the Cistercian spirituality of pure love: cf. Etienne Gilson, *La Théologie Mystique de Saint Bernard* (Paris: J. Vrin, 1934), p. 215.

On St. Bernard and the Song of Songs: cf. Watkin Williams, *The Mysticism of S. Bernard of Clairvaux* (London: Burns, Oates & Washbourne, Ltd., 1931), pp. 30-39. Cf. also Reinhold, *op. cit.,* pp. 293-295.

On nuptial language for stages of prayer: cf. Moretti, *op. cit.,* pp. 30-34, 71-76.

On John of the Cross' view of the Incarnation: cf. Frederico Ruiz, O.C.D., *San Giovanni della Croce* (Roma: Teresianum — pro manuscripto, 1970), p. 18.

"I saw how Jesus . . .": Reinhold, *op. cit.,* p. 292; cf. "Ceremonial for the Consecration of Virgins," *The Roman Pontifical,* in Reinhold, pp. 287-292.

"We do not love . . .": cf. Lacordaire, *op. cit.,* pp. 128-129.

For Vatican II on the Church's nuptial relationship to Christ: cf. *Sacrosanctum Concilium,* No. 7, 85, in Flannery, *op. cit.,* pp. 5, 25. Stanislao Gatto, O.C.D., expresses this point in his study of *Humanae Vitae* and *Gaudium et Spes:* Personal communion with Christ is the ideal and essential goal of every Christian life. Fidelity to love does not remain a pure decision of the will, but must translate itself into a lively sense of friendship which puts us in a state of intimate personal communion with Christ. The soul regards him as friend and spouse, and desires to belong to him entirely, as He has deigned to give himself entirely. Inspired by this love, the soul is solicitous to please him in everything and anxiously takes great pains . . . to bring about its prefect assimilation to its spouse (cf. his *Spiritualità Dei Laici, Attuazioni Esistenziali,* V. II (Roma: Teresianum — pro manuscripto, 1971, p. 100).

185

" 'lead the faithful . . .' ": cf. Venanzio Caprioli, O.C.D., *Spiritualità Sacerdotale* (Roma: Teresianum — pro manuscripto, 1970), p. 36; cf. Thomas Dubay, S.M., *Ecclesial Women* (New York: Alba House, 1970), pp. 25-30 for application of this theme to consecrated women.

"In both man and woman . . .": Andre, *op. cit.*, p. 104; cf. Gerald Vann, O.P., *Moral Dilemmas* (London: Collins, 1965), p. 61.

"This is the role . . .": John Dominic Corcoran, O.P., "The Priest in Church and World," in Jordan Aumann, O.P. (Ed.), *The World in the Church* (Chicago: The Priory Press, 1969), pp. 148-149; cf. Dubay, *op. cit.,* pp. 30-33 for application to consecrated women.

"better able to be . . .": Andre, *op. cit.*, pp. 107-109, *passim.*

10. Cardinal Leo Suenens, "Christian Love and Sexuality Today," in the English edition of *L'Osservatore Romano*, September 23, 1976.

References until footnote 11:

"Our loves do not . . .": C.S. Lewis, *op. cit.*, pp. 19-20, 33.

On a Christian's present state compared to that of original justice: cf. the article "Innocence" in Louis Bouyer, C.O., *Dictionary of Theology* (New York: Desclee, 1965), p. 240.

On the history of physical and sensate loves and consecration to God: cf. Cardinal John Wright, "Christian Theology of the Flesh," in the English edition of *L'Osservatore Romano*, May 20, 1976. This exceptional article contrasts the perennial tendency to extremes in regard to the human body, i.e. pessimism or optimism.

"Of course, . . .": cf. Rock, *op. cit.*, pp. 137-140.

"avoid the two extremes . . .": Aumann, *op. cit.*, p. 5.

"We ought not . . .": Heris, *op. cit.*, pp. 219-220.

"Sexual love . . .": Freible, *op. cit.*, pp. 289, 294.

"From the very fact . . .": Heris, *op. cit.*, p. 230.

Note on the distinction of physical and sensate loves: Authors use a variety of names for these two levels. Some common terms for physical love are generative, sexual or genital love. Terms for sensate love are sentient, sensible, emotional, or psychic love; cf. Heris, *op. cit.*, p. 57. This introduction to sensate love follows several ideas of Fr. Heris, pp. 54-74.

On the "harmony" between physical and sensate loves: cf. Heris, *op. cit.*, p. 192.

On the selfish or generous results of sensate love: cf. *ibid.*, p. 60.

"This group of functions . . .": cf. Perreault, *op. cit.*, p. 7.

"Because sensibility comprises . . .": cf. *ibid.*, pp. 10-12, *passim.*

"the only solution . . .": cf. *ibid.*, p. 13.

On integration of sensate love, chastity and charity: cf. Albert Plé, O.P., "Le Prêtre et la femme," *La Vie Spirituelle, Supplément,* mai, 1969, pp. 228-233.

"This is possible, . . .": cf. *ibid.*, p. 229.

"are essentially the joys . . .": cf. *ibid.,* p. 231.

"There must be . . .": Dom H. Van Zeller, *We Die Standing Up* (New York: Doubleday and Co., 1961), p. 129.

"The human senses . . .": Heris, *op. cit.,* pp. 222-223.

"Eros, . . .": C.S. Lewis, *op. cit.,* p. 153.

"It is important . . .": Aumann, *op. cit.,* p. 16.

"Can God tolerate . . .": cf. Noble, *op. cit.,* pp. 65-67, *passim.*

"Thus, intimate friendships . . .": Heris, *op. cit.,* p. 230.

For those interested in clarifying discussions of signs of morally helpful or harmful "friendships," cf. the series of articles by A. Durand, "Learning How to Love," in *Sponsa Regis,* August, 1964-February, 1965, later reprinted as a booklet, *Friendship in Religious Life* (Collegeville, MN: The Liturgical Press) and the excellent article by Thomas Dubay, S.M., "Celibate Friendship: Illusion and Reality," in *Review for Religious,* V. 36, 1977, pp. 833-843; also Sr. Jane F. Becker, O.S.B., "Overcoming Problems in Friendship," *Sisters Today,* May, 1978, pp. 593-611.

11. Charles Dollen, "In the Service of Life," *Perspectives,* Vol. X, No. 3, May-June, 1965, p. 68; cf. Lawler, Wuerl, and Lawler (Ed.), *The Teaching of Christ* (Huntington, Indiana: Our Sunday Visitor, Inc., 1976), p. 508.

References until footnote 12:

"There obviously exists . . .": *III Summa C.G.,* Ch. 233; cf. also *Summa Theol., Suppl.,* q. 44, a. 2, ad 3.

On the nature and characteristics of Christian marriage: cf. *Gaudium et Spes,* No. 47-8; Lawler and Wuerl, *op. cit.,* pp. 503-512; D.M. Prümmer, O.P., *Vademecum Theologiae Moralis* (Barcelona: Herder, 1947), pp. 476, 481-482, 487; also *Summa Theol., Suppl.,* q. 44, a. 1; and Heris, *op. cit.,* p. 186; the Congregation for the Doctrine of the Faith, *Letter to Bishops of the United States of America,* April 11, 1973.

On current theology of Christian marriage: cf. the stimulating article by Cormac Burke, "Marriage in Crisis," published in *Catholic Position Papers* (12-6 Funda-Cho, Ashiya-Shi, Japan: Seido Foundation, Sept. 1976), and the penetrating treatment of William E. May, "Sexuality and Fidelity in Marriage," *Communio,* Fall, 1978, pp. 275-293.

On the five essentials of Christian marriage: cf. Peter Ketter, D.D., *Christ and Womankind* (Westminster, Maryland: Newman Press, 1952), pp. 98, 127; also *Gaudium et Spes,* No. 47-48.

"It is a wise . . .": cf. Pope Paul VI, *Humanae Vitae* (Rome: *L'Osservatore Romano,* prima edizione, 29-30 luglio, 1968), p. 1, parag. 8; also Sacred Congregation of Rites, *Rite of Marriage,* published by authority of Paul VI, March 19, 1969, Introduction, No. 3.

On the mutual possession of marriage partners: cf. *Gaudium et Spes,* No. 48; also *Sacrosanctum Concilium,* No. 77.

"To surrender oneself . . .": Edith Stein, quoted by Ketter, *op. cit.,* p. 171.

"In itself, sexuality . . ."; cf. Perreault, *op. cit.*, p. 24; also Lawler, Wuerl, and Lawler, *op. cit.*, pp. 506-507.

On the parental dimension of celibate love: cf. Louis Bouyer, C.O., *Introduction to Spirituality* (Collegeville, Minnesota: Liturgical Press, 1961), pp. 173-174.

"Certainly human love . . .": Rock, *op. cit.*, pp. 114-115.

On married partners' interdependence for salvation: cf. Paul VI, Address to Equipes Notre Dame, "The Sacrament of Marriage: A Permanent Source of Grace," in the English edition of *L'Osservatore Romano*, October 7, 1976, pp. 3, 12.

On distractions to prayer arising from married life: cf. 1 Co 7:32-35; also Bouyer, *op. cit.*, p. 135.

"life has its . . .": R.F. Trevett, *The Church and Sex* (New York: Hawthorne Books, 1960), p. 46.

"They [consecrated virgins] reveal . . .": *ibid.*, p. 44; cf. Joseph L. Bernardin, "The Ministerial Priesthood and the Advancement of Women," p. 123, in *The Order of Priesthood, op. cit.*

"Because, in Christian marriage, . . .": cf. Perreault, *op. cit.*, p. 23; cf. *Perfectae Caritatis,* No. 12.

"In this light, . . .": cf. Gatto, *op. cit.*, p. 97.

"Now, the virgin soul . . .": Heris, *op. cit.*, pp. 229-230.

One expression of this teaching on reasonable continence is given by Gatto:

Chastity is not an exigency extraneous to love, imposed from without; it is not a necessity which love submits to and experiences as a violence or constriction.

Chastity is born from within every true and authentic love, and it acts with power and spontaneity to the degree that one's conscience becomes clearly aware of the nature and the laws of love. The fact that Christianity is the religion of love indicates the intimacy and fecundity of chastity together with charity (Cf. Gatto, *op. cit.*, p. 97).

"Celibacy, therefore, . . .": Aumann, *op. cit.*, p. 54.

12. Though not directly pertaining to the matter of this chapter, it would be helpful to note that the two friends themselves would likely be poor judges of the prudence of their relationship, especially in its early stages. Confessors and counselors are aware that emotion can so prejudice one's judgment of his own situation that objectivity becomes nearly impossible. Furthermore, one can be so involved emotionally that he becomes incapable of receiving objective advice.

This is the case in so many poor marriages that were insistently entered into against the wise judgments of others. Consequently it is important for celibate friends to seek reliable counsel early in their relationship and throughout its development to maturity.

188

Final references:

"The more exquisite . . .": cf. St. Francis de Sales, *Devout Life,* Part III, C. 19.

"There can be . . .": Rock, *op. cit.,* p. 131.

"Be prudent . . .": Gerald Vann, O.P., *To Heaven with Diana!,* p. 57.

Select Bibliography

(These works are meant to supplement those referred to in the chapter notes.)

Babbage, Stuart Barton. *Sex and Sanity — A Christian View of Sexual Morality*. Philadelphia: The Westminster Press, 1965.

Barrosse, Thomas, C.S.C. *Christianity: Mystery of Love*. Notre Dame, Indiana: Fides, 1964.

Benda, Clemens, E., M.D. *The Image of Love*. New York: Crowell-Collier, 1961.

Bertine, Eleanor, Dr. *Human Relationships: Family, Friendship, and Love*. New York: Longmans, Green, 1958.

Bertocci, Peter A. *Sex, Love, and the Person*. New York: Sheed & Ward, 1967.

D'Arcy, Martin C. *The Mind and Heart of Love — A Study in Eros and Agape*. New York: Henry Holt and Co., 1947.

Donum Dei. *Religious Chastity: Its Conditions*. Ottawa: Canadian Religious Conference, No. 6, 1962.

Dubay, Thomas, S.M. *A Call to Virginity?* Huntington, Indiana: Our Sunday Visitor, Inc., 1977.

Guitton, Jean. *Essay on Human Love*. London: Rockliff, 1951.

John of the Cross. *The Living Flame of Love*, in *The Collected Works of St. John of the Cross*, Kieren Kavanaugh, O.C.D., and Otilio Rodriguez, O.C.D., (Transl.). Washington, D.C.: Institute of Carmelite Publications, 1973.

Kiesling, Christopher, O.P. *Celibacy, Prayer and Friendship*. New York: Alba House, 1978.

Lull, Ramon. *The Book of the Lover and the Beloved*. New York: Macmillan, 1923.

May, Rollo. *Love and Will*. New York: W.W. Norton & Co., 1969.

May, William E. *The Nature and Meaning of Chastity*. Chicago: Franciscan Herald Press, 1976.

McGoey, John, S.F.M. *Dare I Love?* Huntington, Indiana: Our Sunday Visitor, Inc., 1974.

Pieper, Josef. *About Love*. Chicago: Franciscan Herald Press, 1974.

Rievaulx, Aelred of. *Spiritual Friendship*. Washington, D.C.: Cistercian Publications Consortium Press, 1974.

Teresa of Avila. *The Collected Works of St. Teresa of Avila*, Kieren Kavanaugh, O.C.D., and Otilio Rodriguez, O.C.D., (Transl.). Washington, D.C.: Institute of Carmelite Publications, 1976. (To date only the first volume of this new translation has appeared, containing the *Life, Spiritual Testimonies* and *Soliloquies* of St. Teresa.)

Trimbos, C.J. *Healthy Attitudes toward Love and Sex*. New York: P.J. Kennedy, 1964.

Van Kaam, Adrian. *The Vowed Life*. Denville: Dimension Books, 1968.

Von Hildebrand, D. *Man and Woman*. Chicago: Franciscan Herald Press, 1965.

Wade, Joseph D., S.J. *Chastity, Sexuality & Personal Hangups — A Guide to Celibacy for Religious and Laity*. New York: Alba House, 1969.

INDEX

Bond, Leo, 114, 118
Brancaleone, 60
Bréchard, Mlle. de, 88, 93
Bride, 21-23, 61, 65, 75, 127-130, 162
Bridegroom, 16, 20-22, 64-65, 127-129, 162

Carrel, Dr., 135
Castiglio, Br., 51
Catherine of Siena, 50, 67-75, 78, 95, 118
    and Raymond of Capua, 50, 71-75
    Catherine's friendships, 69-71, 95
    teaching on friendship, 67-69, 95
Cecilia, Bl., 51, 53
Celibate friendship, 98-99, 159, 162
    compared to marital friendship, 92, 99, 148-156
    dangers in, 25, 33, 42, 46, 98-100, 112, 123, 131, 135ff., 145
    in Scripture, 23-25
    in the lives of saints, 49-96
    see complementing love; friendship between men and women; love, celi-
    bate, marital
Celse, 91
Cephas, 24
Cervantes, Lucius, 28
Charity, 9, 68, 99ff., 142, 153
    and celibate friendship, 9, 41, 63, 66-67, 93, 95, 108, 122-130, 142, 160-
    162
    and consecrated chastity, 99, 102-107, 140-141
    and friendship, 112-122
    and love of enemy, 120
    as love of creatures, 100-101, 104, 160-161
    as love of God, 99-101, 103-104, 160-161
    fraternal, 68, 101, 130, 143
    goal of consecrated celibates, 99-101, 160
    nature of, 100, 142
    nuptial dimensions of, 104, 127-130, 153
    parental dimensions of, 129-130
    priorities (or order) of, 99-101, 160-161
    see love, Christian, divine
Charles of France, 73
Charlotte, 91
Charmoisy, Mme. de, 88
Chastity, consecrated, 10, 98, 102ff., 132ff.
    and charity, 99, 102-107, 140-141, 161
    and masculine-feminine friendship, 38ff., 46, 49-96 *passim,* 98, 131-157,
    160-162
    and temptation, 81, 135, 137-140, 144-145, 156
    and Vatican II, 103-105

197

198

Intimacy, with God, 15, 21ff., 101, 103-104, 117-118, 121-122, 149, 151-152, 159
    see Trinity, indwelling; union, with God
Isaiah, 18, 21, 130
Ivory of Chastity, 54

Jacobina, Sr., 53
Jacqueline Coste, 88
James, St., 19, 22
Jane de Chantal, 60, 87-94
Jansenism, 13
Jarrett, Bede, 50
Jehoshaphat, 19
Jeremiah, 21, 23
Jesus, 11, 17, 19-20, 22, 25, 33, 45, 64, 71, 73, 79, 82, 92, 98-99, 102, 112-113, 118, 127-128
    and friendship with women, 25, 33, 102
Joana, 25
John Chrysostom, 118
John d'Acqs, 51
John of Navarre, 51
John of the Cross, 14, 45, 78, 128, 142
John the Baptist, 20, 22
John the Evangelist, 19-20, 25, 102, 159
Jonathan and David, 18
Jordan of Saxony, 50, 56-67
    and Diana d'Andalo, 56-67
    apostolate with women, 58-59
    range of friends, 57-59
    "Siren of the Schools", 57
"Joseph" (the Lord), 80
Joy, 57, 59, 62, 65, 76, 79, 88, 129, 132, 149, 152, 154
    and friendship, 32, 34, 61, 64, 69, 71, 82, 87, 92, 95, 108, 116, 120, 136, 154, 161
    and self-restraining love, 34, 41-42, 141, 145
    see happiness; pleasure
Juana, 83
Julia, 25
Jung, C.G., 30, 110

Ketter, Peter, 147

Lacordaire, Père, 102-103, 128
"Laurencia" (Teresa of Avila), 80ff.
Lazarus, 20, 25, 33
Lepp, Ignace, 28-29, 33, 39, 45
Lewis, C.S., 113, 121, 131-132, 142

199

masculine-feminine; love, complementing
Love, Christian, 10, 29, 43ff., 99ff.
  and celibate friendship, 9, 15-16, 105, 122-130, 160-162
  and complementing love, 43-47, 94-96, 99
  and friendship, 14, 100
  divine object, God, 43, 99-101
  infused gift, 47, 100, 116
  fullness of and consecrated chastity, 29, 41, 98, 101-106, 140, 160
  fullness of, goal of consecrated men and women, 15-16, 45, 94, 99-101,
    130, 152-153, 160-162
  see charity; love, divine
Love, complementing, 32-33, 36, 43ff., 46, 108, 110ff.
  and affective love, 43, 46
  and Christian love, 43-47, 95-96, 124ff., 162
  and fulfilling love for God, 44-45
  and fulfilling love for others, 36-37, 45
  and the saints, 39, 49-96 *passim,* 94-96
  celibate and marital, 41, 99, 112, 148-156
  effects of, 36-37, 43, 46, 110
  exclusive, 37, 150
  quality of communication, 36-37
  unending, 37
Love, divine, 9, 12, 17, 20, 28ff., 44, 47, 66-67, 88, 94ff., 99ff., 104, 117, 124,
    129, 162
  see charity; love, Christian
Love experience,
  adequate, 28, 31, 34-35
  as man or woman, 31
  capability of, for men and women, 23, 46
  fullness of, 41
  inadequate, 31, 33, 35
Love, fulfilling, 34-35, 46, 108, 123-124, 150
  and affective love, 34, 43, 46
  and the saints, 49-96 *passim,* 52, 54, 59, 71, 78, 88, 94-96
  degrees of, 34-35
  primarily for God 44-45
  see friendship; love, functional
Love, functional, 29, 33, 35, 37, 42, 107
Love, human, 12-13, 18-20, 28, 45, 106, 119, 124
  and consecrated celibates, 17, 41, 43, 46-47, 64, 83-88, 94ff., 102-103,
    105, 145, 149-150, 162
  and the Hebrew mind, 45
  limited ability for, 29, 41-43
  see friendship; love, fulfilling
Love, interpersonal types, 34-43
Love, marital, 32
  compared to celibate love, 92, 99, 148-156

201

Navarre d'Acqs, 51
Need-love, 132
    and chastity, 133, 136, 144, 161
    see love, of concupiscence; pleasure; utility
Nereus, 25
Neurosis, 33, 37, 39, 43, 140
Nicolao, 80
Noble, H.D., 120, 143
Noguenza, 52

Obedience, 117, 122, 140, 143, 148-149, 151, 154, 161
    vow of, 72, 77-78, 80-81, 86, 89-90
    see Providence
O'Keefe, Maureen and Evoy, John, 28, 45
Origen, 127

Parental influence,
    for adequate personality, 28, 31, 34, 112, 149
    for celibate formation, 42
    see formative influences
Parenthood,
    of marriage, 129, 149, 156
    spiritual, 129, 149
"Particular friendships", 15
Paternity, spiritual, 111, 129-130, 149-150
    see, charity, parental dimensions of; parenthood, spiritual
"Paul" (Jerome Gracian), 80ff.
Paul, St., 19, 22, 24, 45, 113, 116, 127, 130, 145, 159
Paul VI, 148
Peers, Allison, 78
Peregrinacion de Anastasio, 81
Perfectae Caritatis, 105
Perreault, A.M., 103, 137-140, 152
Person, human,
    adequate, 28, 31, 34-36, 41, 46, 54, 59, 95, 146
    and benevolent love, 137, 144, 160
    mystery of, 44, 111
    related to the Divine Persons, 44-45
    see wholeness, personal; maturity
Petronilla, 53
Philippe, Paul, 14
Philothea, 88
Phoebe, 24
Plé, Albert, 140
Pleasure, as motive for love, 76, 106-107, 112, 116
    sensible, 54, 68, 131, 136ff., 141-142, 144-145
    sexual, 42, 102, 137ff., 161

Summa Theologica, 114, 140-142
Susanna, 25
Suso, Henry, 45

Teresa of Avila, 45, 75-87, 95, 118
    and Jerome Gracian, 78-87, 89
    teaching on friendship, 75-77, 95
    Teresa's friendships, 77ff.
Terruwe, Anna, 28, 33, 39-41, 45
Teutonio de Braganza, 77
Theology, 16-17, 98, 113, 122, 140, 156, 160
    pastoral, 16, 98, 102, 156
Theotime, 88
"Third way", 15
Thomas Aquinas, 14, 106-107, 109, 114, 117, 120, 136, 140-142, 147
Touch, sense of, 142, 144-146, 161
Trevett, R.F., 151-152
Trinity, the Blessed, 15, 20, 44, 121-122, 129, 151
    indwelling of, 20, 100, 118, 162
    see intimacy, with God; union, with God
Tryphaena, 25
Tryphosa, 25

Ugolino, Cardinal, 51
Union, physical (sexual), 38, 136-137
    in friendship, 108
    in marriage, 147-152, *passim*
    see intimacy; love, marital, physical
Union, with God, 16-17, 59, 103-104, 118, 121-122, 125, 128-129, 149, 162
    eschatological, 22, 104, 145, 152, 157
    see intimacy, with God; spousal love and consecration to Christ; Trinity, indwelling
Utilitarian appetite, 43-44
Utility, as motive for love, 106, 110, 112, 116
    see profit

Vann, Gerald, 55, 110, 112, 119, 122, 125, 157
Van Zeller, Hubert, 141
Vatican II, 103-105, 129
Velazquez, 77
Ventura, Fr., 53-54
Vicarious experience, 124, 127
Vincent de Paul, 88, 94
Virginity, 21-23, 52-53, 105, 111, 128-129, 134, 136, 142-143, 151-154 *passim*
Visitation, Congregation of, 92-94

208